Legendary
Texians

Legendary Texians

Volume III

Joe Tom Davis

EAKIN PRESS
Austin, Texas

FIRST EDITION
VOL. III

Copyright © 1986
By Joe Tom Davis

Published in the United States of America
By Eakin Press, P.O. Box 23069, Austin, Texas 78735

ISBN 0-89015-559-3

Library of Congress Cataloging-in-Publication Data
(Revised for volume 3)

Davis, Joe Tom, 1942–
  Legendary Texians.

  Includes bibliographies and indexes.
  1. Texas — Biography — Young adult literature. 2. Frontier and Pioneer
Life — Texas — Young adult literature. 3. Texas — History — Young adult
literature.
I. Title.
Some adult language.
CT262.D38 1986 976.4′009′92 [B] 84-18685
ISBN 0-89015-336-1 (v. 1)
ISBN 0-89015-473-2 (v. 2)
ISBN 0-89015-559-3 (v. 3)

About the Author

Joe Tom Davis is a fifth-generation Texan; his maternal great-great-grandfather, George Lord, was a survivor of the Mier Expedition and the "Lottery of Death."

He attended public schools at Edna, Texas, where his interest in and love of Texas history was whetted by hearing Jackson County tales about the "Wild Man of the Navidad" and the ghost town of Texana, the Allen brothers' first choice for the site of the city of Houston.

Davis, a Navy veteran, earned two degrees from Sam Houston State University, where he was elected to Alpha Chi and Who's Who and received the James Ellison Kirkley Prize as outstanding social science student. After teaching at Sam Houston for two years, he joined the faculty of Wharton County Junior College in 1965 as an instructor of American and Texas history.

While teaching at the junior college, Davis has been elected to Outstanding Educators of America and is a leader in campus beautification efforts. He has a special interest in singing and is a choir member and Sunday school teacher at First Baptist Church, El Campo. He often speaks to school and church groups and to area study and service clubs. Davis is a member of the Texas State Historical Association and the Texas Junior College Teachers Association. He has written two other books: *Legendary Texians,* Volumes I (1982) and II (1985), published by Eakin Press.

*This book is dedicated to
my niece and nephews,
Susan and Stephen Davis,
John Mark and Brent Bonnot,
and
to my pastor,
Reverend Rick DuBroc
of First Baptist Church,
El Campo, Texas*

Contents

Acknowledgments

I could not have written this book without the assistance of many colleagues and friends. I am especially indebted to Mrs. Patsy L. Norton, director of the J. M. Hodges Learning Center at Wharton County Junior College, and two members of her able staff. Much of my reading and research was done in the Hodges Learning Center, where an extensive collection of Texas history titles has been acquired since 1964 through the generosity of the Raymond Dickson Foundation and proceeds from the book, *The History of Wharton County*, by Annie Lee Williams. It is my good fortune that Assistant Director J. C. Hoke is also an outstanding photographer. Mr. Hoke accompanied me on five trips and provided all of the on-site photos in this book along with numerous photographic reproductions; the quality of his work will be apparent to the reader. A special "thank you" is also due Mrs. Mildred Petrusk, the circulation technician, for obtaining reference materials through interlibrary loans.

I also wish to thank two members of the college English Department, Dr. Sandra Coats and Mr. R. L. Cowser, Jr., for advising me on matters of punctuation and usage. Mrs. Genelle Speer of Wharton, Texas, did excellent work in typing a portion of the manuscript. Mrs. Ruby Baty of Wharton was kind enough to escort me to Peach Point Plantation and to points of historical interest in West Columbia, Brazoria, and Clute. I am grateful to Don and Odessa Baylor of Wharton, for letting me use four rare books and journals relating to family history, and to Mike Mitchell of Edna, who allowed me to read an unpublished manuscript, "The Mitchell Family in Texas," for information pertaining to Maj. James Kerr. Mr. Wence De León of Victoria graciously consented to a lengthy interview, allowed me to reproduce the family portrait of his illustrious great-great-grandfather, Don Martín De León, and gave me access to a family document, "Abstract of Title to the Martín De León Survey, A-74, . . ." For the illustrations in this book, I am indebted to Mrs. Baty of Wharton, Mr. De León and the late Admiral A. B. J. Hammett of Victoria, Mrs. Ruth Munson Smith of Angleton, Mr. Stephen S. Perry, Jr., of Peach Point, the late Mrs. Ruth Montgomery Tompkins of Hempstead, and to the cited libraries, museums, and institutions which made available all of the photographs, portraits, and maps I requested. A very special "thank you" is due my talented niece-by-marriage, Mrs. Penny Grissom Bonnot, the art teacher at Edna High School. Penny designed the book cover and drew the likeness of Emily Morgan found in Chapter IV.

My greatest thanks and words of appreciation are due my late father and my mother, Herbert C. and Lorene Smith Davis, and my brother and sister, Cecil and Shirley; it was their steadfast support and encouragement which inspired me to write both this book and two companion volumes.

Joe Tom Davis
Wharton County Junior College
Wharton, Texas

Introduction

In Volume III of this series about legendary Texians, I have continued a biographical approach to the theme of the trilogy: that Texas history is replete with fascinating people whose lives add spice and texture to the flavor and fabric of a unique state's past. In this volume I have reviewed the lives of the "baddest man" in the Republic, a beguiling mulatto who was our first "undercover agent," the Spanish founder of Victoria, the leading black Texian of his day, the priest of Austin's colony, a Baptist pioneer educator, and two families who forged an early Texas dynasty.

Robert Potter was a signer of the Texas Declaration of Independence, the first secretary of the Texas Navy, and a Republic-era senator. Because of these achievements, he is buried in the State Cemetery and has a Texas county named in his honor. One finds many dark corners, however, when delving into the checkered career of this brilliant but erratic statesman. A heinous crime committed in a fit of jealous rage sent Potter to prison and ended a promising political career in North Carolina. Ever the opportunist, Potter made a fresh start in Texas revolutionary politics even as he took on a bitter new rival, Sam Houston. After rescuing a deserted wife during the Runaway Scrape, Potter sought to escape gossip by whisking Harriet Page away to a seemingly idyllic life at remote Potter's Point. At times he revealed a nobler side, as when he used his powerful oratory to quiet a rebellion or attempted to face down an angry lynch mob. This same man, however, wrote a revolting will that trumpeted his infidelity and shattered the spirit of the faithful Harriet; in fact, his illicit relationship with and deception of this brave woman provided the grist for a best-selling novel. Controversy dogged Potter's every step, and an East Texas feud culminated in the murder of this self-centered "Peacock of the Pines."

Legend has it that Emily Morgan was a beautiful mulatto who gave her all — including her body — in contributing to the stunning Texian victory at the Battle of San Jacinto. When Santa Anna invaded Texas with his Mexican army in early 1836, he brought a well-deserved reputation as a womanizer. By the time he burned New Washington (now Morgan's Point) on April 20, he had gone without sex for two weeks; in looting Col. James Morgan's plantation, he took the shapely servant girl Emily as a personal prize. During their two-day liaison, his lust for her totally distracted the Mexican general. On the afternoon of the historic clash with Sam Houston's Texian army, Santa Anna and Emily spent much of the time in bed partying on champagne and gourmet foods. When the Texian attack came at 4:00 P.M. on April 21, the panic-stricken lover was literally "caught with his pants down" and fled undressed from his tent and the scene of battle — conduct which contributed to the total rout of the demoralized Mexican army. After the battle, a grateful Colonel Morgan freed Emily and she soon returned to her home in New York. Fortunately, an English ethnologist took note of her story, a saga which inspired several versions of the well-known folk song, "The Yellow Rose of Texas." In 1985, however, this Yellow Rose tale was uprooted by a reputable Texas historian, who contends that the traditional view of Emily Morgan is a fantasy and myth embellished and romanticized by generations of Texas writers. This scholar debunks what was considered to be the definitive book on the subject and asserts that the author reached "faulty conclusions" in suggesting that Emily Morgan was the "yellow rose." I have included this critique in an annotation and invite readers to draw their own conclusions about a most elusive historical figure.

Martín De León and William Goyens are noteworthy

examples of Spanish and Negro material success in an Anglo world. Don Martín was patriarch of the richest family in South Texas, the greatest cattle baron of his day, and the founder of Victoria. As *empresario* of a Mexican colony, he brought elegance and refinement to a raw, rough frontier area. De León stood his ground when pressured by Green De Witt, a neighboring *empresario*, because of conflicting land claims; in fact, the audacious Spaniard arrested De Witt in settling another argument over contraband trade. Although Don Martín's sons and sons-in-law were politically prominent and staunchly supported the Texas Revolution, the De León family lost all their property and were forced into exile at war's end. William Goyens came to Texas as a penniless "free man of color" and died one of the largest landowners in East Texas. This self-effacing mulatto became a wealthy Nacogdoches businessman and land speculator, a self-taught scholar, and the first black lawyer in Texas. He was both friend and counselor to Sam Houston, who put great faith and confidence in Goyens as Indian agent and interpreter to the Cherokees. After he married a white woman, social ostracism forced William to settle out of town in an area known today as Goyens Hill. In spite of all his achievements, he would have been forced to leave Texas or sold into slavery after the revolution except for the intervention of his white friends.

The early Catholic and Baptist leaders Michael Muldoon and Rufus Burleson are contrasting personalities. Father Muldoon, the resident priest of Austin's colony, was a witty, jovial, fun-loving, hard-drinking Irishman who was equally at home in a planter's "big house" or a crude frontier cabin. Non-Catholics loved him for his tolerance of the host of "closet" Protestants in Texas. The drab monotony of frontier life was always broken by a gala feast whenever Father Muldoon made his rounds conducting mass marriages and baptisms. His concept of pastoral duty led Miguel, as he was affectionately called, to rescue an Indian captive and to twice come to the relief of imprisoned Texas political leaders. Rufus C. Burleson devoted fifty years of his life to Baylor University, first at Independence and then at Waco. The pioneer educator was a self-centered, headstrong, tempermental man of consuming ambition. A stern disciplinarian committed to academic excellence, he served as administrator, full-time professor, and father figure to the male students. After Sam Houston moved his family to Independence, Rufus baptized the general and became his pastor, spiritual adviser, and confidant while Baylor University became Houston's adopted school. In June 1861 a bitter feud with the principal of the Baylor Female Department caused Burleson to resign and accept the presidency of the new Waco University. He made this coeducational institution the preeminent Texas Baptist school while carrying on a long-term personal rivalry with William Carey Crane, the new president of Baylor at Independence. In 1886 the two Baptist colleges merged at Waco with Burleson as president.

The Groce and Wharton families forged a fifty-year dynasty in contributing to the agricultural, political, military, social, and cultural history of Texas. The patriarch of the clan, Jared E. Groce, was the "Cotton King" of Texas and the largest landowner of his day. After his eldest son, Leonard Waller, inherited Bernardo plantation, he stripped it for use by General Houston's Texian army. In 1853 Leonard built "Liendo," an historic mansion that later served as headquarters of a famous general and as the home of a distinguished sculptor. Jared Groce's only daughter, Sarah Ann, married William H. Wharton, and their Eagle Island "big house" became a social and cultural mecca. The Wharton side of the family produced two brothers who played key roles in Texas revolutionary politics. William, the hothead leader of the War Party, chaired the Convention of 1833 and was a member of the commission sent to seek United States aid. He then served as the Republic's first minister to the United States and as a senator before his accidental death. His brother, John A. Wharton, was a founder of Freemasonry in Texas, elected to the Consultation of 1835, and served on its General Council. He was also General Houston's adjutant general at the Battle of San Jacinto before serving as interim secretary of war. At the time of his death, John was a member of the Third Texas Congress. In 1846 Wharton County was created and named in honor of these two brothers. During the Civil War, more laurels were won by the family when William and Sarah's son, John Austin, commanded the famed Terry's Texas Rangers and achieved the rank of Confederate major general.

Writing this series about legendary Texians has been a true "labor of love" for me. If history is biography, the Texas writer is blessed with a treasure-trove. In delving into the drama of our state's past, I found the stage crowded with a marvelous cast of characters. It has been my great pleasure to chronicle the lives and exploits of some twenty-six individuals and families whose colorful threads embellish the unique tapestry of Texas history. I will, of course, take full responsibility for any errors made in the telling of their stories.

As a fifth-generation Texan, I hope that the sense of pride and respect I have for my heritage will be conveyed to and shared by the reader.

IN MEMORY OF
THE FORGOTTEN MAN OF TEXAS HISTORY
FATHER MIGUEL MULDOON
RESIDENT PRIEST OF AUSTIN'S COLONY
TRUE FRIEND OF STEPHEN F. AUSTIN AND
HIS PEOPLE

1823 — 1842

CONTRIBUTED MUCH TOWARDS THE SUCCESS
OF AUSTIN'S COLONIAL VENTURE

ERECTED THROUGH THE EFFORTS OF
MIGUEL MULDOON MEMORIAL ASSN.
SENATOR LOUIS J. SULAK, PRESIDENT
REV. PAUL P. KASPAR, SECRETARY
JOHN L. SULAK, TREASURER
HOUSTON WADE, ADVOCATE

Muldoonmonument on Highway 77 south of LaGrange.
Courtesy University of Texas Institute of
Texan Cultures, San Antonio

I

Michael Muldoon:
That Other Father of Texas

The life of Father Michael Muldoon is shrouded in mystery; his last years and eventual fate are unknown. To Anglo Texians he was the most friendly and sympathetic symbol of Mexican authority; twice he dramatically came to the rescue of imprisoned Texas political leaders. Although he was their Catholic priest, he had a loving tolerance of Protestants in Texas. His religious visits while making the rounds in Austin's colony were gala occasions likened to Roman holidays. Affable and gregarious, he loved such worldly pleasures as a good drink, a good book, or a good conversation. Who was this elusive figure who called Texas "his only home" even though he was only an intermittent visitor over a decade of time?

Michael's father was a native of Dublin, Ireland, but was forced to leave the country for political reasons after a fracas with a British soldier. Fleeing to Spain, he took a Spanish bride and provided their boy Michael with a thorough education in training him for the priesthood. The lad sometimes seemed to love adventure more than religion but was early imbued with such true Christian virtues as friendliness, humility, and unselfish service.

1

Stephen F. Austin
Courtesy of Texas State Capitol, Austin

Replica of Stephen F. Austin's log cabin, Stephen F. Austin State Park (San Felipe).
Courtesy of University of Texas Institute of Texan Cultures, San Antonio

After mingling with the nobility of Europe, the young priest asked for an assignment in Spain's colonies and was sent to Mexico in 1821 as the chaplain of the last Spanish viceroy, Don Juan O'Donojo. For the next twenty-one years, he would appear first in Mexico, then in Texas, equally at home in the best society of Mexico or amid the crudest of surroundings in Anglo Texas. When Stephen F. Austin arrived at Mexico City in April 1822 to seek confirmation of his father's *empresario* grant in Texas, he encountered a complicated political tangle which required him to stay in the capital for an unexpected year. During this time, he met Father Muldoon, who advanced him funds for his room and board and tutored him in Spanish. Thus was born a warm, lifelong friendship.

Austin returned to Texas in the spring of 1823 with his colonization grant confirmed. That grant and the later state colonization law of 1825 required that Anglo colonists be Roman Catholic and that marriage by the church was necessary to legalize the right of inheritance. This requirement created practical problems since Austin's colony headquarters town of San Felipe was a considerable distance from San Antonio and its priests. In June 1824 he wrote to Political Chief José Antonio Saucedo, complaining that a priest was needed for the many couples who wished to marry. After Austin suggested as an expedient that couples be allowed to use a marriage contract and bind themselves to have a church marriage by a priest at the first opportunity, Saucedo authorized such an arrangement in September 1824.

The "Father of Texas" devised the first such marriage-by-bond in his own handwriting on April 29, 1824. In the presence of relatives and witnesses, the bride and groom signed a written agreement containing the traditional marriage vows and providing for a fixed forfeiture sum of money if either party refused to marry legally on arrival of a priest. Many of these colonial marriage bonds in complete form are still on file in the respective offices

3

of the county clerks of Austin County at Bellville, Brazoria County at Angleton, and Gonzales County at Gonzales. Henry Smith of Brazoria County, who served as provisional governor of Texas in 1835 and as secretary of the treasury in President Houston's first administration, wrote a letter of reminiscences on November 18, 1836, and included the following observation about marriage-by-bond:

> . . . Lacking the sanction of law, it lacked everything calculated to constitute a marriage in fact. Many couples, however, not finding the marriage state to possess all the alluring charms which they had figured in their fond imagination, have taken advantage of this slip-knot plan — sought the bond, and by mutual consent committed it to the flames — returned to the world as young as ever and free as the air.

Relief in the form of a convenient means of legal marriage arrived in 1829, when Father Muldoon first set foot on Texas soil and officiated for a time in the Irish colony town of San Patricio before Father Doyle was assigned there in 1830. While Austin was visiting Saltillo, the state capital, in January 1831, he learned that his longstanding request for a priest had been approved by the archbishop in Monterrey and that his old friend, Michael Muldoon, was coming to Texas as vicar general. He then wrote Samuel May Williams and remarked that Muldoon was "so liberal and enlightened on religious subjects," thus assuming that the Mexican government did not with to subject the Anglo settlers of Texas to religious harassment.

Father Muldoon arrived at San Felipe as official resident priest in April 1831 and was evidently well received. On March 1 Frank W. Johnson wrote Austin that all arrangements had been completed for a reception for the priest; then on June 15 Austin and Michael were invited by Thomas Barnett to visit Fort Bend. Since the *empresario* had little cash but plenty of real estate, Mig-

4

uel (as he was known in the colony) agreed to accept repayment of the debt owed him in land. Austin then helped him to secure eleven leagues of land (48,610 acres). Title to the land was issued on May 31, 1831, and surveyor Thomas H. Borden ran the boundary lines. One of Muldoon's first pastoral visits was to present Fayette County, where two of his leagues were located. The land grant was conditional in "that within one year he [Muldoon] shall build permanent landmarks at every angle of the tract" and "must settle and cultivate it as prescribed by law." To satisfy this requirement the priest built a stone hut on his two-league grant at or near the present town of Muldoon.

This itinerant padre was soon conducting marriages, christening children, and baptizing people on his rounds. He was quick to issue an edict forbidding marriages-by-bond and set his own fees at twenty-five dollars for marriages and two dollars for baptisms.[1] It was said that this jovial Irishman delighted in marrying couples joined by bond and, in the same ceremony, baptizing the children of the unions. In one such mass ceremony in Brazoria County, the participants and their offspring filled a room!

Henry Smith, a Brazoria resident who was later the first provisional governor of Texas, observed that the grand wholesale weddings and ". . . the baptism, the wine, the dinner, the dance and the sight of a Roman Catholic priest — was equal to a rare show in Texas." It should be noted, however, that Smith held Father Mul-

---

[1] Years later, W. W. Little of Eagle Lake recalled his baptism and the appearance of the good padre in a letter to Mrs. Julia Lee Sinks of Giddings, who in 1876 was asked to compile a history of Fayette County. Little's letter read in part:

. . . Well do I remember the occasion of receiving the oil and salt. I remember that I cursed and bit his finger when he put the salt in my mouth. He was at the Fort Settlement remarrying those that were married by bond. My father and mother were of the number. They had a gay time, frolicking and dancing the old Virginia reel. Muldoon was a large, red-faced Irishman.

doon in rather low esteem. Henry considered Michael "vain, vulgar and very a scamp as ever disgraced the colony" although it "took up half a column of a newspaper" to list his titles. To Smith the priest was "nothing but a common man — and an Irishman at that" who made "a snug little money making business" out of performing marriages and baptisms. Henry observed that many of the older colonists considered the idea of being baptized by a Catholic priest "an everlasting stigma and disgrace." He causticly recalls Muldoon's mass baptism and marriage ceremony of Brazoria citizens as follows:

> The baptism commenced first, as heretics could not be lawfully joined in matrimony until they were baptized in the true faith. Next commenced a kind of liturgy — that finished, the marriage ceremony, which was short and a mere conjoining in lawful wedlock closed the scene. . . . The scene, take it all in all, was truly ludicrous in the extreme. Most of them had children and some five or six. To see brides on the floor, and while the marriage rites are performing, with bosoms open and children sucking at the breast, and others in a situation realy to [*sic*] delicate to mention, appeared to me more like a burlesque on marriage than a marriage in fact.

After Aylett C. (Strap) Buckner served notice of Muldoon's forthcoming marital mission, a party of thirty, including all Fayette County couples wanting to be married or living together under contract as husband and wife, gathered at the home of a Mrs. Williams at Wood's Settlement near present West Point. The mass rite culminated in a two-day wedding feast.[2]

---

[2] After Texas became an independent republic, the First Congress in 1836 appointed Andrew Rabb as chief justice (county judge) to take Muldoon's place in legalizing marriages in Mina (Bastrop) County. Early one morning, Rabb arrived at Col. John H. Moore's blockhouse (Moore's Fort or present LaGrange) to unite four couples who had earlier signed marriage bonds. It will be recalled that Father Muldoon made these wholesale weddings into gala spectacles. With that in

The baptismal ceremony made one eligible for land ownership and was thus a business rather than a religious proposition to many Anglos. Most of the colonists had a Protestant background but since the law required them to be Roman Catholics, many took vows in a cavalier fashion to become "Muldoon Catholics." This kindly priest did not inquire too closely into the real religious preferences of his new flock; he was simply being pragmatic in certifying as "Catholic" those whose conversion was simply a veneer. In making his rounds, Father Muldoon met only two "exhorters" while delivering a series of religious lectures. One was an old gentleman who admitted to be in the habit of preaching at various places in Austin's colony. Michael attributed this confession less to the old man's arrogance than to "the imbecility of his great age" and let him off with a stern reprimand. The other preacher he encountered was dismissed as an obvious charlatan who had his eyes on a rich widow and her lands. On May 20, 1831, Muldoon wrote a semihumorous, partly poetic account of the parish tour in the local paper, the *Mexican Citizen,* in which he noted:

> . . . With these two slight and impotent exceptions, I have been agreeably surprised to find such order, to receive so much personal respect, and to discover such a *general* and *voluntary adhesion* to the Catholic religion . . . I answer for their religious allegiance.

His broad-minded philosophy and ready wit are revealed in the following toast he composed on the spot at a banquet honoring Stephen F. Austin on January 1, 1832:

---

mind the sensitive Mrs. Moore, stung by the jokes about *young* married people, asked Judge Rabb to "tie the knot" in a quiet, secretive manner. The new "bride" was heard to say, "I was married before an Alcalde. What need is there of repeating the marriage ceremony before a Justice? And if I stand up and acknowledge I have never been married, what is to become of my children?" After Rabb legally married the couples, a merry old busybody asked Mrs. Moore if there had been a wedding that day. "Hush about weddings!" she retorted. "I am sick of them. If a woman marries at eighteen and for ten years is not sure of it, I think it is a poor country to live in."

May plow and harrow, spade and fack
Remain the arms of Anahuac
So that her rich and boundless plains
May yearly yield all sorts of grains.
May all religious discord fall
And friendship be the creed of all.
With tolerance your pastor views
All sects of Christians, Turks, and Jews.
We now demand three rousing cheers
Great Austin's health and pioneers.

Such tact and good judgment quickly reassured the colonists and made Father Muldoon a loved and respected figure. Since he embodied the powers of church and state, Michael's influence was second only to that of Austin during his official Texas stay of little more than a year.

The fun-loving padre did not always project the image of godliness that Anglo-Americans of Methodist or Baptist persuasion expected. In 1831 Moses Lapham, a Puritanical young surveyor and schoolteacher at San Felipe, accused him of fornicating "with blackamoors." Miguel was also addicted to alcohol, and he claimed pioneer newspaperman Godwin Brown Cotten as a favorite drinking crony. In his book *Evolution of a State,* Noah Smithwick wrote that Father Muldoon had an "unlimited capacity for drink" and told of the following incident. It seems that Michael and a "General" Walker were carousing around San Felipe and stepped into a tavern of Frank Adams, who asked the newcomers to join him at the bar. When the priest turned up his nose and replied, "No, I never drink with any but gentlemen," Adams drew back and socked him between the eyes. At first the stunned Michael considered seeking redress for this assault on the authority of the state church, even though the townspeople rallied around the saloon keeper. Rather than protest to the Mexican government, the good-natured Muldoon chose to overlook the matter, apologize for his offensive language, and accept Adams's next drink offer as a way of "taking his medicine."

8

This gray, rotund, jovial priest became a familiar sight trudging the Texas frontier, oblivious of the financial potential of his 50,000 acres of land in present Fayette, Wharton, Lavaca, and Galveston counties; in fact, on March 9, 1836, he sold the eleven leagues to Austin, who then transferred the land to Peter Grayson for $5,000 — only a fraction of its value.

Muldoon was an intelligent, polished man of the world who spent much of his time in Brazoria County enjoying the elegant surroundings and splendid library at Eagle Island plantation, the home of William H. and Sarah Groce Wharton, where his wit and charm made him a welcome guest. There was, however, a not-so-frivolous side to this European charmer. In the spring of 1836, a Mrs. Juergens and her two little boys were carried off by raiding Indians at Post Oak Point in Fayette County. She was held for two months before Muldoon, alone and unarmed, tracked the raiding party to a trading post on the Red River and ransomed her release. The boys were never found, but Michael brought the wife back to the arms of her grieving husband.

Father Muldoon had no successor when he first returned to Mexico in the summer of 1832. Before leaving Texas, however, he twice took the side of the Texians in their looming showdown with Mexican authorities. Prior to the Anahuac insurrection of early June, he and Thomas Jefferson Chambers helped draft, in Spanish, the colonists' protest against the new Mexican customs house at Anahuac; as further proof of his personal courage, he then offered himself as hostage to Mexican troops against the "good behavior" of the imprisoned William Barret Travis. Before the Battle of Velasco of June 26–27, 1832, Michael's efforts almost averted bloodshed. Before the Texians successfully attacked the Mexican fort at the mouth of the Brazos River, he visited Mexican commander Ugartechea in hopes of mediating the dispute but returned to Texian lines to announce his mission a failure. When Muldoon reported that the Mexican leader was confident that 10,000 riflemen could not dislodge him from his position, John Austin prophetically replied, "Very well, padre, wait till tomorrow and you will see."

After his return to Mexico, Father Muldoon was to come to the rescue of his dear friend, Stephen F. Austin. The colonial leader had been imprisoned in Mexico City on February 13, 1834, after writing an indiscreet letter to the town council of San Antonio urging them to form a separate state government for Texas even without Mexican approval. For three months Austin was held in solitary confinement and incommunicado in a thirteen-by-sixteen-foot windowless cell in the old Inquisition prison. He received enough light from the ceiling skylight on fair days to read between ten o'clock and three and was allowed two hours a day to take sun on the roof. The first person to reach him was Miguel Muldoon, who had become a close friend of Santa Anna and was then living on the general's Vera Cruz *hacienda*. The two embraced warmly but were allowed to talk only in Spanish; they continued to see each other and communicate by what Austin called the use of "priestcraft." Muldoon tried unsuccessfully to arrange for Austin to stay at Casa Mexicana, a boardinghouse, but did persuade the commandant to allow meals to be brought in for the Texas leader. Austin then gave the Mexican officer a $200 order through his personal agent, William S. Parrott — enough money to provide good meals, wine, and cheese for some six months.

During these three difficult months, Father Muldoon worked to provide books, writing materials, better conditions, and word from Texas for his old friend. It was Muldoon who arranged for his release from solitary confinement on May 9, 1834, and then led the efforts that finally resulted in his release from Acordada prison in July 1835. In a letter to his brother-in-law, James F. Perry of Brazoria, Austin stated that Michael had been "firm and unwavering" in his friendship during eighteen months of imprisonment.

10

Muldoon was to perform one last service for Texas. On April 17, 1837, a ship bringing William H. Wharton back from Washington, D.C., was captured by two Mexican gunboats off the mouth of the Brazos River. Wharton, the Texas minister to the United States, was placed in a prison at Matamoros, Mexico. Since priests had easy access to the prison, Father Muldoon soon appeared and asked to see his old planter friend, then helped him to escape. On his third visit Miguel smuggled in a priest's garb and said, "Mr. Wharton, . . . If you are accosted, simply extend your right hand with the first two fingers elevated and say 'Pax Vobiscum.' Remember that you are a Catholic priest until you reach Texas." The disguised diplomat was thus able to walk unchallenged from confinement to freedom.

Michael Muldoon was back in Texas for a brief time in 1839, still thinking of himself as the spiritual leader of Texas Catholics. When performing a marriage ceremony at Houston on March 18, he used the title of "D.D. Vicar General of the Catholic Communities of the free and Independent Republic of Texas." Miguel returned to Mexico on the same ship that brought Barnard Bee there as the diplomatic agent of the Republic of Texas. When Muldoon left the Texas capital, Anson Jones gave the priest a letter on behalf of President Houston and the people of Texas thanking him for services rendered Stephen F. Austin and wishing him future happiness and prosperity. Frank W. Johnson and E. M. Pease testified that Muldoon was in Texas again as late as 1842. Tradition has it that a vengeful Santa Anna was awaiting his return and imprisoned the priest for helping Wharton escape. Nothing is known of Father Muldoon from this point forward, although there is conjecture that he lived to return to Spain.

A little town in southwestern Fayette County was settled in the 1830s and named in his honor. In 1886 the townsite of Muldoon was built on the San Antonio and Aransas Pass Railroad ten miles south of West Point on one of the leagues of land granted the good padre. Today there is a gray granite monument just north of Schulenburg on the shoulder of U.S. Highway 77 which reads:

IN MEMORY OF THE FORGOTTEN MAN OF TEXAS HISTORY.
FATHER MIGUEL MULDOON,
RESIDENT PRIEST OF AUSTIN'S COLONY.
TRUE FRIEND OF STEPHEN F. AUSTIN AND HIS PEOPLE.

Portrait of Don Martín De León, by Leonardo De León.
Courtesy of Wence De León, Victoria, Texas

13

II

The De León Family:
Riches, Race, Rapine, and Rags

When Martín De León died in 1834 at the age of sixty-eight, he was the patriarch of the richest family in South Texas and the founder of Victoria. His Mexican colonists started the post-mission cattle business in Texas and brought a touch of elegance and refinement to the raw, rough South Texas frontier. Don Martín's four sons and four sons-in-law were men of political prominence and would actively support the Texas Revolution, yet within three short years after his death, the De León colonists became victims of the most flagrant racial prejudice and abuse in Texas history. One of his sons would be murdered, another would be wounded and arrested, the family lands and livestock would be stolen by Anglo adventurers, and the De Leóns driven into exile. Even the achievements of the De León colonists between 1824 and 1836 were ignored and forgotten until the city of Victoria paid these Latin pioneers belated recognition in April 1972. This is the De León story, a Texas epic of riches, race, rapine, and rags.

The parents of Martín De León, Bernardo and María Galvan De León, headed a wealthy and aristocratic Spanish family when in 1760 they moved from Burgos,

De León Plaza with county courthouse in background. (From 75 Years in Victoria *by Booth Mooney).*

Courtesy Victoria Bank and Trust Co., Victoria, Texas

De León Shrine, Evergreen Cemetery, Victoria, Texas

Spain, to Burgos, Tamaulipas, Mexico. There the De León family enjoyed high rank and prestige. Don Martín, one of five children, was born at Tamaulipas in 1765 and grew into a tall, erect, handsome horseman. Since his father was a man of means, he could have received a classical education at Monterrey and the universities of Europe but chose instead to become a rancher-businessman at age eighteen. Supplying pack-mule trains for the San Nicolas mines was his first business venture. Then in 1790 he joined the regiment of Fieles De Burgos to fight the Tamaulipas Indians and was promoted to captain, the highest rank a native could attain.

In 1795 Don Martín married twenty-year-old Patricia de la Garza, a beautiful and cultured Spanish native of Soto La Marina. Patricia was a near kinsman of Gen. Felipe de la Garza, commandant-general of the Eastern Internal Provinces. The newlyweds immediately started ranching at Cruillas near the Rio Grande and their first son, Don Fernando, was born there in 1798, the only child of ten who would not be born in Texas.[1]

Fortune smiled on the couple in January 1801 when Patricia De León was given livestock valued at $366 by her father, Don José de la Garza, and $9,800 in cash by her godfather, Don Angel Pérez. Such generosity enabled the De León family to settle in Texas in 1806 on the east bank of the Aransas River, where they stocked an extensive ranch with cattle, horses, mules, and goats. The next year Don Martín petitioned Spanish Governor Salcedo at San Antonio for the land between the Aransas River and Cheltipin Creek; twice rejected, he relocated on the east bank of the Nueces River just below present San Patricio in 1809.

Protecting his family from Lipan Comanche attacks

---

[1] The other children and their birthdates are as follows: Candelaria, 1800; Silvestre, 1802; Guadalupe, 1804; Felix, 1806; Agapito, 1808; María Jesús, 1810; Refugio, 1812; Augustina, 1814; Francisca, 1818.

became a concern for De León after the Hidalgo uprising in September 1810 caused the Spanish garrison at Presidio La Bahía to withdraw to Mexico. The young rancher decided to take his family to the comparative safety of San Antonio, where he cooperated with the Republicans in resisting the Royalists. After sending his family back home to Burgos in 1816, Don Martín made frequent trips to his Nueces ranch. By then he owned five or six thousand head of cattle and was selling his livestock at New Orleans.

While driving mules to New Orleans in 1823, he discovered an ideal location for a Mexican colony between the lower Guadalupe and Lavaca rivers. Don Martín met a French pirate named Ramón La Fou at New Orleans and the two made a deal whereby La Fou's ship would be chartered to deliver supplies to De León's proposed colony; in return the Spaniard was to obtain a pardon for the French buccaneer from the Mexican government. On April 8, 1824, Don Martín petitioned the Provincial Deputation of San Fernando de Bexar for the right to establish forty-one Mexican families from Tamaulipas in a town to be called Nuestra Señora de Guadalupe de Jesús on the lower Guadalupe River. The petition was approved and a colonial charter granted on April 13 with the *empresario* being authorized to occupy any vacant land he might choose between the lower Guadalupe and Lavaca rivers. As the De León colony evolved, its informal boundaries became Mission Valley on the north, Coleto Creek on the west, the Lavaca River on the east, and ten leagues up from Matagorda Bay on the south. His settlement was unique in that it was authorized before the passage of the state colonization law, which sanctioned the grant the following October. Thus there were no designated boundaries, specific number of families, or time limits for settlement. De León's colonists were to be exempt from duties on every import except tobacco for seven years.

In October 1824 Don Martín founded his capital

Margaret Wright — photo from Pictorial History of Victoria and Victoria County *by Leopold Morris*

John J. Linn, ca. 1883 — Photo by Cecile Morris Price, courtesy of University of Texas Institute of Texan Cultures

Plácido Benavides —Courtesy of the late Adm. A.B.J. Hammett, Victoria, Texas

Portrait of Silvestre De León —Courtesy of the late Adm. A.B.J. Hammett, Victoria, Texas

town and named it in honor of his personal friend and first president of Mexico, Guadalupe Victoria. The town was located on the site of an earlier trading post called Cypress Grove by the Anglos and El Sabinal or Las Sabinas by the Mexicans. De León hired engineer and surveyor Gen. J. M. J. Carvajal to plat the town streets, plazas, and church. Carvajal, a native of San Antonio, later married one of the *empresario's* daughters, Refugia. The capital city was laid out in a four-square-league area with a main street that De León called "Calle de los Diez Amigos" or "The Street of the Ten Friends." ² The town's public square was to become known as De León Plaza, while the market square would become the city hall square. A courier service with Stephen F. Austin's colony town, San Felipe, was also established.

An Anglo pioneer and woman of mystery known locally as Margaret Wright came to the Victoria area in late 1826.³ Marguerite Theresa Robertson was born of an

---

² Victor M. Rose, the pioneer historian of Victoria, later asked one of Don Martín's grandsons, Patricio De León, the origin of the street name and he replied:

> I do not know, unless in an implied union of the ten principal citizens, who conducted the bulk of the business and had direction in matters of policy, defense against Indians, and general welfare of the community. These were: Don Martín De León, Fernando De León, Valentin Garcia, Pedro Gallardo, Rafael Manchola, Leonardo Manso, J. M. J. Carvajal, Julian de la Garza, Plácido Benavides, and Silvestre De León, the two last named being captains of militia in case of need against the Indians.

³ There is local conjecture that Margaret Wright may have been Theodosia Burr, the lost daughter of former Vice-President Aaron Burr. Portraits of Theodosia do reveal a striking similarity between her facial features and those of Margaret and her descendants. Theodosia was born in New York in 1783. Her mother, Theodosia Bartow Prevost, was the widow of a British officer when she married Aaron. The daughter was devoted to her father and presided over the family household after Mrs. Burr's death. In 1801 this brilliant, talented young woman married Joseph Alston, the future governor of South Carolina. It was rumored that Theodosia loved another man and had an unhappy home life. After her ten-year-old son died in June 1812, the sick, heartbroken Mrs. Alston decided to join her father in New York after a four-year separation. On December 30, 1812, Theodosia

19

English father and French mother in New Orleans in 1789. Madame Trudeau, as she was first called, lost two husbands in Louisiana before leaving Natchitoches at age thirty-six to start a new life in Texas. Marguerite had a son, Peter, and two daughters by her first husband, James William Hays, who was probably killed in the War of 1812. The widow then had two more daughters from a common law marriage with Felix Trudeau, a merchant, trader, and civilian commander of Natchitoches, Louisiana, before he died at age fifty-eight. Nearly three years later, Marguerite, Peter, and her two youngest daughters went to Texas. After a short stay around Gonzales in 1825, Madame Trudeau arrived on the Guadalupe and settled in the Mission Valley area on the west bank of the river six miles above Victoria, land that was later the ranch of Edward Power. Although Don Martín recognized her as one of his colonists, he did not grant the title to her league of land.

In 1828 Margaret married a much younger man, John David Wright, at a chapel in Victoria and they soon had two daughters of their own. By 1834 Wright had secretly obtained title to his wife's land. The Texas Revolution found him in hiding near Matamoros due to a bad debt in Mississippi, leaving Margaret and the children to fend for themselves at Mission Valley. At that very time

---

sailed from Charleston on the *Patriot,* but the ship was never seen again. Most likely the vessel was sunk during a violent storm off Cape Hatteras, but some think it was seized by pirates. According to the latest story, Theodosia was the only survivor of a pirate ship destroyed by a hurricane when she was washed ashore near Matagorda years later. Although suffering from amnesia, she told of being the daughter of "a great white chief" and displayed a locket with the name Theodosia on it. Is it possible that this same mystery woman made her way to the Victoria area?

The reader may wish to refer to "Possible Solution of Age-Old Mystery: Was Pioneer Victorian Theodosia Burr?" in *Pictorial History of Victoria and Victoria County* by Leopold Morris. This local legend, however, is convincingly refuted by author Bettye Welborn Cole (a descendant of Margaret Wright) in *A Passing of the Seasons, The Story of Marguerite Wright.*

Mrs. Wright became a legend and Victoria's "Angel of Mercy" after risking her own life and property by hiding, nursing, and feeding a number of Fannin's soldiers who escaped the Goliad Massacre. After finding these survivors when she went to the river to draw water, Margaret daily supplied them with food and other necessities based on written requests they left in the hollow of a tree. Remarkably, she kept them safe and gave them a gun she managed to steal from a Mexican soldier, even though her home and property were fruitlessly searched several times by Mexican patrols. One of the soldiers she helped was William A. Hunter, later a judge and representative from Refugio County in the Texas Congress. In his deposition in her divorce case, he said, "I had been badly wounded at Goliad [he was bayoneted, shot, and clubbed with the butt of a gun] and was carried to Mrs. Wright's house by Juan Reyna, remaining there until I recovered — about three weeks." Because of these heroics and since she was such an early settler, Sam Houston in 1857 called Margaret the "Mother of Texas" while campaigning at Diamond Hill in Victoria. She owned 300 head of cattle by 1836; the census of 1840 showed the Wrights as owning 6,642 acres of land.

Twelve of the Mexican families settled with De León at Guadalupe Victoria in October 1824; the other twenty-nine families arrived by 1829. Each head of family was entitled to a league (4,428 acres) of grazing land, a labor (177 acres) of farm land, and a homestead building lot in the townsite. The original land grants to the forty-one families were issued under terms of the state colonization law of 1825 and included some grants to Irish and Anglo settlers.[4]

---

[4]   The original colonists were Fernando De León (commissioner); Silvestre, Felix, and Agapito De León; J. M. J. Carvajal (surveyor); José Luis Carvajal; Fulgencio Bueno; John D. Wright; J. M. Escalera, Sr.; J. N. Escalera; J. M. Escalera, Jr.; Valentin Garcia; Leonard Manso; Nicolas Benavides; Desiderío Garcia; Rafael Chovel; Julian de la Garza; Pedro Gonzales; J. Guajardo; Carlos Holguin;

All of the settlers were carefully screened to make sure they were honest, moral Christians and adaptable to the life of pioneer cattlemen. They built their first homes (*"jacals"*) by digging rectangular trenches a foot deep, then setting posts in vertically and tying them at the top with rawhide. The posts were then chinked with rocks and sticks before being plastered inside and out with caliche. The primitive, temporary houses had built-up tamped dirt floors, mud-and-stick fireplaces, and thatched roofs.

Martín De León was entitled to five leagues (22,140 acres) of land after he settled the forty-one families. He located his grant in the eastern extreme of present Victoria County, with Arenosa Creek forming his property line. This land, with Garcitas Creek running through it, became his main cattle ranch. He and Doña Patricia built their first home facing the market square but later built a house of hand-hewn logs nine miles from town on the Guadalupe River. The house, dominated by a large center hall leading to several rooms, contained fine, beautiful furniture including an ornate four-poster bed. It was the most handsomely furnished home in South Texas and was enhanced by the needlework of the De León women.

Ygnacio Mayón; Rafael Manchola; Manuel Dindo; Francisco Cardenas; Francisco De León; Pedro Gallarda; Bonifacio Rodriguez; Alejo Perez; Alvino Cabazos; Agatón Cisneros; Estevan Cisneros; Hipolito Castillo; Estevan Galvan; Simón Rios; John McHenry; Joseph Ware; Plácido Benavides; Ysidro Benavides; Eugemio Benavides; Francisco Vallarreal; Carlos Laso; Manuel Solis; John Linn; J. J. Linn; Edward Linn; Charles Linn; Manuel Dindo (a physician); and Francisco Cardenas (a schoolteacher).

One of the Anglo settlers, John McHenry, was a renowned character in early Victoria. After joining Jean Lafitte's band of pirates on Galveston Island in 1818, McHenry enlisted in Dr. James long's filibustering expedition that briefly captured La Bahía in October 1821. When Dr. Long surrendered to the Spanish, John and the others were briefly imprisoned. After their release, Captain McHenry drifted to the Victoria area, became a De León colonist, and served as first county judge of Victoria County in 1838.

It seems the female De Leóns were very fashion-conscious. Doña Guadalupe De León bought three silk dresses, a pair of earrings, and a gold chain with locket during a New Orleans shopping trip. The family also traveled in style, using coaches or carriages with gold hubs and trim. Private tutors were imported for their children, while the grandchildren were educated in Paris, London, and Madrid. From such travels an impressive picture portfolio of famous family friends still survives, including those of Napoleon Bonaparte, Queen Victoria, Queen Isabel of Spain, Emperor Maximilian and Carlotta, and President Juarez of Mexico.

In 1824 Don Martín founded St. Mary's Catholic Church, a temporary chapel of hand-hewn logs facing the market square and on the site of the present Post Office. It was thus the second oldest Catholic parish in Texas, with only San Fernando Cathedral in San Antonio being older. At first Father José Antonio Valdez came from La Bahía to provide Catholic services; then Father Eubaldus Estany became the resident priest. The Catholic faith was the only religion authorized by the Mexican government, and public worship in any other form or name was illegal. St. Mary's Church was rebuilt between 1850 and 1853 on the original site of Doña Patricia De León's first house and next to the present Nazareth Convent. At that time, one of the church windows was dedicated to the De León family; Doña Patricia gave a gold and silver monstrance (religious receptacle) that is still in use.

Don Martín quickly came into conflict with Green De Witt, a neighboring *empresario* to the northwest, over the issues of land claims and contraband trade. On April 15, 1825, De Witt, a former sheriff of Ralls County, Missouri, was authorized to settle 400 families between the Lavaca and Guadalupe rivers, beginning ten leagues from the coastline and running north to the Old San Antonio road. Green received this colonial grant at Saltillo

23

Coach similar to type owned by De León family, restored by the De León Club of Victoria.

Photo by J. C. Hoke, Wharton, Texas

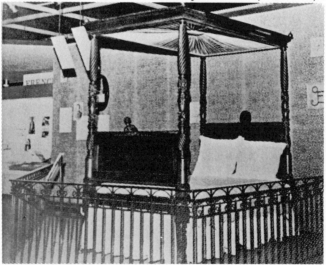

Don Martín De León's bed, now the property of Mrs. Kate Stoner O'Connor of Victoria, Texas.

Courtesy of the late Adm. A.B.J. Hammett,
Victoria, Texas

under terms of the state colonization law but was required to respect the ownership rights of those settlers who were already legally within his grant. En route to inspect his colony capital of Gonzales, he was surprised to find the center portion of his grant occupied by twelve Mexican families of the De León colony, who had already cultivated crops and organized a town. When De Witt wrote the governor suggesting that De León be given lands along the Guadalupe in exchange for his claims along the Lavaca, Don Martín defended his position to the governor, who ordered the land commissioner to approve titles of the De León colonists in October 1825.

Tensions increased between the two *empresarios* after July 1826, when Gonzales was destroyed during an Indian raid and the De Witt colony surveyor-general, Maj. James Kerr, moved to a safer site near the coast.[5]

---

[5] James Kerr, the first Anglo-American settler west of the Colorado River, has been called the Daniel Boone of Texas. He was born near Danville, Kentucky, on September 24, 1790. After his mother Patience died, he moved to St. Charles County, Missouri, with his father, a Baptist minister, in 1808. Reverend Kerr died three years later, and all four surviving sons served as volunteers in the War of 1812. James joined a company of mounted militia and was second in command to Capt. Nathan Boone during several Indian campaigns. After the war, Kerr was sheriff of St. Charles County, then married Angelina Caldwell in July 1818 and moved to St. Genevieve County to be near her father, Gen. James Caldwell. Kerr was very popular among young voters and was twice elected to the state House of Representatives. In 1824 his enthusiastic supporters put him up against his own father-in-law, the incumbent state senator, and James won without even campaigning for the post. When the dictatorial, indignant old general refused to speak to the winner or his own daughter, Kerr resigned from the Missouri Senate. His close friend, Stephen F. Austin, persuaded him to come to Texas, and he accepted the post of surveyor-general for Green De Witt's colony.

Soon after the Kerr family arrived at Brazoria in 1825, the frail Angelina died at Perry's Landing in June and was buried in a hollowed oak log. Within weeks the two boys, Ison and John James, died en route to San Felipe. Their father left his only surviving child, three-year-old Mary Margaret, there to live with a Mrs. Pettus. In August 1825 Kerr and six young helpers, including Deaf Smith, built some crude cabins and laid out the De Witt colony capital of Gonzales

25

He chose to relocate in present Jackson County some miles up the Lavaca River, where he built some block-houses on the west bank and his own permanent home nearby on the east side of the river. This temporary receiving station for the De Witt colonists was referred to by Kerr as the "Old Station" and was well under way by September 1826.

In April 1826 De Witt and his family left Missouri for Texas and reached the mouth of the Lavaca in July.

---

on Kerr's Creek, near the junction of the Guadalupe and San Marcos rivers; this site was a mile east of the present town, and Kerr named it for Rafael Gonzales, the state governor. While Kerr was away on business at San Felipe, Gonzales was destroyed by marauding Comanche and Wichita warriors on July 2, 1826. The attack caused James to relocate nearer the coast on the Lavaca River, where he built a fort called "Old Station" and continued to survey De Witt's colony. His permanent home there also became a general rendezvous for new arrivals.

In May 1827 James received title to a league of land in present Jackson County as one of the "Old Three Hundred" and raised the first crop in the county. That August, Ben Milam executed a power of attorney to Kerr to manage the adjoining colony in his absence. After Green De Witt and his colonists were ordered to move back to Gonzales in late 1827, James was left alone with little Mary Margaret at their home on the Lavaca. He remarried in September 1833, taking Sarah Grace Fulton, the foster daughter of John J. Linn of Victoria, as his bride.

Major Kerr played a leading role in Texas revolutionary politics. He was a delegate to both the Convention of 1832 and 1833 and presided over the protest Lavaca-Navidad Meeting of July 1835. James was also elected to the Consultation at San Felipe in November 1835, but did not attend; at the time he was in the successful expedition against Lipantitlan, a Mexican fort on the Nueces River. Upon returning from the frontier, Kerr was appointed a member of the General Council by the Consultation. He and his neighbor, Elijah Stapp, were elected delegates from Jackson municipality to the convention meeting at Washington-on-the-Brazos on March 1, 1836. The two drew straws to see which one would go or stay behind and lead their families to safety. Elijah won and went on to gain fame as a signer of the Texas Declaration of Independence. After interim President David Burnet appointed him a major in the Texas army in March 1836, James sent his family to Missouri.

In 1838 Major Kerr represented Jackson County in the House of

Convinced that the Old Station was the only convenient port of entry for his colonists, he contracted for the schooner *Dispatch* to bring immigrants and cargo to the colony and built a large flatboat and warehouse near the mouth of the Lavaca. De León became suspicious when Major Kerr maintained that De Witt should be granted both banks of the Lavaca. In July 1826 Kerr wrote Stephen F. Austin and alleged that a small boat of a De Witt colonist had been destroyed either by Martín De León or his sons. The next month Major Kerr levied a more serious charge against Don Martín. Writing to Austin from San Antonio, he said:

> . . . Delion [De Leon] has committed some atrocious outrages on some American travelers, who were on their way here on business with the Gov't. . . . I shall lay the memorial of Mr. Stout before the Chief today relative to Delion's ill-treating and robbing him. . . . It appears that the Chief is determined to consider Delion an empresario over an undefined District for 40 families, and wishes the bounds between De Witt and Delion to be agreed upon by themselves. I have proposed to let Delion go Eastward to the Grassite [Garcitas] and up and down the Guadalupe for quantity: giving De Witt all the Labacca [Lavaca]: but will not make an order to that effect without the consent of Delion. . . .
>
> It appears that De Witt will have to appeal to the Gov't to obtain his rights. This however will, I presume, depend on the advice you may give on the subject. . . .

---

the Third Congress and introduced bills to prevent dueling and to remove the capital from Houston to Austin. He then retired from public life to devote more time to his growing family; Thomas Richard was born February 15, 1841. Late in life James Kerr went to New Orleans to study medicine and spent his last years as a physician. After a brief bout with pneumonia, Dr. Kerr died at his old Lavaca home on December 23, 1850, and was buried on the premises beneath a handsome marble vault. On January 26, 1856, Kerr County was created by the state legislature and named in his honor, with Kerrville as the county seat. A state historical marker has been placed near the old Kerr cemetery eight miles north of Edna on Farm Road 822.

It was the issue of contraband trade, however, that triggered an open conflict between De León and De Witt. In October 1826 Thomas Powell, a De Witt colonist from Missouri, landed at the mouth of the Lavaca and received permission to store his cargo at Old Station. Powell's trade goods included a large quantity of prohibited tobacco, which was not exempt from import duties. After someone informed the political chief at Bexar, he authorized Don Martín to investigate the matter. De León, his son-in-law Capt. Rafael Manchola, and some troops from La Bahía then paid a visit to the Old Station. The aroused founder of Victoria took his sword along and was heard to say that he intended to come with De Witt's head tied to his saddle. Upon reaching their destination, Don Martín's search party disarmed all the De Witt colonists, confiscated *all* of Powell's cargo, arrested Green De Witt, and took him and the goods to La Bahía. Evidently, Austin intervened and acted as mediator, for the entire matter was dropped and De Witt was back at the Old Station by December 1826.

This contraband controversy did irreparable damage to the De Witt colony. The unnerved De Witt blamed De León for the whole affair, contending that Don Martín was trying to ruin his colonial efforts. In July 1827 De Witt left Old Station for two months to recruit settlers in the United States. He gave Major Kerr power of attorney during his absence. On August 29, 1827, Political Chief Saucedo ordered all of De Witt's colonists to leave Old Station and move to Gonzales, an action that was completed by that December. Saucedo also "suggested" that no more De Witt settlers arrive by way of the Lavaca River, knowing full well that the alternative of overland immigration was much longer and more arduous. After De Witt's contract expired on April 15, 1831, and was not renewed, De León was given freedom to colonize all De Witt colony vacant lands near his own.

Noah Smithwick, a blacksmith and gunsmith from Tennessee, first visited Texas in the summer of 1827.

After spending time at De Witt's Old Station, he next visited the Victoria area. In his published reminiscences Noah had this to say about De León's colony:

> We struck out on foot and reached Victoria, or De León's town, as it was then called. There was but one white man in the place, and with him we stopped. . . . Martín De León had settled his grant with Mexicans, most of them being his peons and vaqueros. He had a large stock of both horses and cattle, . . . Señor De León was the very essence of hospitality, as, indeed, I found the Mexicans everywhere to be. He had his caballada driven in for us to choose from. The vaqueros rode in among them caracoling and swinging their lariats, the horses reared and snorted, and we concluded walking would be pleasant pastime compared to riding such steeds, so we continued our journey on foot.

The favorable impression Don Martín made on visitor Smithwick contrasted with the opinion of adjoining *empresarios* who thought that the cultured, aristocratic old grandee was a disagreeable neighbor, one who was favored by Mexican officials and who openly resorted to petty, spiteful, or violent acts against Anglo colonists.

The principal source of wealth for the De León colony was trade in branded cattle, horses, and mules driven to the New Orleans and Opelousas markets. "Bronchos" or wild, unbroken mustangs by the thousands were rounded up, broken, tamed, and sold in Louisiana. Such volume sales could quickly make one rich. The large Mexican ranches in the area also teemed with wild mission cattle (soon to be called Texas cattle or Longhorns) left behind when Mission Espíritu Santo was moved from Mission Valley to Santa Dorotea (Goliad) in 1749. These cattle grazed on waving prairie grass that grew from four to six feet high. Massive "cowhunts" by the many fine *vaqueros* in the colony were common; it was a simple matter to secure title to a piece of land, register a brand, and then claim and brand any mavericks.

Martín De León's largest holding of ranch land was a 25,000-acre spread on Garcitas Creek near the site of LaSalle's old Fort St. Louis. After De León's family was forced to flee Texas, the ranch was eventually purchased by John Newbanks Keeran. Renamed the California Ranch, it is still intact today nine miles east of Inez. Don Martín's centuries-old Jesuit cattle brand (the connected letters "E" and "J" which stands for "Espiritus de Jesus") is the oldest one in Texas, dating from 1807. He even had his own special formula for curing cowhides and drying leather.

Since his cattle ranch was in the midst of Karankawa country, raids were a constant concern. The first time a "Kronk" war party visited his ranch, only Don Martín, his wife, and two servants were at home. The *empresario* quickly planted his big cannon at the front door, with Doña Patricia standing by holding a firing match. The armed servants were stationed at portholes while De León stepped outside to confront the warriors, rifle in hand. Intimidated by this show of force, the Karankawa chief agreed to a friendly powwow and was given a beef for their dinner. From then on, Don Martín maintained an uneasy truce by raising a white flag, butchering some Longhorns, and feeding the raiding party all the beef they could hold. It is no wonder that the Karankawas called him "Vaca Mucha" or "plenty of cows."

In early 1827 Stephen F. Austin initiated a general campaign against the Karankawas, whom he described as follows:

> . . . the Karankawas may be called universal enemies of man — they killed all nations that came in their power, and frequently feast on the bodies of their victims — the [approach of] an American population will be the signal of their extinction for there will be no way of subduing them but extermination.

During this bloody campaign, the majority of the military forces were from Austin's colony. However, a number of De León's colonists participated as did a few from De Witt's Old Station. Austin also had the assistance of Gen. Anastacio Bustamante and a large number of Mexican regular troops who had been sent to Texas to suppress the Fredonian Rebellion. The greatly outnumbered "Kronks" were hounded ruthlessly and finally driven into Matagorda Bay, where half of them were killed or drowned. The hundred survivors had no choice but to sue for peace. On May 13, 1827, a peace treaty was concluded at Victoria with Green De Witt, James Kerr, and Martín and Fernando De León among the signers.

After a series of Karankawa attacks around Victoria in 1834, the De León colonists decided to try a new tack by poisoning their enemy. They ordered a supply of arsenic but received cream of tartar instead. Hominy laced with the supposed poison was "charitably" given to the red men, who took it to their camp and ravenously devoured it. The next morning Don Martín was astounded when they returned asking for more. The *empresario* then determined to fight "fire with fire" by forming an alliance with the Tonkawa Indians and persuading them to assassinate their former friends. The scheme involved having the two tribes meet near Goliad, supposedly to discuss a joint attack on the De León colony. During the feast, all of the Karankawa warriors fell into a drunken stupor while a small Tonkawa boy went through the camp cutting the strings of their long bows. After twelve of the defenseless Karankawa braves were stabbed to death, the Tonkawa chief took their scalps to De León and proceeded to hold a "scalp dance" on the market square. Late in 1834, militia captains Plácido Benavides and Silvestre De León led a company of Mexican and Anglo colonists to victory over the Karankawas in a pitched battle at Green Lake in Calhoun County.

The four De León sons were issued land titles between January 1833 and September 1834. The youngest son, Agapito, located his league just north of his father's ranch while the eldest, Fernando, took land east of Agapito's with Arenosa Creek as his boundary. The second oldest son, Silvestre, located his league up the Guadalupe River from Victoria in the present Nursery area, with brother Felix located just to the west across the river. Felix De León was a stockman supplying the New Orleans market. When he married Doña Sálome Leal in 1827, the event was recorded in the capitals of Europe and Mexico. As commissioner of the colony, it was Fernando's responsibility to issue land titles; however, in practice most of the actual work was done by his secretary, Plácido Benavides, who came to the colony with his older brothers Ysidro, Nicolas, and Eugenio in 1828. Silvestre and Plácido also served as militia captains charged with protecting the colonists against Indian attacks. They once pursued some Tonkawas to their peninsular retreat and brought back eighteen Tonkawa children who were divided among the citizenry and baptized.

The studious Silvestre was elected to the office of alcalde in 1830 and proved his impartiality by ruling against his father. It seems that a poor man complained to the new alcalde that Don Martín had wilfully killed his hog. However, the elder De León justified the act on the grounds that the hog had destroyed his garden. When his son asked if he had a "lawful fence," Don Martín admitted that it was not the best, then asked if the alcalde would give judgment against his own father. Silvestre replied that although he remained the dutiful son off the bench, he must rule with strict impartiality in performing his official duties. He then assessed damages of twenty dollars. Don Martín promptly paid that sum and remarked that he was proud of such a son.

Silvestre's influence on a Mexican officer may have affected the outcome of the Battle of Velasco of June 1832. Before the Texian assault, Colonel Ugartechea sent a courier to Victoria seeking reinforcements. Mexican Captain Artiaga sought the advice of Silvestre, who convinced him that none of his men would reach Velasco alive, that the Texians hidden in the dense "Caney Swamp" could pick them off with impunity. Thus the beleaguered Ugartechea received no help from Victoria.

In 1829 Martín De León was authorized to settle 150 more families on the ten littoral leagues along the coast, an area that had earlier been off-limits to settlement. Among the more notable newcomers was John Joseph Linn, an Irishman the Mexicans called Juan. He was born in County Antrim, Ireland, on June 19, 1789. After his father, a college professor, was involved in a rebellion and forced to flee to New York, the family joined him at Poughkeepsie in 1800. John Joseph started a mercantile business at New Orleans in 1822 and caught the Texas "bug" while on a visit to Mexico. He reached Victoria in the summer of 1829 but never accepted the league of land he was entitled to; instead, he took a town lot fronting the market square and built a substantial native cypress house there in 1829, the home he lived in until his death.[6] Quick to master the Spanish language, Juan started a mercantile business and built a Victorian warehouse. A man of great tact and diplomacy, he was liked and trusted by his Mexican neighbors and became their liaison with Anglo settlers. In the spring of 1831, Juan's parents and younger brothers, Charles and Edward, joined him at Victoria. He married Margaret C. Daniel at New Orleans in April 1834, a union that produced fourteen children. In 1836 he founded a port on Lavaca Bay called Linnville, where he built a warehouse and wharf. (This port of entry for goods from New Orleans to San Antonio was attacked and destroyed during the great Comanche raid of August 1840.) Juan Linn's bridging of two alien cultures was demonstrated when he was elected the last alcalde of Victoria, then its first mayor.

---

[6] Linn's house has long since disappeared. The site is now occupied by the McCabe-Carruth Funeral Home, 301 South Bridge Street, which faces the Victoria City Hall Square.

All of the De Leóns were devout Catholics,[7] and it was Don Martín's dream to build a magnificent cathedral in Victoria to rival those of Mexico and Europe. It seemed that this goal would become a reality after he completed sketches and estimates for the project and contracted for construction workers from Mexico and Spain. Then a cholera epidemic swept through Victoria and claimed the sixty-eight-year-old Don Martín as its first victim in August 1834. At the time of his death, Victoria had a population of almost 300, the wealth of the De León colony was estimated at one million dollars, and the De León family was worth at least half of that total. The founder of Victoria was buried in the courtyard behind his beloved St. Mary's Church. Upon his father's death, the eldest son Fernando became at age forty-four the nominal head of the De León family.

Don Martín's sons-in-law were also destined for lead-

---

[7] A remarkable story passed down through generations of the De León family asserts that Don Martín's religious faith actually saved his life. It seems that he once returned to Texas alone after selling a herd of bronchos and mules in New Orleans. When a desperado saw him leave for home with a packed money belt, he decided to trail De León, bide his time, then kill and rob him en route at some isolated camp. After Don Martín crossed the Sabine and reached a stretch of uninhabited East Texas, the robber decided to strike one foggy evening. Even when camping out, it was De León's custom to recite prayers to each of the twelve Apostles just before turning in. It was almost midnight and the campfire was down to embers when the *empresario* said his prayers, then fell asleep. The highwayman was about to pounce on his prone victim when, through the mist, he suddenly saw twelve ghostly figures slowly circling the sleeping cattleman; one member of this eerie guard had only one leg and was hobbling as best he could. An attack seemed out of the question to the startled outlaw so he fled into the night, never to return. Years later he happened to encounter Don Martín and told him of the abortive robbery. De León was truly amazed to hear this tardy confession, particularly when he recalled that night camping out in East Texas. He distinctly remembered falling asleep before finishing the twelfth and final prayer. His conclusion was that the apparition must have been the twelve Apostles guarding him, with the incomplete figure being his unfinished prayer.

ership. In 1831 Plácido Benavides married Doña Augustina De León, and the couple took their league and labor of land on a stream later known as Placido Creek, adjoining the holdings of his brother, Don Eugenio. Plácido was elected alcalde of Victoria in 1832 and 1834; during this time he built his "Round Top House," a fortress that was used by all the colonists during Indian raids and so named because its top story resembled an old-fashioned conical beehive.[8]

It was Alcalde Benavides who led the resistance which prevented another De León son-in-law, Bexar Representative José M. J. Carvajal, from being arrested by Mexican troops at Victoria. After Santa Anna dissolved the state legislature in the fall of 1835, Colonel Ugartechea ordered Carvajal brought to Mexico City to stand trial for treason. At a meeting of Victoria citizens, thirty determined men offered to confront the Mexican troops coming to arrest the legislator. After the soldiers rode into the public square, the armed residents closed in from all sides and alcalde Benavides informed the commanding officer that he would not deliver *any* citizen of Victoria into the hands of the military. The embarrassed sergeant then ordered his men to mount and go to the river, where they camped for the night. The next morning the sergeant visited Juan Linn and confessed that he too was politically opposed to Santa Anna before ordering his men back to San Antonio empty-handed.

A third son-in-law, Rafael Manchola, served as Don Martín's attorney and was also commandant of the Mexican garrison at Presidio La Bahía. After marrying María De Jesús De León, they settled at La Bahía and Rafael was elected alcalde. While serving as a deputy to

---

[8] During the great Comanche raid of August 6, 1840, which took the lives of fifteen settlers near Victoria, the families in town found a safe haven in this stronghold. The Round Top house stood at 302 South Main, a site occupied today by the old Fossati's Delicatessen on the opposite end of the block from the present Post Office and Federal Building.

the state legislature, he petitioned that body to change the name of the town to Goliad, an anagram for the revolutionary hero Hidalgo, and the request was granted on February 4, 1831. A fourth son-in-law, José Miguel Aldrete, and Manchola took turns as alcalde of Goliad during the colonial period.

As advocates of the federal Constitution of 1824 and enemies of military dictator General Santa Anna, the De León colonists took the Anglo side when the Texas Revolution erupted in 1835–36. After driving horses to New Orleans in November 1835, Fernando De León purchased $35,000 worth of supplies, arms, and ammunition for use by Texas volunteers and chartered the schooner *Anna Elizabeth* to bring the munitions to Texas. However, the ship was spotted by the Mexican revenue cutter *Montezuma* near Matagorda, run ashore at Pass Cavallo, and seized. (Later, some enterprising citizens from Matagorda sailed down in the *William Robbins,* recaptured the *Anna Elizabeth* from the Mexican prize crew, and kept the cargo for themselves.) Don Fernando and J. M. J. Carvajal were taken prisoners on board the Mexican ship and thrown into jail at the port of Brazos de Santiago near Matamoros. Although De León escaped during an exercise period and returned to a hero's welcome at Victoria, he lost all of his uninsured investment, even a carriage he had purchased in New Orleans for family use. On February 14, 1836, acting Governor James W. Robinson appointed Don Fernando as an aide-de-camp for the purpose of organizing the Victoria militia. The eldest De León son also donated goods for the Texas army at San Jacinto.

Plácido Benavides and Silvestre De León led a company of thirty Mexican ranchers from the Victoria area which reinforced the Texians during the siege and assault on Bexar in December 1835. Silvestre also provided much of the military equipment and provisions used at the Alamo and San Jacinto. After the taking of Bexar, Captain Benavides and volunteers from Refugio and Goliad joined Dr. James Grant on an expedition toward Matamoros, Mexico. The party of thirty traveled to some ranches near the Rio Grande and captured fifty to sixty good horses for the Texas cavalry. On the way back they were ambushed by some of Gen. José Urrea's dragoons at Agua Dulce Creek on March 2, 1836, with all of Grant's party being killed except Benavides and a man named Brown. After making good his escape and warning Colonel Fannin at Goliad of the approaching Mexican army, Plácido returned to Victoria to protect his family.

Upon hearing news of the Battle of Gonzales, Juan Linn and Captain Benavides went there and joined the company of Capt. John Alley. During the same period, Mexican Captain Saviriago, in command at Goliad, went to Victoria and took possession of a mounted three-pound cannon belonging to the De León family. Linn left Gonzales in November 1835 when he was chosen as a delegate to the Consultation at San Felipe. In early 1836 Juan was elected alcalde of Victoria, defeating a Mr. Garcia by a margin of sixteen votes. One of his first official acts was preparing a reception for the "Red Rovers," Captain Shackleford's volunteer company from northern Alabama. After reaching Dimmitt's Landing, the company marched to Victoria, where they were quartered and entertained before meeting their tragic fate in the Goliad Massacre.

Linn and José M. J. Carvajal were elected as the Victoria delegates to the historic convention meeting at Washington-on-the-Brazos on March 1, 1836. However, both missed signing the Texas Declaration of Independence only because they learned en route that General Santa Anna's army had reached San Antonio; at that point the two turned back to look after their families. Linn was then appointed quartermaster for Fannin's command at La Bahía and forwarded him needed supplies, including corn and twenty yoke of oxen.

Alcalde Linn ordered the evacuation of Victoria on March 17, 1836. His close friend, Fernando De León, provided him with two yoke of oxen for a cart and small wagon to carry his wife, infant daughter, and a few necessities to the safety of Fernando's ranch on Garcitas Creek. After leaving his family there, Juan traveled through a deserted Texana on his way to join Houston's retreating army. Only minutes after his departure, a Mexican officer, Captain Holtzinger, arrived at the De León ranch and informed the owner of Fannin's surrender and Urrea's occupation of Victoria; Fernando was to report there within three days. Upon reaching the encamped Texas army at Groce's Landing, Linn spent three days with General Houston and was asked for his opinion on the military and political situation. After learning that Juan had a schooner due from New Orleans, Houston sent him to join interim President Burnet on Galveston Island where Linn donated his ship's cargo — $3,600 worth of critically needed groceries and supplies — to the indigent Texian army after the Battle of San Jacinto. President Burnet asked Juan to interview the prisoner Santa Anna, then charged him with supplying the vanquished Mexican army on their retreat toward the Rio Grande.[9]

After the battle of Coleto and the Goliad Massacre,

---

[9] In his book *Victor Rose's History of Victoria,* the historian describes Linn's interview with Santa Anna as follows:

> . . . The disconsolate president-general was found in a tent alone, apparently immersed in his own gloomy reflections, and oblivious to all surrounding objects. But when the name of his visitor was announced, he looked up with a degree of animation, and exclaimed: "Ah, you come from Guadalupe Victoria!" He proved quite voluble, and entered freely into a discussion of pending issues. "We were mutually mistaken," he said. "Mexico and Texas did not understand each other. We must become acquainted, when confidence will necessarily result. . . ."

The first newspaper correspondent report of the Battle of San Jacinto and interview with Santa Anna was the one sent to the New Orleans *Bee* and *Bulletin* by John J. Linn. It was dispatched from Galveston on April 28, 1836, and appeared in the *New Orleans Bulletin* on May 11.

Victoria was occupied by Gen. José Urrea's Quautla Dragoons from March 31 to May 14, 1836. Since most of the De León colonists were native Mexicans and had supported the Texian revolutionary cause, they were branded traitors and made to suffer by the Mexican occupying forces. Fernando De León was singled out for vengeful treatment. He was arrested and forced at gunpoint to lead Mexican soldiers to a ravine at Dimmitt's Landing, where contraband, corn, beeves, and horses were hidden. It was his alleged complicity in the seizure of these goods that caused Fernando to be hated and distrusted by newcomers and hounded by lawsuits for the amount confiscated in his later years. After the Battle of San Jacinto, General Urrea released Fernando upon the condition that he and his brothers would leave Texas and retire to Mexico. During the occupation, the abandoned home and premises of Juan Linn were also plundered; even the piano of Mrs. Linn was carted off to Matamoros.[10]

---

[10] Capt. Teleforo Alvarez and his saintly wife Francisca resided in Linn's house during the Mexican occupation. They had arrived at the port of El Copano on March 17, 1836, just after Maj. William P. Miller and his Nashville Battalion of seventy-five volunteers were captured there. The Mexican garrison had hidden behind the bluff, making it appear that the port was deserted, so many of Miller's unarmed men jumped overboard to swim to shore. When the Mexican cavalry suddenly dashed into view, the surprised Nashville volunteers surrendered without resistance. Señora Alvarez ordered that the American prisoners be given refreshments and have their tight arm bonds removed before they were taken to Goliad. Since they had landed in Texas *without arms in their hands,* Santa Anna used this technicality to separate Miller's men from those of Fannin and to exempt them from the massacre. When Francisca learned the night before that Fannin's men were going to be shot, she interceded with Colonel Garay, who promised to save all he could. The brave *señora* also visited the fort that night, managed to spirit some prisoners away, and concealed them on a fort parapet until after the massacre. As the doomed United States volunteers were filing out to their death on that Palm Sunday morning, Francisca persuaded a Mexican officer to give her custody of a young boy, thus saving one more life. For these exploits she became known as the "Angel of Goliad."

Señora Alvarez undertook an even more dangerous mission of

39

The situation went from bad to worse for the De León colonists when the Texas army "liberated" Victoria. Don Fernando was again arrested on unspecified charges and suffered a painful wound when shot by a sniper named Brantley while bathing in the Guadalupe River. Gen. Thomas J. Rusk established his headquarters at Victoria and took defensive measures anticipating a Mexican invasion. After cancelling all furloughs and leaves in late June 1836, he issued orders for the detention and removal of all Mexicans suspected of being sympathetic to Mexico. John J. Linn and members of both the De León and Plácido Benavides families were arrested. Linn was promptly released, but it was decided to send the others to New Orleans until the emergency was over.

Most of General Houston's army after San Jacinto were adventurers from the United States who looked upon those with Spanish surnames as enemy aliens. At Victoria these newcomers filed on their lands and took the homes and livestock of the De León settlers as payment for armed services. After they removed all officeholders of Mexican descent, Victoria changed overnight from a Spanish culture town to an English-speaking town. It was during this time that twenty-eight-year-old Agapito De León caught Mabry "Mustang" Gray and his gang in the act of rustling his cattle. When Agapito pointed out his brand on the cattle, Gray killed him. No charges were ever filed for this base murder. Ironically, this is the same killer whose name is enshrined today as

mercy when her husband was ordered to Victoria. After seven members of Col. William Ward's ill-fated Georgia Battalion made their way there, three of them were killed and the others captured. The next day the four were taken out to the market square to be executed. Their lives were dramatically saved when Francisca rushed out to the square from the Linn house, spread her skirts wide to protect the captives from the guard, and announced her willingness to die with them if the Mexicans opened fire. After Santa Anna's surrender, the four were released. Before leaving Victoria, Señora Alvarez received a letter from Major Miller at La Bahía, thanking her for the great kindnesses to his men and for saving his life.

a Texas hero on the San Jacinto Monument (although the name inscribed is Maberry B. Gray).

In late 1836 the De León, Benavides, and Carvajal families went to the port of Linnville and booked passage on a ship bound for New Orleans, taking their jewels and a limited supply of clothing but leaving behind several hundred thousand dollars worth of lands and livestock in the Victoria area. They first settled at Opelousas, Louisiana, where on January 24, 1837, Doña Patricia De León sold her five-league ranch and building improvements to Pleasant Branch Cocke for the paltry sum of $10,000.[11] Plácido Benavides died at Opelousas in 1837 and was buried there. The three families then moved to New Orleans and lived there three years, fending off poverty through manual labor and fine sewing before returning to Soto Del Marina, Tamaulipas, Mexico, in 1839.

Tragedy continued to strike the De León and Benav-

---

[11] Although this deed is on file at St. Landry Parish, Louisiana, descendants of Doña Patricia insist that she never actually sold the De León ranch. In an interview with the author, Wence De León, a great-great-grandson, questioned the authenticity of the deed by pointing out that an "X" was used in place of her signature even though the highly educated Mrs. De León could certainly read *and* write. If she had received the $10,000, why would the family be so financially hard-pressed when they moved on to New Orleans?

In July 1837 records show Mr. Cocke selling the De León ranch to Isaac Franklin of New Orleans for $11,000. In order to satisfy a claim of $1,992.60 in back taxes against the De León estate, this land was sold at public auction to the highest bidder, William Patterson of Victoria, for the incredibly low price of $45.60 in November 1841. As a result of a district court decree of partition in August 1859, one of Don Martín's daughters, Candelaria Aldrete, and two grandsons, Martín and Francisco, claimed Silvestre De León's interest and were awarded two-twentieths of the old De León ranch with the other eighteen-twentieths going to the heirs of Isaac Franklin. By May 1861, all of the De León descendants had sold their interest in the ranch. In a series of six piecemeal transactions between 1875 and 1886, all of Martín De León's original ranch was purchased by Capt. John N. Keeran.

ides families. In 1842 Silvestre was robbed and murdered while returning from a business trip to New Orleans. Plácido's brother, Ysidro Benavides, came back from Louisiana in 1838 and settled on his Chocolate Creek land. In 1843 seven of his friends traveled from Mier, Mexico, to Ysidro's ranch, where they exchanged trade goods for bales of tobacco. The Mexicans were camped on Zarco Creek nine miles beyond Goliad en route home when they were attacked and robbed by the Victoria "cowboys," a group of desperadoes led by "Mustang" Gray. After being tied together, stripped, and blindfolded, the hapless victims were allowed a few minutes to pray before being shot in the head at point-blank range. The only survivor of the massacre was Manuel Escoban, a cousin of Benavides, who miraculously lived through the gunshot barrage despite a terrible face wound. One of the dead was Regalado Moreno, brother of Don Ysidro's wife. Escoban was found wandering about the vicinity and taken first to the Benavides ranch, then to Victoria where his evidence was given. When he was able to travel, Benavides conveyed him to Mier where Manuel later died from the wound's effects. Unfortunately, no attempt was ever made to bring the Anglo murderers to justice although their ringleader, "Mustang" Gray, died of malaria fever at Matamoros in 1847.[12]

---

[12] Gray, the worst Texas badman of his day, became the subject of a book written in 1858 by the Honorable Jeremiah Clemens, United States senator from Alabama. Clemens came to know Mustang when they served together in the Texas army and under Gen. Zachary Taylor in the Mexican War. The senator titled his book *Mustang Gray; A Romance,* and claimed it was based on facts although John J. Linn denounced the book as "imagination" and "mock-heroic fiction." According to Senator Clemens, Mabry Gray came to Texas from South Carolina at age twenty after killing a rival suitor in a duel. Using the Carlos Ranch along the San Antonio River as his hangout, Mustang rustled cattle and horses while serving as the "hit man" for a notorious Corpus Christi smuggler. Author Clemens adds an interesting twist in telling of the Benavides massacre by contending that President Sam Houston had declared Gray an outlaw and put a price on his

In 1844 Fernando De León decided that the family should return to Texas, only to find his lands occupied and cattle confiscated under various false pretensions. His mother also returned to Victoria that year, bringing the Benavides grandchildren with her. She died there in 1849 and was buried beside her husband in the St. Mary's courtyard; Felix De León joined them there the next year.

Don Fernando found a home on his smallest ranch, "Escondida" or "hidden treasure," seven miles north of Victoria in the Mission Valley area. He spent his remaining years there fighting old lawsuits which stripped him of much of his estate.[13] In spite of all his financial trav-

---

head. According to this story, Mustang responded by threatening the life of every Mexican entering Texas who carried an official permit; the Benavides party had permits from Mayor A. M. Wiginton of Victoria.

The book even clothes Gray with some redeeming qualities. During the great Comanche raid of August 1840, he and his "cowboys" were stealing horses in the area when the marauding Indians killed Johnstone and Mary Gilleland at their home on the San Antonio River. When the Comanches took as captives the two Gilleland children, eight-year-old Rebecca and seven-year-old William, a volunteer posse of ranchers chased the raiders to a mott called Willow Grove where the Texians were reinforced by a Ranger company led by Albert Sidney Johnston. In the fierce battle that followed, the Comanches held their own in the timber shelter until Gray and his rustlers joined the fray by attacking them from the rear. Before fleeing, the Indians ran a lance through the white boy and struck his sister a heavy blow to the head, leaving them for dead. Both recovered, however, with Rebecca eventually becoming president of the Daughters of the Republic of Texas and William a distinguished poet.

According to Clemens, a lovely señorita from Mier was with Mustang at the end, and she died while hugging his lifeless body. The two lovers were buried in a double grave on a low mound where the woods and prairie meet along the San Antonio River.

[13] On this Escondida ranch are some unique ruins: a cellarlike excavation walled with solid masonry, located four miles from the site of the old Mission Espíritu Santo and on the opposite bank of the Guadalupe. When hostile Indians forced the mission to relocate at present Goliad in 1749, tradition has it that the padres hid the church valuables in this walled hole before abandoning the Mission Valley area,

ails, the federal census of Victoria County in 1850 listed him as owning land valued at $30,000. This dignified and portly gentleman died at Escondida in 1853 at the age of fifty-five. Later that year, the Catholic church reinterred the bodies of Don Martín, Doña Patricia, and their four sons in one common grave. It is a sad irony that the surviving members of the once-richest family in South Texas had no money to buy a tombstone at the time.

Two of the earliest De León colonists, Margaret Wright and Juan Linn, were to live out their last years in Victoria. After a stormy married life with John David Wright, Margaret filed for divorce in March 1848, the first contested divorce suit in Texas history to reach the Texas Supreme Court. This nasty legal battle covers 153 pages of court records with Mrs. Wright's grounds including desertion, abuse, laying claim to her headright without her knowledge, and the unproven charge that John David ambushed and killed her son, Peter Hays, in September 1847 in a squabble over her land rights. The divorce was granted in 1851 and the property divided according to the court's instructions, but Margaret soon fell on economic hard times. On September 14, 1876, her old friend, John J. Linn, wrote the following article in the *Victoria Advocate:*

> We are informed that Mrs. Margaret Wright, an old and respected citizen of this city, is now suffering for the want of proper care at her home in the upper part of town.
>
> Mrs. Wright is connected with the early history of our town, coming here among the first American settlers, some 50 years ago and in other days has given with an open and generous charity and to many of a sufferer. She is now old and feeble and her condition excites the pity of all.
>
> We suggest that the town authorities pay some at-

---

hence the ancient name of the ranch. The precious cache was later exhumed and moved to the cathedral of Zacatecas.

tention to this matter and give the aid required by this helpless person.

Margaret was to suffer through one final tragedy. One of her daughters, Emma Ann Wright, married Gen. José Ramirez and both were murdered near Eagle Pass in late September 1877, leaving an estate valued at $50,000. It seems that none of this money reached Margaret; she died in an impoverished state at the Victoria home of her youngest daughter, Tennessee Wright Noble Bennett, on October 21, 1878, and the eighty-nine-year-old ranchwoman was buried in Evergreen Cemetery.

John J. Linn served as a member of the House of Representatives in the Second and Third Texas Congress from 1837 until 1839, then was elected first mayor of Victoria that April. He lost much of his fortune when his settlement on Lavaca Bay, Linnville, was burned to the ground during the great Comanche raid on August 8, 1840. The war party of Chief Buffalo Hump burned Juan's wharf and looted his warehouses, fleeing with a two-year supply of merchandise. After statehood, Linn retired from his mercantile business and periodically served as mayor or alderman of Victoria. In the late 1840s he caught "railroad fever" and was one of the stockholders in the county's first railroad, the San Antonio and Mexican Gulf line, which was chartered on September 5, 1850. The first five miles of track were laid at Port Lavaca in 1856, with the first train reaching Victoria on February 20, 1861. During the Civil War, however, Confederate troops ordered the destruction of the railroad and all port city wharves, fearing that the facilities might become a springboard for a Union inland invasion.

Juan Linn spent his last decades in his Victoria home and lived to see his memoirs, *Reminiscences of Fifty Years in Texas,* published in 1883. When this pioneer Irish merchant died at age eighty-eight on October 27, 1885, he was the oldest member of the St. Mary's congregation. His obituary was written by his third son Edward, who served five terms in the state legislature before becoming editor-in-chief of the *Victoria Advocate*. In 1936 the Texas Centennial Commission erected grave monuments in memory of Martín De León and John Joseph Linn in the Evergreen Cemetery at Victoria. At the same time a marker was placed on the Victoria City Hall Square facing the site of Plácido Benavides's Round Top House across the street.

After 120 years of neglect, apathy, and silence, historical and memorial services were held at Victoria on April 8, 1972, to honor the De León family. One service was held at City Hall, where Don Martín's great-granddaughter, Patricia De León, and Dr. Ricardo Victoria, great-grandson of the first president of Mexico, were presented engraved plaques and gold keys to the city. This observance marked the first reunion of these two historical families since 1824. The De León Historical Shrine, framed by a beautiful Spanish iron fence, was also dedicated that day at Evergreen Cemetery. Speakers including U.S. Senator John Tower and U.S. Congressman John Young helped to dedicate five Texas State Historical Markers to Doña Patricia De León and her four sons.

There is a fitting footnote to this story. The many descendants of the original De León colonists who still live in Victoria now send their children to an elementary school named in honor of Martín De León. The Victoria Independent School District Board of Trustees announced the naming of the school in March 1979.

William H. Wharton
Courtesy of Mrs. Ruby Baty,
Wharton, Texas

John A. Wharton
Courtesy of Mrs. Ruby Baty,
Wharton, Texas

Sarah Ann Groce Wharton
Courtesy of Mrs. Ruby Baty,
Wharton, Texas

John Austin Wharton
Courtesy of Mrs. Ruby Baty,
Wharton, Texas

III

The Groces and the Whartons:
Two Generations of Texas Leaders

From 1822 until 1878, the Groce and Wharton families played key roles in the agricultural, political, military, social, and cultural history of Texas. Joined by bonds of marriage, they contributed the "Cotton King" of Texas, a hero at San Jacinto, the Republic's first minister to the United States, two members of the Texas Congress, the hostess for President Lamar, a Confederate general, and the builder of an historic mansion. The families left an indelible mark on the Texas past, and their grand old house has a history of its own.

Jared E. Groce, the patriarch of this remarkable clan, was born on a Virginia plantation in 1782. After moving to Lincoln County, Georgia, in 1804, he married Mary Ann Waller. In 1814 he settled in Alabama, where he founded a settlement and plantation called Groce's Fort.

After being attracted by the generous land terms, Jared became one of Stephen F. Austin's "Old Three Hundred" families and started for Texas in the fall of 1821. He brought a caravan of fifty covered wagons, farm implements, tools, seeds, building materials, a train of livestock, and ninety slaves. Crossing rivers on pontoon bridges, he first came to present Brazoria County but soon concluded that the Gulf Coast climate was too unhealthy. Groce then moved up the Brazos River and founded a settlement called Groce's Landing (or Ferry) four miles south of present Hempstead in January 1822. Because "of the property he brought with him," Jared in 1824 received title to ten leagues of land from Austin — a total of 44,284 acres. Five of the leagues were in present Waller and Grimes counties; the other five in present Brazoria County were divided into three plantations: Eagle Island, Evergreen, and Lake Place. Evergreen was later sold to Alexander Calvit, while Lake Place was purchased by Maj. Abner Jackson and renamed Lake Jackson.

In 1822 Groce built "Bernardo," a house of cottonwood logs hewed and counterhewed as smooth as glass. The rooms were twenty feet square and the fifty-five-foot porch was framed by polished walnut columns. In the backyard was a thirty-by-thirty-foot "Bachelors' Hall" for guests and a cabin for the doctor. For many years Bernardo was considered the finest home in Texas, and Jared was renowned for his lavish displays of hospitality.[1] Mrs. Jane Long was a frequent house guest while

---

[1] There were contrasting views, however, as to the courtesies extended visitors by Jared Groce. In writing of a trip to Texas in 1828, a proud Mexican official, José María Sanchez, recorded the following scathing remark about his reception at Bernardo plantation:

> They did not deign to offer us shelter in the house, even though they saw us camping under the trees. Later, they asked us into the house for the sole purpose of showing us the wealth of Mr. Groce and to introduce us to three dogs called Ferdinand VII, Napoleon, and Bolivar.

For three days in March 1836, interim President David G. Burnet and his cabinet stayed at Jared's last home, Groce's Retreat, in Grimes County. Among the hangers-on was William Fairfax Gray, a well-to-do land speculator and money lender from Virginia. In his diary, Gray made the following caustic comment about their host:

> Some gents had expressed an unwillingness to remain at Groce's, because they thought it imposing on the hospitality of a gentleman too

she lived at nearby San Felipe. The quarters for Groce's hundred slaves were located about three-fourths of a mile from the "big house." These one-room log cabins were twenty feet square and fronted on a large lake. The cabin for each slave family had a door, windows with wooden shutters to keep out the elements, dirt floors covered by animal hides, and a fireplace for cooking and heating. Nearby was the overseer's house, a large kitchen, a dining hall, and a day nursery to care for slave children while their mothers worked.

The daily preparation of food for this slave army was a formidable task. When the wake-up call came at 4:00 A.M. on Bernardo plantation, the men first fed the mules while cooks brewed pots of coffee. Another bell sounded at daylight and all hands assembled at the dining hall for an "eye-opener" cup of coffee. All then headed to the fields, the men to plow and the women to hoe. At 7:00 A.M. a breakfast consisting of ham or bacon, hot biscuits or corn bread, and fresh steak or chicken was packed in tin buckets, placed on carts, and sent to the fields for distribution. Dinner was cooked and served at noon following the same procedure. At either 6:00 P.M. or sundown, all the slaves came to the dining hall for a hot meal.

The Groce family eventually built five princely homes in Texas: Bernardo, Pleasant Hill, and Liendo in Waller County, Groce's Retreat in Grimes County, and Eagle Island in Brazoria County. Jared Groce earned the titles of "Father of Texas Agriculture" and "Cotton King" of Texas after producing the first cotton crop in 1822 and building the first cotton gin in 1828. He eventually owned hundreds of slaves and received an average of $80,000 for his yearly cotton crop. Groce took his first two cotton crops to Mexico by mule caravan in 1824 and

---

much. This delicacy was cured when, on starting, he presented each with a bill for $3 per day, man and horse. My bill was $8 from Friday night to Monday morning.

When he paid off the rich planter, the angry Burnet said in a cool voice, "Here is your money, Mr. Groce."

Wharton flat silverware made from Mexican silver coins.
Courtesy Mrs. Ruby Baty, Wharton, Texas

Desk used by Stephen F. Austin at Peach Point.
Courtesy Stephen S. Perry, Jr.,
Peach Point Plantation

1825 and sold them for Mexican silver dollars. This currency was of little value, however, since the closest stores in which to spend it were at San Antonio and Nacogdoches. For the time being, Jared stacked the bags of silver dollars in the closet under the stairway at Bernardo Starting in 1826, he shipped his cotton to New Orleans.

In 1827 the only Groce daughter, Sarah Ann, graduated from a finishing school in New York City at age seventeen and her oldest brother Leonard brought the "Princess," her lifelong name in Texas, home to Bernardo. (She was named for Jared's mother; also, Sarah is a biblical Hebrew name meaning princess.) The doting father wanted a special touch of elegance for Sarah's homecoming dinner, but most of the family china had been broken or cracked en route to Texas. His problem was solved when a Mr. White, a house guest and silversmith, offered to convert some of the Mexican coin to silver dishes. Colonel Groce surely beamed when Sarah was seated at a dinner table set with shiny new silver plates, cups, and bowls.

While attending a boarding school at Columbus, Tennessee, she had fallen in love with a young lawyer, William H. Wharton, who came from an old but impoverished Nashville family. William and his brother John A. had been orphaned as boys and raised by their uncle, Jesse Wharton, in that city. William studied under Dr. Horace Holley at Transylvania College in Kentucky before graduating in the first class of the University of Nashville. When he and Sarah were married on December 5, 1827, the bride asked her father if she could convert the remaining silver dollars into flat silver dining pieces as a wedding gift. For their wedding trip to Nashville, one of Sarah's three leather trunks was packed with the silver bags beneath her beautiful New York party dresses. While they visited William's married sister, Elizabeth (Betsy) Washington, and Uncle Jesse in Nashville, the silver bags were sent to a New York silversmith along with a letter of instructions as to the number of pieces for the silver place settings. Once the task was completed, a Nashville jeweler provided a leather case lined with velvet dividers for each silver piece. The Whartons stayed at his sister's home for an extended period, and Sarah had her baby there in July 1828. Little John Austin was named after William's brother.

In addition to the silver dollars, Colonel Groce also gave Sarah forty slaves and Eagle Island plantation — 16,000 acres of the finest land in Brazoria County — as wedding presents. The Whartons' new Texas home was located on Oyster Creek in present Clute some twelve miles inland from Velasco. The plantation's name apparently originated when an eagle built her nest in a large live oak tree on the grounds. In early 1828 Jared Groce wrote his brother-in-law, William Waller, at Mobile, Alabama, asking him to supervise the construction of a home for Sarah. The colonel wanted to duplicate a Mobile house he had admired while living at nearby Groce's Fort. Every plank of this white two-story Southern mansion was sawed and numbered at Mobile, then shipped to Texas to become the first frame house and most elegant place of residence in Austin's colony. It was completed by the time the Whartons returned from their long honeymoon trip in 1829.

The Eagle Island "big house" was the size of an ordinary city lot. This mansion was ninety-eight feet long, fifty-two feet wide, and contained twelve rooms with most being twenty feet square. The doors, window facings, and stairway were of solid mahogany. The furnishings included velvet carpets, silk and wool damask curtains, brass chandeliers with crystal prisms, and large full-length gold-framed mirrors in the parlor and dining room. Each bedroom had a four-poster bed with tiesters and silk drapes along with china washstands, bowl and pitcher, slop jars, and commodes. Colonel Groce's slaves made brick from the Brazos clay for the foundation, fireplaces, and walkways. Another ornament of the house

53

was William Wharton's extensive library of books on history, fiction, and poetry; a special prize of the collection was a series of leatherbound books, "A Portrait Gallery of America," about the lives of great Americans. A frequent quest and library user was the urbane Father Michael Muldoon, the resident priest for Austin's colony.

Eagle Island was also said to have the finest gardens in Texas. A landscape gardener was imported from Scotland to tend the figs, oranges, pears, plums, melons, and quince. The grounds comprised some twenty acres shaded by large live oaks and colored by a variety of flowers and shrubs brought from Natchez, Mobile, and Nashville. One could stroll along brick walks bordered by pink and white striped lilies and gaze upon white bridal wreath, yellow jasmine, and pink crape myrtle. Apart from the showplace grounds, Eagle Island was basically a sugar plantation complete with a brick sugar house, a double set of kettles, and frame cabins for the overseer and slaves.

In 1834 the Wharton family took in a motherless little girl. It seems that a Mr. Cleveland, his wife, and their five children had just arrived in Texas from Natchez, Mississippi. Shortly after landing at Velasco, Mrs. Cleveland died of cholera. News of the helpless husband's plight soon reached Eagle Island. Sarah, who had lost her own mother at age two, offered to take ten-year-old Annie Cleveland as her foster daughter. Although Annie was never legally adopted, she continued to live with the Whartons, cared for and educated as if she were their own child. The proud young lady took the family name and always signed her name as "Anne Wharton Cleveland." She later married District Judge Edward T. Branch, a former member of the Texas Congress, in her home at Eagle Island.

William and Sarah soon had some prominent neighbors across the river at Peach Point plantation: Stephen

F. Austin's only sister, Emily Margaret, and her husband James F. Perry.

Emily had married James Bryan at Potosi, Missouri, in 1813 but he died in 1822, leaving her with three small sons: Joel, Moses Austin, and Guy. Two years later, Margaret married Perry, a prosperous Potosi merchant, and they had three more children. After Stephen's younger brother, Brown Austin, died on August 19, 1829, while on a business trip to New Orleans, the "Father of Texas" felt very much alone. Later that year he began to pressure the Perrys to emigrate to Texas as soon as possible. Austin requested an eleven-league grant (48,830 acres) in the names of both Emily and James Perry in order that one-half of the land would benefit her children by the deceased Mr. Bryan.

By June 1831 the Perrys were ready to pull up stakes in Missouri. Traveling overland, they reached San Felipe on August 14. James left his family there and started improvements on his large "stock farm" between Pleasant and Chocolate bayous near present Alvin. Emily and the children followed him there in mid-April 1832. This site, however, was quite isolated and offered no school opportunities for the young Perrys, so Austin chose a better location near Brazoria which afforded both river access and rich soil. On December 27, 1831, he wrote Mr. Perry telling him to "remove all your stock to Peach Point, make corn there in the cane brake — let the work at Chocolate go and begin down here at once . . . The idea of a good house for this year must be abandoned, log cabins must do." In another letter Stephen noted a fresh incentive for relocating: "Mrs. Wharton is a fine woman. Emily will be pleased with her."

The Perrys' first Peach Point house was built in November 1832, and the boat landing for both the Perry and Wharton plantations became known as Perry's Landing. James Perry bought the 1,908 acres from Austin, who drew plans for the house and his own quarters which were not followed.[2]

William Wharton's brother, John A., was practicing law in New Orleans when he wrote to Sam Houston in Washington, D.C., on June 2, 1832, and invited him to come to Texas. This intriguing letter read in part:

> . . . I gave Dr. Branch T. Archer of Virginia a letter of introduction to you; Dr. Archer has been in Texas for upwards of twelve months, is intimately acquainted with matters and things, there, and is in the confidence of all of their leading men. He is of the opinion that there will be some fighting there next fall, and that a fine country will be gained without much bloodshed . . . he is very desirous that you should go there, and believes that you can be of more service than any other man; he left for Virginia today, and should you fall in with him, I expect that he will put you in the notion of going. Texas does undoubtedly present a fine

---

[2] While Austin was imprisoned at Mexico City, he sent his power of attorney to James Perry so that colonists could continue to receive deeds to their lands. After the capital of the Republic of Texas was moved to Columbia, Secretary of State Austin made frequent visits to Peach Point, where a bedroom and study in the Perry home were reserved for his use. In December 1836 a severe cold developed into pneumonia and Austin was put to bed in an unheated shed room in the Columbia home of Judge George B. McKinstry. As his condition worsened, Mr. Perry and Moses Austin Bryan were summoned to his deathbed. The end came on December 27. The last words of the "Father of Texas" were: "Texas recognized. Archer told me so. Did you see it in the papers?" Austin's body was carried to Perry's Landing on the steamboat *Yellowstone,* and he was buried in the family Gulf Prairie Cemetery as the grieving President Sam Houston sprinkled a handful of the rich Peach Point soil over the coffin. Austin rested at Peach Point until 1910, when his body was reinterred in the State Cemetery; an empty tomb still marks his original burial place.

Today only the Austin bedroom and study of the original large Perry home are preserved; the rest of the plantation house was destroyed by the 1909 storm. The tiny two-room white structure contains a variety of memorabilia and serves as a private Perry family museum to Austin's memory. Stephen Samuel Perry, Jr., the present owner of Peach Point, is a fifth-generation direct descendant of the original 1832 settler.

field for fame enterprise, and usefulness, and whenever they are ready for action, I will be with them. I expect to visit my Brother [William H. Wharton] in August, and as matters are getting worse there every day I should like to be provided with a pass port, if you will procure one for me, I will be very thankful, and should it ever lay in my power to confer a favour on you, I will not forget your kindness.

In 1833 John A. Wharton left New Orleans to join William in a law office at Brazoria and to make his home at Eagle Island. John was soon the owner of an anti-Austin newspaper, *The Advocate of the People's Rights,* which he published until March 1834. Sometime that year he was also involved in a rather mysterious duel with William T. Austin. There seem to have been two possible causes for Austin's challenge: either a Wharton remark ruined William's romantic prospects with a young lady or else he made a disparaging comment about Austin's dead brother John. In any case, the field of honor was Battle Island on the present Jack Phillips ranch. Wharton was obviously unfamiliar with dueling pistols; his second lamented that he handled the weapon like he used an axe. When the two combatants fired simultaneously at ten paces, John's right arm was shattered in the exchange and he was carried to the home of Dr. James Phelps, where Dr. Branch T. Archer attended him.

In the meantime, Jared Groce's eldest son, Leonard Waller, had taken over much of the family business in 1825 after being called home from school to go to Texas with his father. His younger brothers, Jared, Jr. and Edwin, followed in 1830. Edwin drowned in the Brazos River the next year at age sixteen. Jared then divided the two leagues on the Brazos between his surviving sons, with Leonard taking the lower league, Bernardo plantation, and Jared, Jr. receiving the north league, where he built a mansion called Pleasant Hill for his bride, Mary Ann Calvit, a niece of Jane Long. On August 11, 1838, he ran the following advertisement in *The Telegraph and Texas Register* at Houston:

> NOW OR NEVER! I am compelled on account of bad health to travel, and offer for sale (to raise money) any of my land lying on the Brazos, Bernard or Colorado Rivers. Those on the Brazos are scattered on both sides of the river from tide water to the old Bexar Road; and I will also include my plantation where I now reside, which is well known. Bargains can now be had — but delay and all chance is lost.
>
> Pleasant Hill, June 28, 1838

After dividing his estate, Colonel Groce took the three-league place in present Grimes County, naming it Groce's Retreat because he moved there to escape the malaria along the Brazos bottoms. Keeping only ten slaves for himself, he built a "big house" there on Wallace Prairie in 1833. Since he was crippled in both hands, Groce could not fight in the Texas Revolution but did outfit many men for the cause. While on their way from Washington-on-the-Brazos to Harrisburg, interim President David G. Burnet and his cabinet stayed at Groce's Retreat from March 18 to March 21, 1836. Jared's last home thus served briefly as the temporary capital of the Republic of Texas. He died there in retirement on November 20, 1836.

In March 1829 Leonard Groce was chosen as a sublieutenant when a militia company was elected at San Felipe. He married fifteen-year-old Courtney Ann Fulton in November 1831, inherited Bernardo in 1835, then purchased most of his father's original grant; by 1838 he was paying taxes on 67,000 acres. Leonard first achieved political prominence by serving as a delegate to the Convention of 1833. During the revolution, General Houston's Texian army of 1,400 camped and drilled for twelve days on the west bank of the Brazos at Groce's Landing. During this time, Leonard stripped Bernardo plantation for army use by providing the beef and corn for Houston's forces and offering the troops a hospital facility. The "Twin Sisters," two six-pound cannons sent as a gift by the people of Cincinnati, Ohio, were mounted at Bernardo on April 11, 1836. Groce later served as a private in Capt. William Ware's company from June 4 to September 4.

The Wharton brothers were also active in Texas revolutionary politics. At a Brazoria meeting on June 20, 1832, William was among the hundred citizens who signed on "to become a part of the military of Austin's colony and to hold themselves in readiness to march to any point on the shortest notice." A showdown was triggered when the schooner *Brazoria* sailed down the Brazos with two cannons intended for use at Anahuac. After the vessel was turned back by Colonel Ugartechea and Mexican troops at Fort Velasco, 112 Texian militiamen gathered at Eagle Island plantation and organized into three assault companies. On June 25 Wharton took part in the Battle of Velasco, a successful Texian attack on the fort, and he was one of two emissaries who witnessed the Mexican surrender of the fort on June 29. William, a hothead leader of the War Party, was elected chairman of the Convention of 1833 which sent Stephen F. Austin to Mexico City with a petition demanding separate statehood for Texas within the Mexican federal system. Wharton often clashed with the more conservative Austin, but when news of his imprisonment reached Texas, the *ayuntamiento* of Brazoria drafted a petition on July 31, 1834; this strongly worded defense of Austin was signed by Alcalde Edwin Waller and First Regidor William Wharton.

On August 15, 1835, William presided over a meeting at Columbia which sent out a call for a consultation of all Texas citizens. The next month he and James F. Perry were among those in Brazoria County who subscribed $500 each to the war effort. After the Battle of Gonzales, Wharton distributed a broadside at Brazoria which began, "Freemen of Texas. TO ARMS!!! TO ARMS!!! Now's the day, and Now's the hour!" When Austin was elected commander in chief of the Texian army at Gonzales on October 11, 1835, he selected William as his judge advocate. Both took part in the Siege of Bexar but left for San Felipe on November 25 after being chosen as commissioners to seek aid in the United States. While serving in this fund-raising capacity, the two settled their past differences and were soon "on the best of terms," according to Austin.

John A. Wharton was a founder of the Freemason movement in Texas. In March 1834 the state legislature of Coahuila-Texas passed an act declaring that no person should be molested for religious or political opinions, provided he did not disturb the peace. Although the all-powerful Catholic priesthood in Texas had strongly opposed the Masonic order, this liberalization of the law emboldened the Masons of Brazoria to start a lodge. At ten o'clock on a March morning in 1835, Wharton, Anson Jones, Asa Brigham, James A. E. Phelps, Alexander Russell, J. P. Caldwell, and Warren D. C. Hall met to organize the first Masonic Lodge in Texas. They chose a secluded place near Brazoria, a little grove of wild peach or laurel near the family cemetery of John Austin. Meeting under a two-hundred-year-old oak tree, they decided to apply to the Grand Lodge of Louisiana for a dispensation to form and open the Holland Lodge, named in honor of John Henry Holland, the Most Worshipful Grand Master of Louisiana.[3] The seven then took up a collection to defray the expenses of John Wharton, who delivered the petition to Alexandria, Louisiana.

After receiving the dispensation, Dr. Anson Jones called the first meeting of Holland Lodge No. 36 on December 27, 1835, in the old courthouse building in Brazoria. Holland Lodge met for the last time in February 1836, with James Walker Fannin, Jr., serving as senior

---

[3] The acre on which the Masonic Charter Oak stands was given to the Grand Lodge of Texas by Mrs. Jane Ballowe Holt in 1952. This historic tree is located at Pleasant and Wood streets in Brazoria.

Oration at the funeral of John A.
Wharton by David G. Burnett.

———————◊———————

The keenest blade on the field of San Jacinto
is broken! —— the brave, the generous, the talent
John A. Wharton is no more! His poor remains
lie cold and senseless before you, wrapped in the
habiliments of the grave and awaiting your kind
offices to convey them to the charnel-house appointed
for all the living. A braver heart never died.
A nobler soul, more deeply imbued with the pure
and fervent spirit of patriotism, never passed from
its tenement of clay to the more genial realms of
immortality. Though he was young in years
and at the very threshold of his fame, yet every
heart in this assembly will respond, in painful
accordance, to the melancholy truth that a mighty
man has fallen among us. Many princes of the
earth have perished in their prime, surrounded
with all the gorgeous splendors of wealth and
power, and their country has suffered no damage.
But surely it will be engraven on the tablets
of our history, that Texas wept when John A.
Wharton died.

The brief time permitted us to linger about

Oration at funeral of John A. Wharton by David G. Burnet.
Courtesy Mrs. Ruby Baty, Wharton, Texas

61

deacon. The next month Brazoria was abandoned during the Runaway Scrape and occupied by Mexican general José Urrea.

On January 27, 1836, Grand Master Holland granted the formal charter to the Holland Lodge. The next day the charter was dispatched to Brazoria by John M. Allen of Louisiana Lodge No. 32, who had been recruiting soldiers for the Texas army in New Orleans. Allen also brought the following deputation to John A. Wharton, authorizing him to install Holland Lodge:

> . . . Know ye, that reposing special Trust and Confidence in the Masonic zeal and integrity of Brother John A. Wharton, I do hereby appoint the said worthy Brother to act as my Proxy at the installation of Holland Lodge of Master Masons . . .
>
> And to hereby empower the said Worthy Brother to perform all the duties which devolve on a Grand Master in relation to such installation . . .

Allen finally caught up with Anson Jones just before the Battle of San Jacinto. After receiving the charter on the prairie between Groce's plantation and the battlefield, Dr. Jones carried the prized document in his saddlebags during the historic clash with Santa Anna's army. The day after the battle, the Mexican general was captured and brought before the sleeping General Houston, who was nursing a shattered right ankle. Fearing that he was about to be hanged or shot, Santa Anna awakened him with the Masonic handclasp and "filled the air" with the secret Masonic distress signal. The first to recognize the sign was fellow Mason John Wharton, who used his influence to help save the Mexican dictator's life.

John Wharton first emerged as a political leader when he was chosen as Columbia's delegate to the Consultation of 1835, where he chaired a committee that drafted a statement of the causes for taking up arms against Mexico. He personally favored a declaration of independence, but the Consultation chose instead to endorse the Mexican Constitution of 1824, the position of Austin and Houston. John also served as a member of the provisional state government's General Council of fifteen. It was this same Consultation that selected his brother as one of three commissioners to the United States.[4] After the Consultation chose Sam Houston as the new commander in chief on December 7, 1835, he selected John as his adjutant general, the chief staff officer. Colonels Wharton and Sidney Sherman were the only high-ranking officers on Houston's staff who had full uniforms. John wore a well-tailored blue woolen outfit with brass buttons and a pair of fine boots but completed his outfit with a nonregulation Mexican sombrero. In 1832 he had written his old Tennessee friend, Sam Houston, and urged him to come to Texas and lead the revolt, but their relationship was strained by Sam's decision to lead the Texian army on a controversial retreat. Interim President David G. Burnet strongly criticized Houston for not standing and fighting General Santa Anna, and Wharton was influenced by David's friends and spies in the army. The proud, sensitive adjutant general was also

---

[4] It was William H. Wharton who safeguarded one of our most treasured documents. After the signing of the Texas Declaration of Independence at Washington-on-the-Brazos on March 2, 1836, the original was taken to Washington, D.C., along with the Treaties of Velasco, as de facto evidence of Texas's independence. Five copies of the declaration were also penned and sent to various Texas towns, but none of them survive today. William Wharton, one of three official Texas representatives to the United States, left the Declaration of Independence at the U.S. State Department with the following handwritten note on the back of the document: "Left at the Department of State, May 28, 1836, by Mr. Wharton. The original." For sixty years this priceless eleven-page document gathered dust in the State Department archives, with most Texans assuming that it had gone up in flames when the state capitol burned in 1881. After the declaration was "found" in the State Department in 1896 and returned to Texas, it was permanently displayed in the capitol rotunda from 1929 until 1940, then turned over to the state library due to concern for its safety and preservation. Since 1962, the declaration has been kept locked in a fireproof filing cabinet in an archives stack room of the Lorenzo de Zavala State Archives and Library Building in Austin.

hurt by General Houston's unwillingness to confide in him.

John Wharton's assertiveness and gallantry caused him some anxious moments during the Battle of San Jacinto. As the Texians passed the Mexican breastworks and engaged the enemy in hand-to-hand combat, several company leaders attempted to stop and reform lines and commands. Seeing this, the alarmed Colonel Wharton cried out: "Regulars, why have you stopped? On! On!" When General Houston reacted by shouting, "God damn it; quit trying to command," the mortified Wharton said nothing and galloped away. Once the conflict became a rout, John's most noteworthy effort was an attempt to restore discipline and spare the lives of those Mexicans trying to surrender. When he saw old Uncle Jimmy Curtis poised to slit the throat of a Mexican colonel, Wharton grabbed the officer and yanked him up behind on his horse; undaunted, Uncle Jimmy shot his adversary right off John's mount, oblivious of the raving and ranting of his superior officer. Many of the retreating Mexicans waded into Peggy's Lake, where their bobbing heads became inviting targets for Texian riflemen. Seeing no sport in this, John ordered his men to hold their fire. But Private J. H. T. Dixon retorted, "Colonel Wharton, if Jesus Christ were to come down from heaven and order me to quit shooting Santanistas I wouldn't do it, sir!" Wharton put his hand on his sword, the obstinate Dixon backed off and cocked his rifle, and John discreetly wheeled his horse and fled the face-off.

The evening after General Houston's right ankle was shattered by a Mexican copper ball during battle, the suffering Sam cried out: "Have I a friend in this world? Colonel Wharton, I am wounded, I am wounded; have I a friend in this world?" John was not in a magnanimous mood when he replied, "I wish I was. Yes, General, I hope you have many friends."

It was John Wharton who, by correcting his superior, gave the name to the site of one of the most telling victories in the annals of military history. When Houston sent prisoner Santa Anna's dispatch to General Filisola calling for the limited withdrawal of Mexican troops, Colonel Almonte asked how the dispatch should be dated. Sam replied, "Lynchburg, I believe, is the name of this place." Wharton interjected, "No, sir. It is called San Jacinto." Houston proclaimed, "Then let it be dated San Jacinto." Two days after the battle, John made a rash suggestion, offering to ride to Filisola's camp to propose armistice terms. General Rusk nixed the proposal, however, by convincing Houston that negotiating such terms was the proper responsibility of interim President Burnet and the civil government.

Wharton was to provide a final footnote to the Battle of San Jacinto. It was he who received Santa Anna's farewell letter to the Texas Army written at Velasco on June 1, 1836, when the defeated general thought he was about to be returned to Mexico. John later gave this historic document to his sister-in-law Sarah.

After San Jacinto, Texas commissioner and War Party leader William H. Wharton was less than proud of many of his planter associates. The paucity of big landholders and slaveowners on the combat rolls of the Revolution caused him to make this caustic comment:

> In glancing over the list [of those who fought at San Jacinto], I am surprised and mortified to find that very few men of property had any part in the perils of that glorious day [April 21, 1836]. I do not see on the roster a single one of the wealthy merchants of Matagorda or the opulent planters of Old Caney. . . . The planters were taking care of their cattle and slaves and the merchants were minding their goods . . .

William and Sarah Wharton hosted many prominent political leaders at Eagle Island plantation after the infant Republic of Texas chose nearby Columbia as its first temporary capital. The First Congress assembled there on October 3, 1836, with President Sam Houston taking the oath of office on October 22. The most frequent quest at Eagle Island was President Houston, who had known both Wharton brothers at Nashville while he was governor of Tennessee. William even promised Sam one of the puppies of a fine pair of hunting dogs the president admired. Col. Mirabeau B. Lamar loved to browse among the books of poetry in the Wharton library; he had written a book of poems, and Sarah found him fascinating. Other house guests of the Whartons included Stephen F. Austin, Henry Smith, James Collinsworth, E. M. Pease, Anson Jones, Edward Burleson, David G. Burnet, Thomas J. Rusk, and Albert Sidney Johnston.

On October 28, 1836, a ball was held at Brazoria to celebrate the first anniversary of the Battle of Concepción. President Houston, still limping from his San Jacinto wound, was wearing moccasins when he crowned the beauty queen. Guests were served French confections from New Orleans. The highlight of the glittering affair came when the radiant Sarah Wharton presented Houston with a silk flag inscribed with these words: "Texas is and shall be free while supported by brave Tennessee."

After William Wharton was appointed by President Houston as the Republic's first minister to the United States, Sarah and little John accompanied him when he sailed for Washington, D.C., on November 22, 1836.[5] Once he achieved U.S. recognition of Texas independence on March 3, 1837, the Whartons came home to celebrate

---

[5] Wharton was expecting a better position and told a friend that the president was sending him into "honorable exile" just to get him out of the way. Some months later, Houston heard of William's remark just when he was about to appoint three commissioners charged with purchasing a navy for the republic. Among the candidates recommended for the post was John A. Wharton. Political observers were surprised when he was not among those chosen. President Houston soon had a casual meeting with William; with a childlike, bland smile, he offered this explanation for the snub: "I did not appoint your brother one of the three naval commissioners because I did not wish to drive any more of the Wharton family into exile."

that diplomatic victory. En route Sarah remained in Nashville for several weeks due to an eye problem. On April 10, William boarded the *Independence,* the flagship of the Texas navy, at New Orleans for what was to be the last cruise of that vessel. On April 17, 1837, the *Independence* was attacked and captured by two Mexican warships, the *Vincedor del Alamo* and the *Libertador,* just offshore from Velasco. The diplomat and the entire crew were taken as prisoners to Brazos Santiago, the port of Matamoros, Mexico. William's imprisonment afforded an opportunity for Austin's nephew and sister to vent their bitter feelings toward Wharton for his earlier criticism and opposition of Stephen's conservative policies. On August 6, 1837, Moses Austin Bryan wrote his stepfather, James F. Perry, and made the following comment about William's incarceration: ". . . He will now know what uncle suffered — I am glad they have put him in the dungeon and hope they may keep him three months and then let [him] go home and make his report . . ." Emily Perry was also in a vindictive mood when she observed that "he [Wharton] will be able to judge how our poor brother felt, I do not pity him; I hope that they will keep him until his Proud Spirit is completely humbled —"

Sarah Wharton learned of her husband's fate when she arrived at Eagle Island. The resourceful, devoted wife and Dr. Archer immediately began a horseback journey to Washington, hoping to pressure the U.S. government to insist that Mexico grant William the traditional diplomatic immunity. Their mission was aborted in the woods of East Texas when Sarah's leg was broken when her horse fell. She was carried back to Eagle Island on a litter, spent a week recuperating, then boarded a boat at Velasco bound for Washington. Just before the ship sailed, she heard from her husband. William sent her a small book of poems with some secret message words underlined as a code alphabet. He mentioned being treated with kindness and suggested a possible prisoner exchange, saying that the Mexicans might "require Gen-

James E. Perry
Courtesy Stephen F. Perry, Jr.
Peach Point Plantation

eral Cos in exchange for me." The reassuring message halted Sarah's plans and gave William's brother John an idea. Initially, he chartered a schooner for $4,000 at New Orleans with the idea of leading a rescue expedition, but Father Muldoon was the first to intervene. Since priests had easy access to the prison at Matamoros, William's old friend paid him a visit and brought him a change of clothes — the garb of a Catholic priest. The good father then took his place while Wharton dressed as a padre and casually walked out of prison to safety. Brother John soon arrived at Matamoros as President Houston's emissary on a prisoner exchange mission, only to find that William had already escaped. John Wharton was also imprisoned, but President Bustamante set all the Texian captives free in October 1837.

Both Wharton brothers remained active in politics after the revolution. John A. served as interim secretary of war from March until October 1836, then was elected by Brazoria to serve in the House of Representatives of the Republic. When the capital was moved to Houston, he practiced law there for two years before being elected to the Third Congress. He was suddenly taken ill, however, and died at Houston on December 17, 1838. W. Y. Allen, chaplain of the lower house, kept a diary at the time and made the following reference to John's death:

> . . . The attack of fever was severe. I was sent for to visit the sick brother. . . . I had a few words with him on the subject of religion. I was requested to repeat my visit, which I did, when he requested me to pray for him, and to instruct him as to the way of life, saying he had been brought to think of the great subject as he had never done before. I was not allowed by his physicians to see him again. He soon afterwards died.
>
> Wm. H. Wharton, who died the following summer, though professedly skeptical, was a scholarly gentleman, and made a beautiful speech in favor of the circulation of the Bible, at the organization of the Houston Bible Society. And now they are all gone. . . .

Upon hearing of John's demise, all officers of the Texas army then in Houston resolved to wear a mourning band on their sleeves for thirty days. Led by Colonels Sherman and Hockley, these officers assembled in front of the Wharton residence and marched in procession to the burial site, the city cemetery. Former interim President David G. Burnet delivered the eulogy at John's funeral; the eloquent, effusive tribute read in part:

> The keenest blade on the field of San Jacinto is broken! — the brave, the generous, the talented John A. Wharton is no more! . . . Though he was young in years and at the very threshold of his fame, yet every heart in this assembly will respond, in painful accordance, to the melancholy truth that a mighty man has fallen among us. . . . But surely it will be engraven on the

69

tablets of our history, that Texas wept when John A. Wharton died. . . . He was among the first to propose the independence of Texas; and true to the frankness of his nature, he was foremost with those who nobly bared their bosoms to the storm when that declaration . . . was pronounced. . . .

To you he furnished ample evidence . . . that when his mind was turned to politics, it seemed as if nature had fashioned him for a statesman. . . . That eloquent tongue is hushed in death, . . .

To you, soldiers! . . . You have witnesed . . . his patient endurance of fatigue and suffering in the tented field, his agonized indignation at ever successive retreat before the invading foe. Many of you retain, in vivid recollection, his burning impatience for the conflict when on the great day of San Jacinto his buoyant spirit congratulated his companions-in-arms on the near prospect of a battle; and you have marked his gallant bearing when the shock of arms fire sounded on the plain, . . .

After first being buried in Houston, John's body was later reinterred at his beloved Eagle Island.

In 1838 Mary Austin Holley, the widow of William's former law professor, visited Eagle Island. While enjoying the Wharton's hospitality, Mary made the following diary entry on Monday, February 26:

Spend my time delightfully in conversation and books which make the ornaments of the parlor together with . . . shells and fossils — Beautiful editions of poetry and philosophy. . . .

Mr. Wharton lives as *gentlemen* do in other countries with the associations of literature and taste. Is fond of declaiming and reasoning, . . . Mrs. Wharton is all that a lady should be — Having a cultivated inquiring mind. Converses well.

Some two weeks later, Mrs. Holley wrote to Mrs. William M. Brand of Lexington, Kentucky, and made the following reference to her Eagle Island stay:

. . . I became acquainted with Mrs. Wharton, who in-

70

Orizimbo Plantation, home of Dr. J. A. E. Phelps.
Courtesy Mrs. Ruth Munson Smith, Angleton, Texas

Liendo Plantation
Photo by the late Mrs. Ruth Montgomery Tompkins, Hempstead, Texas

Stephen F. Austin's bedroom and study at Peach Point.
Photo by J. C. Hoke, Wharton, Texas, Courtesy Stephen S. Perry, Jr., Peach Point Plantation

Peach Point Plantation
Courtesy Stephen S. Perry, Jr., Peach Point Plantation

71

vited me to go home with her next day, which I did, in a barrouche & four . . . I spent several days very agreeably. They live more like people elsewhere, at Mr. Wharton's than any where in Texas . . . seemed like Col. Meads. They have a Scotch gardner — & a charming garden. A lake and island, it of which I made a drawing. Mr. Wharton had much to say of old times. Is fond of declaiming & reading poetry . . . They have a great many beautiful books & other curiosities — center table, woolen damask curtains — sofa, silver pitcher, white china, etc. etc. I hated to leave so agreeable a place — and Mrs. Wharton, — really a charming woman.

Their house is always full of company. . . .

Late in 1838, William moved his family to Houston after being elected to the Senate of the Republic. During this time, the gracious Sarah served as the hostess at social functions for widower President Mirabeau B. Lamar.

After Jared E. Groce, Jr., died at Pleasant Hill on February 3, 1839, William had to spend several weeks there as an executor of his will. On March 4, the morning of his departure at Bernardo, Wharton drew a pistol from his holster as he was dismounting and accidentally shot himself in the left breast and hand. After lingering for ten days attended by his dear friend, Dr. Branch T. Archer, he died in Sarah's arms on March 14, 1839, and was buried beside his brother on the grounds at Eagle Island. One can imagine Sarah's sense of pride when Wharton County was created in 1846 and named in honor of her husband and brother-in-law. She was pleased to have widower Dr. Archer spend his last years at Eagle Island; the grateful doctor in turn gave all the jewelry of his deceased wife and daughter to Sarah's grandchild, Kate Ross. He died at Eagle Island in September 1856 and was buried beside the Wharton brothers.

After William's untimely death, the lonely Sarah was invited to stay at brother Leonard's Bernardo plantation. During this extended period, she felt a real sense of peace and consolation whenever she held Leonard and Courtney's eighteen-month-old boy, Edwin Waller, in her lap. Since the blond-haired, blue-eyed tyke was being called either Buddy or Sonny, his Aunt Wharton had an inspiration: would the parents consent to change his name to William Wharton Groce to honor her deceased husband? A loving brother readily complied, recording in the margin of the family Bible that the change was "by request of his sister." Thus was born a special bond between aunt and nephew. When Sarah Wharton went back to Eagle Island, she took little William Wharton with her for a visit that stretched into months; in fact, he spent part of each year there until he was of school age and later recalled that he "hardly knew which was his real home, Bernardo or Eagle Island." This special nephew first started drinking coffee at age two and fondly remembered the daily ritual of jumping in bed with Aunt Wharton to share in her early morning coffee.

During this time Sarah's own son, John Austin, was receiving his first formal education at Bernardo where he, Fulton Groce, and their two Waller cousins were tutored in the "Little White School House" by a Mr. Dean of New York City. John Austin was a freckled, auburn-haired lad who resembled his mother. After completing his education at the University of South Carolina, he married Penelope Johnson, the only daughter of Governor David Johnson of that state, in 1848. Sarah Wharton traveled to Columbia for the wedding, then had the ell or wing at Eagle Island refurnished in rosewood as a bridal suite for the surprised, delighted couple. Once they settled in, the newlyweds began to compose little poems for each other and leave them scattered about the house. After reading law with his cousin, Jack Harris, John received his license and opened a practice with attorney Clint Terry of Brazoria. Aunt Wharton's first grandchild, Sarah Ann, lived only a short time, but John and Penny had little Kate Ross in 1854.

Sarah Wharton retained an interest in politics after William's death. In July 1845 she invited her friends in Brazoria County to spend the day at Eagle Island and discuss an important matter. She suggested that they send a token of appreciation to ex-President John Tyler for his role in the annexation of Texas. (Sarah was related to him on her mother's side through the Chiles and Page families of Virginia.) The response was enthusiastic. Mrs. Wharton offered to donate her prized silver pitcher and have a Lone Star emblem engraved on it. In addition to this elegant gift, Sarah penned an eloquent letter assuring Mr. Tyler of their gratitude and pride. The note read in part: ". . . We firmly believe that to you, Texas is indebted for the success of this great measure. Texas, no longer a lost Pleiad, has returned to take her place in a bright and beautiful constellation." The former president received the gift and letter at his Virginia home, Sherwood Forest, on January 1, 1846, and wrote a reply to Sarah that very day, saying that the gift was

> . . . a highly valuable New Year's offering, to be handed down to my children, . . . Be pleased . . . to make known my grateful homage to the ladies . . . and to accept for yourself my cordial salutations. . . . Woman's heart is the shrine of virtue and her tongue the oracle of truth. To have my name registered in the first, and repeated with a commendation by the last is an honor which I highly appreciate.

Evidently, Sarah Wharton was also quite successful in the man's world of sugar planting. Crop records for 1852 list her as the eleventh largest sugar producer in Brazoria County, with 240 hogsheads that year.

With the Civil War looming on the horizon, John Austin Wharton was chosen as a presidential elector in 1860, then served as Brazoria County's delegate to the secession convention at Austin. In 1861 a Fort Bend County sugar planter, B. F. (Frank) Terry, was authorized to recruit a regiment of mounted volunteers, a unit named the Eighth Texas Cavalry but more commonly called the famed Terry's Texas Rangers. When ten companies of 100 men each met at Houston in September 1861, the twenty-four-year-old Captain Wharton was leading Company B from Brazoria and Matagorda counties; with him was cousin William Wharton Groce. The young men of this regiment were skilled marksmen and splendid horsemen. Their ranks included sons of leading families, college graduates, professional men, merchants, stockmen, and farmers. When John Austin went off to war, he moved his family to the Shelton Oliver home near Leonard Groce's new "big house," Liendo, just east of present Hempstead.

After Colonel Terry was mortally wounded in the Battle of Woodsonville (Kentucky) on December 17, 1861, Captain Wharton was elected to take his place and was promoted to colonel. In April 1862 an incident occurred before the stand-off Battle of Shiloh which revealed his depth of character. It seems that a heavy rain fell all night before the battle; fearing that their wet arms would fail in action, the men asked to fire them off the next morning. Giving no thought to the possible consequences, Colonel Wharton agreed, pointed to a wooded hillside, and said, "Go off there and shoot." Since the exercise sounded like a brisk skirmish, Wharton was summoned to headquarters and severely reprimanded. Upon his return the perturbed leader admitted to a serious blunder and made a speech asking his men to "wipe out the stain by our gallant behavior in the coming engagement" and to "ride further into the enemy's ranks than any other regiment."

John was promoted to brigadier general seven months after Shiloh, and William Wharton Groce was promoted to captain and joined his staff. While Murfreesboro was being taken in July 1862, General Wharton suffered a broken arm but put his reins between his teeth and fired his revolver with the other hand until the enemy surrendered. In November 1863 he was appointed major general for his extraordinary conduct at Chicka-mauga. In early 1864 Wharton was placed in command of all cavalry forces in the Department of the Trans-Missis-sippi. In the Battle of Mansfield (Louisiana) fought that April, Confederate General Richard Taylor and 11,000 troops routed a Union army of 25,000 intent on occupying East Texas. As the bluecoats retreated down the Red River, they were harassed by General Wharton and his cavalrymen. After this campaign, John's health became "quite impaired from constant and hard service" and he was granted a brief leave to visit his wife and mother in Texas, his first time away from the front line in three years. Among the aides who came with him was Col. Francis R. Lubbock, the former Confederate governor of Texas. In his memoirs, *Six Decades in Texas* (1900), Colo-nel Lubbock recalls the trip from Louisiana to Liendo:

> . . . The journey was a very pleasant one. General Wharton was in a buoyant humor, full of fun and sen-timent, and often relieved the tedium of the way by re-citing snatches of verse, and in some instances entire poems. His literary taste was excellent, his mind well stored with masterpieces of British and American poets that had strongly impressed him, and his talents as a speaker were of a high order. Consequently, these recitations in each instance apropos, were much en-joyed by his auditors. A favorite of his was "Bingen on the Rhine," and he recited it in a manner that fully brought out its beauties and suggestive meanings, . . .

According to Lubbock, "there was quite a dinner party, and we were kindly and cordially received" at Liendo, with General Wharton carving the turkey for family and friends. Another of John's men, L. B. Giles, wrote his memoirs, *Terry's Texas Rangers,* in 1911 and had this to say about his wartime leader:

> Wharton was a man of ability, of a distinguished fam-ily, liberally educated, a lawyer and a captivating pub-lic speaker. Enterprising and ambitious, he never for-got during a wakeful moment that the soldier who

survived this war would be a voter. He distinguished himself on many fields. . . .

A feud, however, was to snuff out Wharton's life and political promise. In 1865 he renewed his law practice at Brazoria and made a fateful business trip to Houston that April. George W. Baylor, one of his subordinate officers during the war, was also in town. Baylor was reputed to be the first man to raise a Confederate flag in Austin and had started as a lieutenant in the Second Texas Cavalry. In the spring of 1864, he was strongly recommended for promotion to brigadier after the battles of Mansfield and Pleasant Hill (Louisiana) but Wharton, his commanding general, delayed the promotion, prompting ex-Governor Lubbock to observe that the two had "unpleasant misunderstandings" growing out of "military matters." On April 6, 1865, Wharton and Baylor exchanged "hot words" on a Houston street; both were still fuming when they met a few minutes later at Maj. Gen. John Magruder's headquarters in the Fannin Hotel. When they renewed their argument, Wharton called his critic a liar and slapped his face; the enraged Baylor instinctively pulled his revolver and fired, killing his antagonist.

John was first buried at Liendo, but the body was eventually reinterred in the State Cemetery at Austin. A portrait of him now hangs in the Texas Senate Chamber, presented by surviving comrades of Terry's Texas Rangers. George Baylor never stood trial since there were no credible witnesses to the tragic incident; the only other person in the room at the time was a near-deaf officer. Baylor went on to serve as an officer in the Texas Rangers for twenty years and grew repentant in old age, admitting before his death that the Wharton shooting had been a "lifelong sorrow."

Penelope Wharton never recovered from the loss of her husband. She became quiet and somber and went into virtual seclusion at Eagle Island, placing all family responsibilities on the tired shoulders of her mother-in-law Sarah. The sugar plantation did not generate income after the war; in fact, all Aunt Wharton had in the way of assets was property. When money was needed she turned to William's cousin, Col. Jack Harris, a Galveston lawyer who mortgaged pieces of her land. Sarah was forced to borrow money to send granddaughter Kate Ross to college at Nashville. Kate, a talented artist and musician died at age eighteen on August 8, 1872, and was buried at Eagle Island. Her obituary in the *Galveston News* read in part:

> ... highly educated, a fine musician, a graceful poetess, beautiful in person, gentle and charming in manners, and lovely in character, in the very bloom of apparent health too, the pale messenger came, and after an illness of but a few hours, her spirit was taken to her Father's. . . .

This latest sorrow was too much for Miss Penny to bear. She grew thinner and more wane, staying in bed most of the time. After her eyesight began to fail, household members took turns reading to her.

Sarah Wharton could no longer bear this load alone. Needing both help and someone to brighten a gloomy house, she asked her nephew William Wharton Groce to bring his family and live once more at Eagle Island. Captain Groce had a very lucrative cotton compress business in Houston, so pulling up stakes was a great financial sacrifice; nevertheless, he brought his beautiful wife Katie and their three children to live in the ell at Eagle Island. Their arrival was a tonic to Sarah's spirits, and she celebrated in 1874 with a Christmas dinner feast of raw oysters, stuffed turkey, wild ducks, turnips and greens, sweet potatoes, rice and plum pudding. Each night after supper the family would gather in the parlor to recite the Lord's Prayer, hear the captain read Bible passages, and listen to Miss Katie sing hymns. This ever-smaller circle was broken on May 15, 1876, when the totally blind Miss Penny died in her sleep, bringing an end to this line of the Wharton family.

Since Aunt Wharton had not had a respite from family obligations in years, she was persuaded to go to Galveston to visit friends and relatives after Christmas 1877. Miss Katie spent weeks having some of her old party dresses altered into fashionable frocks for this much-deserved holiday. The matriarch of the Wharton clan seemed to be healthy and in good spirits, promising the baby girl, "Little Miss" Sarah Wharton Groce, that "Aunty is going to bring her baby something nice when she returns." [6] While visiting in Galveston, Sarah Wharton died suddenly at age sixty-eight on February 11, 1878, and her funeral was held there at the home of Judge J. W. Harris. As a fitting historical tribute, members of the Texas Veterans Association escorted her body to the steamer *Thomas;* that same boat taking her remains home to Eagle Island also carried that special gift for Little Miss, a rocking horse.

In her will, Sarah Ann Wharton left Eagle Island plantation to her beloved nephew, Capt. William Groce. The new owner later moved his family to Richmond and in 1884 sold the estate to Harris Masterson, who transferred it to a northern syndicate for division into small farms. The Eagle Island "big house" was destroyed by the Galveston hurricane in 1900; the grounds where it stood were eventually purchased by the Brazoria County Cemetery Association and is known today as Restwood Memorial Park. On the cemetery grounds are state markers locating the graves of William and John A. Wharton and their dear friend, Dr. Branch T. Archer; tombstones nearby mark the graves of Sarah, Penelope, and Kate Wharton. All of the Groce and Wharton interest in this

---

[6] It was this "Little Miss," Sarah Wharton Groce Berlet, who wrote a book, *Autobiography of A Spoon,* telling of the five generations of family members who owned the Wharton silver between 1828 and 1956.

land has long passed, and the only reminders of those bygone days of grace and glory at Eagle Island are some stately oak trees and the Wharton family burial sites.

Now let us return to Liendo, the only one of the five Groce family mansions that survives today. In 1849 Col. Leonard Groce purchased a 3,000-acre cotton plantation five miles southeast of present Hempstead that José Justo Liendo had received as a land grant in the 1820s. Leonard moved his family there in 1853 and built a sixteen-room, two-story mansion using Georgia longleaf pine hauled from Houston and red clay Brazos bricks made by his own slaves.

Built in the Colonial Greek-Renaissance style, this stately white frame house was trimmed with green shutters and had four tall columns across a front veranda which supported an upstairs balcony. In honor of the "Lone Star state," Colonel Groce positioned a bronze star on the roof gable above the front entrance. On the first floor of this showplace home was a large entrance hall with two parlors to the left having brick fireplaces; across the hall was a large dining room that could seat twenty-four guests. Upstairs were several spacious, sunny bedrooms with eleven-foot ceilings. A runway connected the "big house" with a large, detached kitchen featuring a huge oven that could roast an ox whole. Adjoining the kitchen was the "spring house" enclosing a cistern where the milk, butter, eggs, and meat were kept cool. A fountain in the front lawn which never worked came to be called "Groce's Folly"; the piping was later taken up and made into bullets.

Running this plantation required an army of some 300 slaves, and Leonard even maintained a schoolhouse for his ten children.[7] He was renowned for his lavish din-

---

[7] Wharton Collins and Frances Spriggs were among the slaves born on the Liendo plantation in the 1850s. Wharton recalled that the

ners, and Liendo soon became a center of entertainment and hospitality for southeastern Texas. The mansion served as a stopover for stagecoach and horseback riders bound from Houston and Galveston to Austin and was the scene of one seemingly prolonged house party before the Civil War. Many political notables visited from Austin and Houston; a frequent guest was U.S. Senator Sam Houston, who admired Groce's fancy vest and received it as a prized gift.

A dramatic change in the function and mood of Liendo came in early 1863, when the plantation became the site of a Union prisoner of war camp. The first prisoners brought to Camp Groce were captured in the Battle of Galveston; they were joined months later by Union sailors taken from the federal gunboats *Clifton* and *Sachem* at the Battle of Sabine Pass. Camp Groce was a series of long, narrow buildings patrolled by Confederate guards. Although the camp had a cook stove and prisoners were allowed to bathe in nearby Clear Creek, sickness and death were still common. Malaria was a constant threat, and a typhoid outbreak in the fall of 1864 resulted in sick prisoners being cared for in a Hempstead hotel. The camp was also used by Colonel Groce's son William as a place to recruit and train troops for the Confederate army.

---

boys stayed in flimsy, scanty shirttails until they were twelve and ready to take up field work. When they were hoeing, a stiff breeze caused the work crew to resemble a flock of white cranes with flapping wings, a "pretty sight" to young Collins. His slave wife Frances was given by Leonard Groce to his son Fulton as a wedding gift when Groce married Acenath Jackson. Although the slave couple spoke with affection of the rest of the Groce family, Frances Spriggs Collins had this to say of her new mistress:

> Miss Cennie whipped me hard. She had nothing else to do. She whipped me when I stopped rocking Miss Courtney, and she beat me when I did not come running when she called me. She had the worst temper. She used to yell and scream at Mr. Fulton but he paid her no mind.

Wharton Collins agreed with his wife's assessment, saying, " 'Deed, Frances had it rough with Miss Cennie."

81

On August 26, 1865, the reality of defeat and Reconstruction reached Hempstead when Maj. Gen. George Armstrong Custer rode into town. He had been placed in command of all federal cavalry forces in Texas by Gen. Phil Sheridan and brought a regiment of 4,000 troopers from Iowa, Wisconsin, Illinois, and Indiana. Custer soon chose Liendo plantation as a camping ground and stretched his tents in front of the mansion gate on September 1. Since four of Leonard Groce's seven sons had served as Confederate soldiers, the sight of all those bluecoats made him furious. However, two gracious women breached this wall of hostility. Libbie Custer had come to Texas with her husband, but her only furniture was a bucket and two campstools. When she sent a servant to Liendo to borrow a rocking chair, Courtney Groce volunteered the use of her finest parlor rocker; she also offered the Custers a room in the mansion, but the general refused it and his family camped instead in a new hospital tent. When Libbie became very ill, however, she was invited to the house, put in a comfortable bed, and nursed to recovery by Mrs. Groce. This kindness was so appreciated by General Custer that he forbade his soldiers to molest Colonel Groce's grounds or fields and encamped them on an unused part of the plantation. For two months, Mrs. Groce supplied the Custers with milk, jelly, vegetables, and roast of mutton while the general was invited to go deer hunting with the planters and given five hounds. George and Libbie also enjoyed many long rides in the beautiful countryside. After receiving orders to proceed to Austin, Custer and his entire command left Liendo plantation behind on October 30, 1865.

After the war, the abolition of slavery made Leonard Groce's holdings an economic liability so he sold out and moved to Galveston. When the payments were not met, Liendo reverted to him and he was forced to declare bankruptcy in 1868. His wife died at Galveston the next year, and Leonard passed away at his beloved Liendo on August 29, 1873. Shortly before his death, he sold the plantation to two prominent newcomers, the Scottish Dr. Edmund Montgomery and his German wife, Elisabet Ney.

Elisabet, the daughter of Alsatian-Polish parents, was born in 1833 at Munster, Westphalia, Germany. When she was eighteen, the tall, red-haired beauty shocked her father, a stonecutter, by announcing that she intended to study sculpting. She won her point by going on a hunger strike and was enrolled in the all-male Academy of Art at Munich. Two years later she met Edmund Montgomery, a young medical student and prospective model, and the two began a ten-year courtship. Elisabet's career as a sculptor was launched when the old philosopher, Arthur Schopenhauer, agreed to sit for her. She later executed the busts of such European notables as Jacob Grimm, Richard Wagner, Giuseppe Garibaldi, Otto von Bismarck, King George V of Hanover, and King Ludwig II of Bavaria. During this time, Edmund received his M.D. degree at Wurzburg and accepted a post as lecturer of physiology at St. Thomas Hospital in London, where he conducted original experiments in biology. Even after Edmund and Elisabet married in a secret civil ceremony on the island of Madeira in September 1865, she insisted on retaining her maiden name and he referred to his wife as "Miss Ney" or "my best friend."

Dr. Montgomery contracted tuberculosis while performing an autopsy in London, so the couple moved to America in 1871, seeking a better climate and fleeing from political difficulties triggered by the Franco-Prussian War. They first joined a Utopian farm commune of Bavarian aristocrats called "The Brotherhood of Man" near Thomasville, Georgia, but the malarial swamps drove them away after two years; in the meantime two sons, Arthur and Lorne, had been born to them.

After Elisabet went alone to Galveston seeking a depresed plantation home, the German consul there put her in touch with Robert Leisewitz of Brenham, who knew of Liendo. The place met all of her requirements: a warm, dry climate that would be good for Edmund's

Elisabet Ney
Courtesy Perry-Castaneda Library,
The University of Texas

84

health; enough acreage to insure privacy; and a location close to a cultured, German-speaking town (Brenham). The vagabonds reached lawless Hempstead (nicknamed "Six-Shooter Junction" and the "Hell Hole of Texas") in late February 1873. On March 4, Dr. Montgomery purchased the Liendo big house and 1,100 acres for $10,000 with a one-fourth down payment in gold.

When Miss Ney first stood on the upstairs balcony of the clapboard mansion and gazed out upon a huge live oak hung with Spanish moss, she remarked, "Here will I live, and here will I die!" The beauty of the setting inspired her to observe that "the place is something in a dream." Edmund chose the largest southwest bedroom for his study and laboratory, with Elisabet's bedroom opposite his housekeeper Fraulein Cresentia Simath ("Cenci") down the hall across from the nursery. Unlike the former wealthy owners, Miss Ney could not afford to furnish Liendo, so the house contained only narrow plank beds, crude makeshift tables and benches, folding chairs, and one tin sit-in bathtub. The couple did plant a grove of live oaks on the west side of the mansion, named it their "Sacred Grove," and vowed to be buried there, side by side.

While her brilliant husband, the "hermit philosopher," spent most of his time in a laboratory conducting microscopic examinations of living cells and writing articles for leading scientific journals, Elisabet took on the management of the plantation and practiced no serious sculpting for twenty years. Wearing "breeches" and with two pistols strapped on, she rode her rounds astride like a man. It frustrated her to pay generous wages to a work force of former slaves, illiterate and unskilled tenant farmers and field hands whom she regarded as lazy and ignorant. When Edmund inherited 1,000 pounds ($5,000 at the time) in the spring of 1874, he used much of it to buy adjoining acreage, only adding to plantation losses; eventually he was borrowing money simply to cover operating costs for twenty-two tenant families on a 2,200-

acre spread. Since Miss Ney was a novice in agriculture, shunned by other planters and chronically short on funds, the plantation soon fell into hopeless decay and disrepair.

In the early fall of 1873, macabre rumors began to circulate after two-year-old Arthur ("Arti") Montgomery died in his mother's arms of diphtheria. Elisabet took the body to an improvised studio upstairs, spent the night modeling his figure in clay, then cremated the corpse on a stack of logs in the "Sacred Grove" the next morning. As the flames leaped skyward, the distraught mother raced to the upstairs balcony and watched silently for an hour. It should be noted that a Dr. Conway Nutt from Houston ordered the fire since he feared the spread of the highly contagious disease. Elisabet put Arti's ashes in a leather pouch, hung it on the side of the fireplace in the southeast parlor, locked the door, and never entered that room again. When Dr. Montgomery died many years later, the pouch was put into his coffin. The sculpted death mask of Arthur was stored in his mother's small private trunk at her bedside, then placed in her casket when she died. There was much murmuring among the plantation Negroes as to why these "queer furriners" held no funeral or burial services, while Hempstead residents gossiped about the atheists, murderers, and "blasphemous pair" at Liendo.

The plantation became an even greater curiosity to townspeople and travelers because of the strange, eccentric behavior of Miss Ney; in fact, local blacks dubbed her "the witch woman." It was rumored that she and the doctor were free-lovers living together unmarried. On her few trips into Hempstead, Elisabet dressed in Grecian robes, wore a heavy veil, and talked as little as possible. Her black servant, Jim Wyatt, said she looked "like an Ayrab" or like "folks in Bible stories." In her heavy German accent, she denigrated the neighbors as "peasants" or "the common herd" and invited only politicians, educators, and scientists to visit Liendo. When she threw pe-

86

riodic tantrums, her husband would ride out the storm by pitching a tent in the yard.

As their youngest son Lorne ("Lore") grew up, Elisabet made him play alone or just with plantation black boys. She hired numerous tutors for the defiant and unruly student and designed all his clothes, including a court suit of satin and lace, a Scottish kilt, and a tunic. Once when he went into Hempstead with his mother, Lorne had to wear a white woolen Grecian toga and sandals, prompting the kids in town to ridicule the "little bastard" with the "nightshirt" on. From then on he insisted on wearing *regular* clothes. When Lore was fourteen, Dr. Montgomery decided to send his rebellious son away to boarding school. By this time the lad hated his mother and had become estranged from her for life. In early 1887, the handsome, powerfully built teenager enrolled at Swarthmore College in Philadelphia but failed in his studies within a year. After attending school in New York and Switzerland, Lorne ran off to Italy.[8]

---

[8] After four years, Lorne returned to Liendo and eloped with Daisy Tompkins of Hempstead in July 1893. His infuriated mother referred to the marriage as "nothing but animal instinct turned loose without conscience" and refused to recognize the union. When Elisabet first encountered Daisy at Liendo, she acidly remarked, "So you're the hussy who stole my son." Upon hearing that, Lorne retorted, "You're no mother, I hate you," while she rejoined, "And I no longer have a son," and stormed out of the house bound for Austin. During the Spanish-American War, Lore went to San Antonio and enlisted as a private in Theodore Roosevelt's Rough Riders on May 18, 1898. When his worried mother visited the encampment and he was summoned to see her, he told the officer-in-charge, "I don't want to hear anything she has to say," abruptly turned heel, and left her standing there in the tent. While his famed cavalry regiment was charging up San Juan Hill in Cuba, Private Montgomery was confined to a hospital bed with measles and dysentery, although he did win recognition as a skilled interpreter and orator.

Less than two years after the war, Daisy divorced Lorne; his second wife, Alma, died in November 1904. During this trying period, Miss Ney refused to accept his three children. Perhaps the cruelest cut of all occurred after Edmund and Elisabet paid all expenses to have 500 copies of the doctor's book published and invited Lore to dinner to

Once he left home, Elisabet's artistic interest re-
vived after ex-Governor Oran Roberts, a warm friend of
her husband and frequent visitor to Liendo, invited her
to Austin to sculpt. Through his influence a woman's
committee in October 1890 commissioned Miss Ney to
create likenesses of two great Texas heroes, Sam Houston and Stephen F. Austin, for the Texas Pavilion at the
Chicago World's Fair Columbian Exposition of 1893.
Since Elisabet had empathy for Houston, she chose to
sculpt him first; in fact, the Austin statue was not finished in time to be exhibited at Chicago. Needing a studio in Austin, she purchased a seven-acre tract called
Hyde Park just north of The University of Texas campus.
Her studio, called "Formosa," was located at 304 East
Forty-Third Street. Constructed in 1892, it had a distinc-
tive German touch and was modeled after a miniature
medieval castle complete with battlements and a watch-
tower; her balcony bedroom included a hammock and sit-
in tub. Miss Ney's eclectic tastes in architecture were realized with exterior native limestone, furnishings from
the Sears & Roebuck catalogue, a desk purchased by saving soap coupons, unfinished cedar posts in the studio in-
terior, and mass-produced millwork for the wooden trim.

In 1901 the state legislature appropriated $32,000
and commissioned Elisabet to finish the marble statues

---

help celebrate the achievement. After they finished eating, he
browsed through his father's lifelong effort, uttered a hollow laugh,
and said,

> You mean you two spent all that money for *this,* and you're selling it
> for two-and-a-half dollars? I'll bet no more than forty persons, includ-
> ing the two of you, will ever read it.

Although Dr. Montgomery gamely took the contemptuous remark as
a joke, his sobbing wife suffered a heart attack as she jumped from her
chair; she was in bed for six weeks at Liendo. Incredibly, Lorne never
apologized for the incident. After his third wife Sarah died, he remarried Daisy before suffering a painful spinal injury. House, keeper
Cenci nursed him through months of suffering before Lore died on
June 15, 1913, and was buried with Roosevelt's Rough Riders in Arlington National Cemetery.

of Houston and Austin which now stand in the national and state capitols. After they were unveiled in January 1903, the legislature authorized her to sculpt the "Memorial to Albert Sidney Johnston" above his grave in the State Cemetery at Austin. Lorado Taft, author of a history of American sculpture, described the Johnston memorial as "a work of high order." She was also commissioned to do busts of many famous Texans including governors Roberts, Lubbock, Ross, and Sayres. In her life Miss Ney modeled some 100 people. Her last and finest showpiece, a statue of Lady Macbeth, was finished in 1905 and now stands in the Lincoln Gallery of the Smithsonian Institution in Washington, D.C.

Such a burst of creativity made Formosa the cultural center of Austin, a gathering place for visiting artists and patrons of the arts. Elisabet would entertain with sparse, plain suppers of clabber, cheese, vegetables, fruit, "wind-dried" bread, and tea served on rough tables and benches under a live oak. The main fare for the lucky invited guest was "high thinking." She had her own studio garden and private pond, "Bull Frog Lake," to furnish a cool canoeing diversion. Visitors included such notables as dancer Pavlova, pianist Paderewski, and singer Enrico Caruso. During these years, Dr. Montgomery stayed at Liendo but the couple wrote weekly; doubtless, their long separations contributed to the local rumors about her alleged sexual appetites.

Miss Ney arranged to have one of her husband's manuscripts, *Philosophical Problems in the Light of Vital Organization,* published by G. P. Putnam's Sons of New York. Five hundred copies of this 462-page book were printed, an elegant edition bound in maroon cloth with gold lettering. Edmund became active in civic affairs while living alone. He served as a volunteer academic consultant when Prairie View State Normal School was founded in 1878–79 and delivered the commencement address for Hempstead High School in 1894. Dr. Montgomery also served two terms (1894-1898) as Waller

County road commissioner and was elected chairman of the county Democratic Executive Committee in 1892. His scientific achievements were recognized with his selection as president of the Texas Academy of Science in 1903.

Years of inhaling marble dust took an inevitable toll on Elisabet. By the time she finished the Lady Macbeth statue in 1905, she was suffering from exhaustion, experiencing difficulty in breathing, and had several minor heart attacks. In her last months the weak artist was confined to her chair in the upstairs room at Formosa, and Edmund moved in to care for her. Miss Ney was sitting alone in her chair when she died of a heart attack on Saturday, June 29, 1907. A large crowd of devotees saw the body off at Austin, but only Lorne and a wagon awaited her final return to Hempstead. She was buried at Liendo in the "Sacred Grove," a hundred feet west of the house. After being partially paralyzed by a stroke and confined to bed, Dr. Montgomery died at home on April 17, 1911, and was buried beside his famed wife.

Formosa was eventually purchased by the Texas Fine Arts Association and became a museum of Elisabet's artworks in 1928. The Ney Museum is now operated by the Austin Parks and Recreation Department. In March 1973 it was designated as a State and National Historical Landmark. In 1931 Edmund's extensive library, writings, and letters were presented to the De-Golyer Library at Southern Methodist University, and the university placed a bronze plaque on his gravestone.

In 1961 the Liendo property was purchased by Carl and Phyllis Detering of Houston. Since that time they have occupied the mansion and restored its original 1853-era appearance. This grand old house is just off the Wyatt Chapel Road five miles southeast of Hempstead. In recent times the home was used as a backdrop in the NBC television soap opera "Texas." It is a recorded Texas Historic Landmark and serves as a graceful, fitting monument to the Groce and Wharton families of early Texas.

Likeness of Emily Morgan, by Penny Grissom Bonnot, Edna, Texas.

IV

Emily Morgan:
The Yellow Rose of Texas

The legendary Emily West Morgan spent less than two years of her life in Texas, yet in that brief time she became a folklore figure as our first "undercover agent" and a heroine of the Texas Revolution. General Santa Anna paid a huge, historic price when he was totally distracted by her favors during a two-day liaison. His lust for and desire to impress Emily caused the spellbound Mexican dictator to issue erratic orders and make careless mistakes that defied all military logic. After the story of the comely mulatto's contribution at San Jacinto was passed on by her owner, she was destined to become the namesake of a hit song performed by Mitch Miller and Chorus in 1955. It all makes a great tale, but was she *really* the "Yellow Rose of Texas"?

Emily D. West was a beautiful, intelligent mulatto girl born in the vicinity of Albany, New York. At age nineteen she sailed from New York City on the schooner *Flash* on November 2, 1835, bound for Galveston Bay in the company of Mrs. Lorenzo de Zavala. Although Emily had free papers, she came to Texas as an indentured servant of Col. James Morgan of New Washington, now Morgan's Point.

92

After visiting Brazoria in 1830, Morgan was inspired to leave Philadelphia and open a mercantile business in Texas. At the time, the area was a part of the Mexican state of Coahuila-Texas and slavery was prohibited. However, a state law of 1828 allowed immigrants to "liberate" their slaves and then make them indentured servants for life. Morgan thus bound his sixteen slaves for ninety-nine years, then set out for Anahuac, Texas, with his wife Celia and their three children. In 1835 James became the local agent of the New Washington Association, a New York real estate company; in this capacity he purchased huge tracts of land in Liberty and Harrisburg municipalities, including the point at the mouth of the San Jacinto River where he laid out the town of New Washington. To populate the colony he imported Scotch Highlanders along with blacks from Bermuda and New York. Two company-owned schooners, the *Flash* and the *Kosciusko,* were dispatched from New York City and arrived at Morgan's warehouse on the San Jacinto about December 15, 1835.

Emily West probably lived for a time with the Zavalas on Buffalo Bayou before becoming Colonel Morgan's housekeeper and taking her master's name. She arrived in Texas during the early phases of the Texas Revolution, a time when Anglos were resisting the tyrannical rule of Gen. Antonio Lopez de Santa Anna. Starting in April 1834 and extending over a period of months, Santa Anna had forced his liberal vice-president into exile, dissolved the Mexican Congress, and disbanded state legislatures. In October 1835 he abrogated the federal constitution and established a central system of government for Mexico — in effect, a military dictatorship. That month this "Napoleon of the West" marched an army northward to reassert his authority in Texas. As the war clouds gathered, Emily's master was commissioned a colonel and assigned as commandant of Galveston Island, serving from March 20, 1836, until April 1, 1837. In addition to guarding Texas government officials and refugees there, Colonel Morgan built fortifications on the island, gave provisions to the Texas army, and donated the use of his two company ships.

When General Santa Anna marched on Texas, he already had a well-deserved reputation as a ladies' man. The forty-two-year-old dandy had handsome features, wore expensive clothes, and had elegant tastes; even while on military campaigns, he slept on silk sheets and dined with crystal stemware and silver serving dishes. When he began his fateful Texas expedition, he left behind in Mexico a matronly, long-suffering wife and a succession of expensive mistresses favored with lavish estates.[1] During the Mexican thirteen-day siege of the Alamo at San Antonio, his sexual passions were aroused by a seventeen-year-old beauty named Melchora Iniega Barrera. After her mother prevented his efforts to seduce Melchora, the resourceful Santa Anna arranged a mock marriage conducted by a Mexican sergeant impersonating a priest. After the fall of the Alamo on March 6, 1836, the newlyweds on March 31 left San Antonio in a royal coach pulled by six white mules. On April 2, high water at the Guadalupe River forced the general to return his bride, the heavy carriage, and a trunkload of silver to Mexico City. According to legend, Melchora later had his child before legally marrying the Mexican sergeant "priest."

When Santa Anna reached San Felipe on the Brazos River, he decided to turn *down* river and chase the interim government of Texas President David G. Burnet then at Harrisburg, only a few miles northwest of New Washington. General Sam Houston, the commander in chief of the Texian army, had earlier retreated *up* the Brazos from San Felipe, encamping for twelve days at Groce's Landing to drill his ragged army. On April 12,

---

[1] Santa Anna had five children by his wife Doña Inés; of the two daughters and three sons, one died in infancy and another was retarded.

94

General Houston crossed the Brazos on the steamboat *Yellowstone* and marched his army toward the coast.

At sundown on April 15, Santa Anna reached deserted Harrisburg and learned from three of Gail Borden's printers that President Burnet had left two days earlier to join his family at New Washington after ordering the ad interim government to Galveston Island. The stymied Mexican general burned Harrisburg and dragged the printing press of Borden's revolutionary newspaper, *The Telegraph and Texas Register,* into Buffalo Bayou. In the meantime, Mexican soldiers were looting houses on the opposite side of the bayou, taking women's apparel, fruits, preserves, chocolates, and a fine piano as booty. On the morning of April 17, Col. Juan Almonte and a company of dragoons rode down to New Washington to find the town deserted except for the indentured servants minding Colonel Morgan's plantation; their master was away serving as commandant of Galveston. At the time, Emily Morgan may have been helping President Burnet and his family to store their personal effects in Morgan's warehouse before boarding the *Flash* anchored offshore. The Burnets managed to escape by rowboat to the schooner, but Emily and the other servants were captured by Almonte. Santa Anna and 750 infantrymen arrived at New Washington at noon on April 18. After burning and sacking the town, the Mexican dictator emptied Morgan's warehouses of James's prized orange grove. Santa Anna had been without a woman for two weeks, so when he first noticed Emily Morgan, he took the pretty, shapely, golden-skinned servant as his personal prize.

While the Mexican general was at New Washington, he also nabbed a mulatto boy named Turner, a printer's apprentice and excellent horseman, who was bribed and sent ahead with some Mexican dragoons to scout for Houston's location. Before he departed, Emily pulled Turner aside, told him that General Houston was camped near Lynchburg, and persuaded him to warn the Texian leader of Santa Anna's approach if he had the chance. Turner then used his faster horse to outdistance the dragoons and reach the Texian camp on the morning of April 20. Emily was thus able to send an indirect alert to General Houston before reaching the battlesite herself. When the mulatto boy returned, he misled Santa Anna into thinking that Houston's army was on the Trinity River.

At 8:00 A.M. on April 20, a false alarm threw the Mexican leader into a state of panic when Capt. Marcos Barragan and his dragoons raced into New Washington shouting that General Houston's main army was right behind them. Two miles back, Barragan had run into Col. Sidney Sherman and a Texian scouting party of forty horsemen; in the exchange of fire, the Mexicans suffered four losses before they broke and ran. Although Santa Anna regained his composure after several slugs of opium, his fear spread to the troops, and Col. Pedro Delgado was able to restore order only after leading a futile search for the enemy. That day the weight of the plunder, a twelve-pound cannon, and the heavy ordnance cases slowed the Mexican army to a snail's pace as they slogged through the boggy marshlands headed west toward Lynch's Ferry on the San Jacinto River.

At two o'clock on the afternoon of April 20, Santa Anna's army reached the perimeter of a large wooded area, a small, rolling prairie where Buffalo Bayou meets the San Jacinto River. Houston's army had reached the area three hours earlier and was encamped only a mile away, hidden by trees and underbrush. By this time the impatient Santa Anna was pining with desire for Emily and determined to march no further. Thus he hastily chose this plain of San Jacinto as a campsite, although it violated all military convention. All the officers of the Mexican general's staff openly opposed the location of the camp; Colonel Delgado later summarized their concern as follows:

We had the enemy on our right, within a wood, at long

96

musket range. Our front, although level, was exposed to the fire of the enemy, who could keep it up with impunity from his sheltered position. Retreat was easy for him on his rear and right, while our own troops had no space for manoeuvering. We had in our rear a small grove, reaching to the bay shore, . . . What ground had we to retreat upon in case of a reversal? From sad experience, I answer — None!

In contrast, Santa Anna's lust for Emily led him to carefully locate his own gaudy silk marquee on a romantic, honeymoonlike spot, a rise overlooking San Jacinto Bay. This octagonal-shaped red-striped headquarters "tent" was carpeted and contained three rooms. Crates of champagne stood at the entrance; inside were medicine chests full of opium for Santa Anna's addiction, the stolen piano, silverware, china, gourmet foods — and Emily. To further impress the comely concubine, her lover foolishly exposed himself to enemy fire, bedecked with medals and ornate headpiece and prancing on his big bay.

When Santa Anna made camp, the only enemy he could see was a tiny force of thirty Texians and two small cannons along the distant fringe of timber. The sight and a fresh dose of opium emboldened him for battle, so he ordered his musicians to play "Deguello," the old throat-cutting song of no quarter played during the Alamo assault. He then ordered Colonel Delgado to engage the Texians in a skirmish from the grove of trees between the two camps. Delgado had been placed in charge of the cannons and took the twelve-pounder, the Gold Standard, with him. In the artillery duel that followed, Mexican cannoneers wounded Lt. Col James Neill while the Texians returned fire with the "Twin Sisters." During the exchange, Santa Anna issued a ridiculous order to Delgado, telling him to unload the cannon powder and ammunition from pack mules and leave it unprotected on the island of timber. Shortly thereafter, a direct hit broke the Gold Standard's limber (the detachable fore part of the gun carriage), partially disabling the cannon. This

97

Texian shot also scattered the Mexican ordnance boxes and killed two pack mules.

For the next two hours, all was quiet; then at 4:00 P.M. hostilities resumed after Lt. Col. Sidney Sherman received General Houston's reluctant permission to attempt to capture the unguarded Mexican cannon. Sherman had specific orders, however, not to engage in a major battle. Just as Sidney and his seventy volunteers approached the island of timber, they saw Colonel Delgado scurry away with the Gold Standard. Awaiting the Texians were fifty Mexican dragoons commanded by Capt. Miguel Aguirre, who shouted, *"Soldados God Dammes, vere usted"* (God Damn Soldiers, come here). Once the Texians accepted the invitation and charged, Santa Anna sent in two companies of riflemen as reinforcements. Sherman's men won the initial clash, then had to retreat to dismount and reload their rifles; at that point the Mexicans attacked before the Texians remounted and forced them back a second time. During the melee, Private Mirabeau B. Lamar saved the lives of both Secretary of War Thomas J. Rusk and Private Walter Lane, a future Confederate general. After General Houston denied Sherman's appeal for infantry support during the seesaw fight, the Texians finally retreated with only two men badly wounded. When the cavalry skirmish was over, Houston had hot words with Sidney but promoted Lamar to the rank of full colonel of the cavalry for his valor. To the men in camp, however, Sherman was a hero and Sam was resented for refusing to reinforce the brash assault leader. As the troops watched Houston's raft being built that night for another possible retreat, there were mutinous mutterings about defying further orders to run. Secretary of War Rusk even told the general that his men would follow some other leader if he did not order an attack the next day.

At 9:00 A.M. on April 21, Mexican general Martín Perfecto de Cos arrived with 500 reinforcements to give Santa Anna a total force of some 1,300. Since Cos's men were weary and sleepy after a long march, they were ordered to stack their arms and go to sleep in an adjoining grove. At about the same time, nine young recruits from the United States reached Houston's camp after rowing an eight-oar cutter from Galveston. One of them later recalled that

> . . . a Scene singularly wild and picturesque presented itself to our view. Around 20 or 30 campfires stood as many groups of men: English, Irish, Scots, Mexicans, French, Germans, Italians, Poles, Yankees, all unwashed and unshaved, their long hair and beards and mustaches matted, their clothes in tatters and plastered with mud. A more savage looking band could scarcely have been assembled. Yet many were gentlemen, owners of large estates. Some were distinguished for oratory, some in science, some in medicine. Many had graced famous drawing rooms. Their guns were of every size and shape. They numbered less than 800.

Early that morning, General Houston climbed a tree and watched Emily serve Santa Anna his breakfast. At 10:00 A.M. he sent scout Deaf Smith to estimate the total number of the enemy by counting tent tops. When the spying assignment was completed, Smith reported that the Mexican officers and soldiers were partying with their campwomen (*soldaderas*); it was customary for Mexican troops to keep women who would cook, forage, and perform conjugal duties. At the end of Deaf's report, Sam Houston remarked, "I hope that slave girl makes him neglect his business and keeps him in bed all day." Around noon, Smith suggested that Vince's Bridge should be destroyed to prevent further Mexican reinforcements. This bridge spanning Vince's Bayou was eight miles back on the road to Harrisburg and was the only exit to the Brazos, where second-in-command General Filisola was encamped with 2,000 men. When Deaf said he could burn the bridge if given six men from the spy company, Houston consented to the attempt although fearful that Smith would be killed. After providing him with two axes, General Houston told his chief scout, "Unless you hasten, you will find the prairie changed from green to red on your return." Early that afternoon, Deaf and his men burned and cut down the cedar timber bridge with Smith himself chopping down the bridge supports. Thus there was to be no means of escape for *either* army later that day.

From noon until 2:00 P.M., General Houston held his first and only council of war of the entire campaign. Surprisingly, only the two most junior members among his eight field officers voted to attack that afternoon; Sidney Sherman, Mirabeau B. Lamar, and John A. Wharton were against the idea. The consensus was that sending raw troops with few bayonets across a mile-long open prairie in daylight was simply too risky. In a diary he kept of the Mexican army's campaign in Texas, Lt. Col. José Enrique de la Peña included the following fascinating bit of intelligence:

> ... A slave appeared before Houston at three o'clock the afternoon of the 21st, informing him that General Santa Anna was sleeping and that his camp had delivered itself over to a feeling of confidence and *great abandon*. [Could Emily have sent Turner on yet another mission?]

At 3:30 that afternoon, General Houston mustered his army of 783 Texians in a two-man-deep line that extended for a thousand yards. There was not a single Mexican sentry in view when the Texians assembled in battle formation.

Leading the charge on his white stallion "Saracen," Houston gave the order, "Trail arms! Forward!" at 4:00 P.M., a time when the April sun was lowering and shining directly into the Mexicans' eyes. Screened by rising ground and tall prairie grass, the Texians silently advanced on the run. When they were within sixty yards of the Mexican breastworks, General Houston shouted the order, "Kneel! Shoot Low! Fire!"; obviously, the Mexican targets were in a horizontal position and were caught either sleeping, lying about, or in afternoon lovemaking. Most of the Texian infantry opened fire with one deadly volley, then turned to rifles as clubs and Bowie knives as daggers rather then take time to reload. Many of the canny Texas frontiersmen, however, acted solo-style in deciding when to shoot. Capt. W. J. E. Heard remembered Houston yelling when they crested the hill, "Halt, Halt! Now is the critical time! Fire away! God damn you, fire! Aren't you going to fire at all?" Once the shooting started the four-piece Texian band, a drummer and three fifers, began to play the only tune that all of them knew. Walter Lane always insisted that the song was "The Girl I Left Behind" but every other eyewitness says it was "Will You Come to the Bower?" [2] This popular love song included the following suggestive lyrics:

---

[2] There is also dispute as to who actually played this song. According to family tradition, the descendants in the Davis-Mc-Cullough-Schwab family line insist that Houston's army had only two musicians, fiddle players Daniel and George Washington Davis, but no fifers or drummers. Although General Houston did have a black freedman, Dick, who beat a tom-tom as a camp wake-up call each morning, he was *not* a military drummer.

Daniel Davis, a native of Georgia, and his son George came to Texas in early 1831 as colonists of Green De Witt and settled near Gonzales. Each received a league of land as head of family while another son, John, received one-third that amount since he was single. All of the Davis men were fiddle players. John was among the thirty-two volunteers from Gonzales who died at the alamo. His father Daniel fought in the Battle of Gonzales, and the famous "Come and Take It" cannon was buried in brother George's peach orchard. After General Houston ordered the burning of Gonzales, Daniel and George Davis joined the retreating Texian army.

According to family lore, here is the scenario on the day of the Battle of San Jacinto. Houston planned to deceive the Mexican army into thinking his troops were carrying out a drill. He thus ordered his two fiddlers to play something that Texians knew that did not sound aggressive; that was good news for the Davis boys since they didn't know a march anyway! In carrying out Sam's wishes, they chose a crude-but-popular frontier love song, "Will You Come to the Bower?" As Daniel and George repeatedly scraped out their waltz tune at an awkward march tempo, the Texian army formed two long columns at

101

Will you come to the bower I have shaded for you?
Our bed shall be roses all spangled with dew.
There under the bower on sweet roses you'll lie
With a blush on your cheek but a smile in your eye.

During the deadly Texian assault, Houston had two horses shot from under him and his right ankle was shattered by a three-ounce copper ball. Sidney Sherman's Second Regiment was on the extreme left wing of the line and was the first to make contact with the enemy. Their assignment was to assault the right side of the Mexican camp, which was in a grove of trees. Sherman's eager men hit the enemy with "hornet hate," and General Houston credited him with being the first to shout the terrible battle cry: "Remember the Alamo! Remember Goliad!" This impassioned, thunderous cry spread down the Texian line like a lighted fuse; coming after dead silence, it probably had a more demoralizing effect on the Santanistas than did the Texian gunfire. The sudden, savage attack caught the Mexicans by total surprise and in the midst of daylong dissipation. Colonel Delgado later implied he was the only officer in camp who wasn't either asleep or having a party and admitted that the Mexican infantrymen were a "bewildered and panic-stricken herd" that offered only token resistance.

When the Battle of San Jacinto began, Santa Anna

3:30 P.M. and started to advance out of Mexican gunshot range. To enemy lookouts the maneuver appeared to be a semicomic parade drill. Up until the first shots and the Texian charge at 4:00 P.M., the wail of the Davis fiddlers could be heard on the left side of the battle line. During the eighteen-minute melee, the two intrepid musicians stayed behind at the tree line and continued to saw away.

George W. Davis received a veteran's grant for participating at San Jacinto, and his name is on the monument there. His father never applied for the bounty since he "only played the fiddle" that historic day. At age sixty, Daniel Davis took part in the Mier Expedition and drew a white bean in the lottery of death. After two years in Perote prison, he went home to Gonzales broken in health. His son George served in the Civil War and died in 1880. Both rest in the burial plot named in their honor, Fiddler's Bend Cemetery, near Yoakum.

was literally "caught with his pants down" having a diverting nap with Emily Morgan. Upon hearing shots, he rushed out of his tent wearing only red slippers, white silk drawers, and a linen shirt. Delgado said,

> . . . I saw His Excellency running around in the utmost excitement, wringing his hands, and unable to give an order. Some cried out to commence firing; others to lie down to avoid grape shots. Among the latter was His Excellency.

Instead of rallying his forces, the "Napoleon of the West" grabbed a bed sheet, a box of Harrisburg chocolates, and a gourd water bottle, then mounted "Old Whip," a fine stallion stolen from Allen Vince, and fled the scene of battle. The Mexican leader later claimed he was asleep at 4:30 P.M. "from fatigue and long vigils when the din and fire of battle awoke me." Circumstantial evidence would indicate, however, that all the action was not outside his tent that fateful afternoon. After the rout, George Erath searched Santa Anna's quarters and found ample evidence of a party interrupted in progress, including baskets of champagne and cooked gourmet food left uneaten. Erath later remarked that the Mexican general's personal effects were such "as a European prince might have taken with him in the field" and that much of the San Jacinto victory was due to "Santa Anna's voluptuousness."

The Mexican soldiers who tried to escape by way of Vince's Bridge were simply slaughtered in the swamps. The greatest carnage occurred in a tidewater bayou called Peggy's Lake just behind the Mexican camp; a Texian soldier said that dead Mexicans and horses made a bridge across it. Frenzied Texas troops bloodthirsty for revenge shot or clubbed enemy heads bobbing out of the water, and some frontiersmen took scalps. This personal, wanton killing upset General Houston, who wanted at least one company under discipline in case a large Mexican column under Urrea or Filisola appeared. Unable to

103

stop the bloodbath and ignored when he ordered his men
to parade, the exasperated Houston finally shouted,
"Gentlemen, I applaud your bravery. But damn your
manners!" According to Private Bob Hunter,

> . . . Gen'r'l Houston giv orders not to kill any more but
> to take prisners. Capt Easlen [William Mosby East-
> land] said Boys take prisners, you know how to take
> prisners, take them with the but of yor guns, club guns,
> & remember the Alamo, remember Labaher [La
> Bahía], & club guns right & left, & nock there God
> Damn brains out.
> The Mexicans would fall down on their knees &
> say me no Alamo, me no Labaher. . . .

When he realized that Houston was severely
wounded, General Rusk assumed command, restored
order, and brought in some 250 prisoners at sundown.
That night the Texians could hear the ghastly din of
snarling packs of wolves fighting over the Mexican
corpses scattered across the prairie.[3]

---

[3] The land where the battle was fought was owned by the widow
Margaret McCormick, called Aunt Peggy by her neighbors. She and
her husband Arthur were natives of Ireland who settled at New Orleans in the 1820s before being drawn to Texas by the prospect of one-
cent-an-acre land. Arthur McCormick was one of Austin's Old Three
Hundred colonists and received his league of land at the confluence of
Buffalo Bayou and the San Jacinto on August 10, 1824. Much of the
4,428 acres was marshland, and the McCormicks built a home near
the southwest edge of a body of water called Peggy's Lake. After Arthur drowned in 1825, Margaret raised two young sons alone and became one of the largest cattle raisers in the area, owning 600 head by
1836. During the Texas Revolution, she joined thousands of other settlers in the panic civilian flight known as the Runaway Scrape.
   When Aunt Peggy returned home a few days after the Battle of
San Jacinto, she was horrified to find the decaying remains of several
hundred Mexican soldiers strewn about her once-beautiful ranch. The
distraught widow went to General Houston's headquarters and demanded that these corpses be removed; in his memoirs, Robert Hancock Hunter reported the following exchange:

> Said Houston, "Madame, your land will be famed in history."
> "To the devil with your glorious history," she retorted. "Take
> them dead Mexicans off my league. They'll haunt me for the longest

The Battle of San Jacinto lasted eighteen minutes. In his official report, General Houston stated that 630 Mexicans were killed, 208 were wounded, and 730 were taken prisoner. Only nine Texians were killed or mortally wounded. Santa Anna, however, managed to elude the victors. When he fled the battlefield, he gave Old Whip his head and the stallion's homing instinct took him to Allen Vince's corrals near burned-out Vince's Bridge. After miring his mount in an attempt to foard the bayou, Santa Anna walked to a slave cabin on the deserted Vince ranch, where he put on a slave's garb. That night he lost his sense of direction and began to walk aimlessly back toward the Texian camp. When Sgt. James A. Sylvester captured the former dandy at 11:00 A.M. the next day, he had bare, bleeding feet and was wearing a filthy blue cotton jacket, domestic cotton pants, and a stinking hide cap. His importance was not known until other Mexican prisoners greeted him with cries of *"El Presidente!"*

At 2:00 P.M. on April 22, Santa Anna was brought before the reclining General Houston, who was nursing his shattered ankle. Before the two-hour interview, the shaken Mexican leader had to chew opium plugs to regain his composure. Unaware that Houston intended to keep him alive, he gave the secret Masonic distress signal.

On May 14, 1836, interim President Burnet and

---

day I'll live."

Old Sam detailed some soldiers to bury the Mexicans, but the stench of death stymied their efforts. Since the general could not bring himself to burn the bodies, nothing more was done and later visitors to the battlefield collected bones as souvenirs. The year after the battle, a bitter Margaret told the Harris County tax assessor that the dead Mexicans had destroyed the value of her land.

Mrs. McCormick was even more agitated after finding about half of her livestock missing, evidently used as a food supply by both armies. She later made an unsuccessful claim to the Texas government for 140 head of cattle, forty hogs, and seventy-five bushels of corn even though a House committee admitted that her claims were "in a considerable extent meritorious." Aunt Peggy lived alone in her twilight years before being robbed and murdered in the 1850s.

Santa Anna signed both public and secret treaties at Velasco. The public treaty declared an end to all hostilities with all Mexican troops evacuating Texas to the southern side of the Rio Grande; the provisional government also pledged Santa Anna's immediate safe return to Mexico. In the secret treaty, the Mexican dictator pledged to use his influence with the Mexican government to secure the recognition of Texas independence with its southern boundary as the Rio Grande. Burnet was severely criticized when the public treaty was made known; angry mutterings arose from Texians who wanted death for this tyrant with the blood of the Alamo and the Goliad Massacre on his hands. It was President Houston who eventually settled the problem of what to do with Santa Anna. In late November 1836, he sent the Mexican general to visit American president Andrew Jackson, who returned him to Mexico and temporary retirement.

But what of Emily Morgan? Immediately after the Battle of San Jacinto, she was escorted back to New Washington, a seven- or eight-mile trip, by a member of the Texian spy company; most likely her escort was either Deaf Smith or his black son-in-law, Hendrick Arnold, since both had used her as a contact at Morgan's plantation. Emily told her story to Colonel Morgan on April 23, and he was so impressed with her notable contribution that he granted her freedom and bought her a house among the tiny free Negro population in the new city of Houston. In 1839 *Houston Morning Star* estimated there were only twenty to thirty free Negroes in the town. Little wonder, then, that Emily was soon issued a Texas passport as "a free woman" in 1837 and chose to return to her home in the free state of New York, where she faded into obscurity. James Morgan later purchased the candy-striped tent of Santa Anna and gave it to Samuel Swartwout, a business partner and the customs collector of New York. Colonel Morgan also told Emily's story verbatim to an English friend, the ethnologist William Bollaert, who visited Texas from December 1841 until April

106

1844 and kept diaries of his experiences. Although Bollaert was among the first to record Emily's account, it was not until 1956 that a major edited part of his writings appeared in a book titled *William Bollaert's Texas.* The book quotes an assertion made by William on July 7, 1842, after he had "gazed with some interest" on the San Jacinto battlefield. After crediting James Morgan in his diary, Bollaert noted:

> The Battle of San Jacinto was probably lost by the Mexicans, owing to the influence of a mulatto girl [Emily] belonging to Colonel James Morgan. She was closeted in the tent with General Santana at the time the cry was made: "The enemy! They come! They come!" She detained Santana so long that order could not be restored readily again.

The saga of Emily Morgan was widely circulated as a part of Texas folklore long before Bollaert's account was published. For years Mexican historians have verified Emily's presence at San Jacinto, referring to her in such terms as Santa Anna's "quadroon mistress during the Texas Campaign." In his 1959 book about the battle, *The Day of San Jacinto,* Frank X. Tolbert also cites the Bollaert account of Emily Morgan. The earliest known copy of the song "The Yellow Rose of Texas" appeared soon after the Battle of San Jacinto. This handwritten version was addressed to "E. A. Jones" and signed by an unidentified "H. B. C." It was written by a mysterious black lover who had deserted his sweetheart and wanted her back. The lyrics are as follows:

> There's a yellow rose in Texas
> That I am a going to see
> No other darky knows her
> No one only me
> She cryed so when I left her
> It like to broke my heart
> And if I ever find her
> We nevermore will part.

Chorus I (of three):
She's the sweetest rose of color
This darky ever knew
Her eyes are bright as diamonds
They sparkle like the dew
You may talk about dearest May
and sing of Rosa Lee
But the yellow rose of Texas
Beats the belles of Tennessee.

Another version of the song soon appeared about "Emily, the Maid of Morgan's Point." The first published edition of "The Yellow Rose of Texas" in sheet music form was copyrighted in September 1858. Confederate soldiers marched to the tune during the Civil War. In 1936 David W. Guion composed a concert transcription of the song to commemorate the Texas centennial and dedicated it to President Franklin D. Roosevelt, who phoned his personal thanks and had Guion play it at the White House. Then in 1955 Mitch Miller and Chorus recorded Don George's arrangement of the folk song for Columbia Records. Miller and his singers quickly made this the best-known version of the tune on his sing-along television show. Former U.S. Senator Ralph Yarborough often used this song to attract voters to his Texas campaign rallies. In the Miller version of the chorus, the lyrics have been amended quite a bit:

She's the sweetest little rosebud,
That Texas ever knew,
Her eyes are bright as diamonds,
They sparkle like the dew,
You may talk about your Clementine
and sing of Rosalee,
But The Yellow Rose of Texas
is the only girl for me!

In 1976 Martha Anne Turner, the author of numerous books on Texas subjects, wrote an account of Emily Morgan titled *The Yellow Rose of Texas: Her Saga and Her Song*. She pointed out that until comparatively recent times, twentieth-century Texas historians tended to ignore Emily's presence at San Jacinto or treat the inci-

108

dent as myth. Turner concluded that several factors contributed to the censorship of Emily: Historians and writers would not permit the idea of sex to tarnish any
account of the celebrated battle; Texas history was usually offered to students of grammar school level, so allu-
sion to sex was avoided; male chauvinism and race prejudice colored some accounts of the battle. Author Turner
best stated the modern-day case for the "Yellow Rose of
Texas" by saying, "Whether or not the mulatto girl wit-
tingly detained Santa Anna — she had little choice — she
deserves to be elevated to her rightful place as a heroine
of Texas history." [4]

---

[4] In 1985 Dr. Margaret Swett Henson, a retired University of
Houston historian, historical consultant, and author of several books,
in her investigation of the Yellow Rose, found that Emily D. West had
free papers when she arrived in Texas. She wasn't a slave and didn't
belong to Colonel Morgan or anyone else, and that there is no link
connecting her with the old song "The Yellow Rose of Texas." Professor Henson notes that two eyewitness Mexican detractors of General
Santa Anna failed to mention his dallying with a woman. Neither
Ramón Caro, Santa Anna's secretary at San Jacinto who wrote a
vindictive exposé of the dictator, nor Col. Pedro Francisco Delgado,
who kept a diary, recorded anything about a woman in the general's
tent. Dr. Henson goes on to say:

> No contemporary at the battle said anything about Santa Anna in
> the tent with Emily. The closest remark was that of George Erath [a
> Texan soldier who later gave his name to a county], who spoke of
> Santa Anna's "voluptuousness," which in the 19th century might as
> well refer to the opium habit as the sexual interpretation by 20th-
> century historians.

She contends that William Bollaert's gossipy footnote about Emily
Morgan "fixed the myth" and that "the story of a woman in the tent
was a popular ribald tale told by men who wanted to believe that
about Santa Anna." Henson does admit, however, that Colonel Morgan possibly employed Emily as a housekeeper, that Santa Anna perhaps acquired her services after arriving at Morgan's house, and that
she did accompany the Mexican army to the battleground.

Kent Biffle has written a feature story about Margaret Henson's
findings for *The Dallas Morning News*. In an article titled "Yellow
Rose Story Loses Its Bloom," he sums up the frustration of the lover of
Texana who must choose between the folklore and scholarly percep-
tions of the Yellow Rose of Texas by saying, "Will somebody please
tell Margaret that overly energetic documentation can sure wreck a
good story."

V

William Goyens:
A True-blue Black Texian

William Goyens came to Texas in 1820 as a penniless "free man of color." When he died in 1856, he was one
of the largest landowners in East Texas, leaving an estate that would make him a millionaire based on present
land values.

After first escaping an attempt at enslavement, he
became a self-taught scholar and the most important
black leader of his era. Goyens was a trusted Indian agent
and an indispensable link between Texas and Cherokee
leaders. He prospered in the business world as a blacksmith, innkeeper, freighter, lawyer, money lender, and
land speculator. His friend and confidant, Sam Houston,
described William as "one of the greatest persons of integ-
rity known to Texas during the 1800s." This is his story, a
chronicle of black achievement amid adversity.

He was one of nine mulatto children and was born
into a free Negro family in the slave state of North Carolina in 1794. His father, William Going, was married to a
white woman and had earned free status as a soldier
after the state assembly promised freedom to any slave
who would serve in the Revolutionary army; in fact, he
later received a pension for his service. However, there
were few practical advantages in being free for the Going

110

William Goyens in front of his blacksmith shop in Nacogdoches, Texas, ca. 1840. Watercolor by M. Emanuel.

Courtesy University of Texas Institute of Texan Cultures, San Antonio

William Goyens, Sam Houston, and John Forbes with Chief Bowles at treaty-making with the Cherokees (1836). Painting by Kermit Oliver, 1960s.

Courtesy Texas Southern University, Houston, Texas

111

family after the American Revolution. They had to wear patches on their left shoulders emblazoned with the word "free"; they could not carry firearms or buy or sell liquor; their only chance to receive an education came by learning to read borrowed books. After reading the life story of Capt. John Smith, young William Goyens (his name an improvisation of his father's) found a model for his life. The magic of the printed page led him to a knowledge of rhetoric and logic, law, philosophy, theology, astronomy, and geometry.

When he was twelve years old, William was told to go to Mexico if he hoped to become more than a slave. After receiving letters from a friend who had gone to Texas, Goyens realized that this far frontier offered real opportunities to a free Negro and decided to go there in spite of his father's opposition. Traveling by sea from North Carolina to New Orleans, he then went overland to Texas on El Camino Real (The Royal Highway) from Natchitoches, Louisiana, to Nacogdoches, Texas, arriving in 1820. He found Nacogdoches nearly abandoned and in ruins, with only five houses and a church standing. Prior to 1812 the town — the only one in East Texas at the time — had a population of nearly 1,000, but the Spanish reaction to a series of unsuccessful filibustering expeditions had taken a vengeful toll on the settlement. Goyens, however, liked the location and decided to make Nacogdoches his permanent home.

When William first came to Texas, his personal freedom was in jeopardy. Although the Mexican Constitution of 1824 prohibited Negro slavery, a state law of 1828 provided that Texas immigrants could "liberate" their slaves, then make them indentured servants for life. In the early 1820s Goyens went before Erasmo Seguin and had himself declared a freeholder of Nacogdoches. However, while he was on a freight-hauling trip to Natchitoches in 1826, a man named Bele English claimed William as his property. Before English would cancel the claim, Goyens was forced to pay 1,000 pesos, buy a slave woman from Señor Llorca, and transfer her ownership to Bele. Ironically, he bought his first slave to avoid slavery himself! Shortly thereafter, the light-skinned mulatto petitioned the Nacogdoches alcalde, who officially ruled that Goyens was in fact a free man.

His first occupation was that of blacksmith, a common trade for a free Negro. On May 7, 1827, he bought a town lot north of Banita Creek near the present county courthouse and built a house there, operating an inn in connection with his home. William's work force in the adjacent blacksmith shop included both slaves and hired white men. He was soon involved in gunsmithing, wagon manufacture and repair, carpentry, and hauling freight between Nacogdoches and Natchitoches. By the time he became a Roman Catholic in 1831, he was a prominent businessman and the owner of four slaves. William was fluent in both English and Spanish and gained a reputation as a learned man, one who could read even better than he wrote. In addition to his intellectual pursuits, he devoted long hours to prayer and Bible study and later lamented to his friend, Sam Houston, that he had no time left for study after devoting his day to other men's affairs and his own family. Even after becoming a wealthy man, he dressed simply and was known to be hospitable, kind, good-humored and even-tempered; a friend remarked that "he [Goyens] seemed to be born and made for friendship."

William was also involved in the making of a local legend. After the ill-fated Fredonian Rebellion in December 1826, a Mexican garrison of 200 commanded by Colonel Piedras was established in Nacogdoches the following June. Local unrest caused by the restrictive state colonization law of 1830 resulted in a Texian attack on the Mexican garrison on August 2, 1832; the Battle of Nacogdoches ended two days later when Piedras surrendered his command to Col. James Bullock. Shortly thereafter, the chastised Mexican leader visited blacksmith Goyens, bringing two large copper pots and a mysterious request:

113

he wanted two large cans with lids, each four feet high and two feet in diameter, to be forged from the pots. After the task was completed, Piedras asked William to seal the cans but not to inspect their contents. That night Goyens recorded in his diary that his handiwork contained Mexican gold and silver pieces, jewels, and church valuables. Piedras later buried the sealed cans on the banks of Ysleta Creek, and the treasure has yet to be recovered.

In 1832 the thirty-eight-year-old Goyens married an attractive white woman, the widow Mary Pate Sibley (or Lindsey), a Georgia native who had one son, eleven-year-old Henry, by her first marriage. Mary and her son had been boarding at William's inn since 1829. The nuptials were conducted by Father Deus, the local Roman Catholic priest. After this wedding, Henry became Goyens's ward; the couple would have no children of their own. Since Texas laws forbade racially mixed marriages, William always faced the possibility of legal harassment and a charge of moral turpitude; nevertheless, such local notables as Sam Houston accepted Mary as his wife.

The newlyweds in 1832 purchased over a thousand acres of land four miles northwest of Nacogdoches on El Camino Real (now State Highway 21) and built a large two-story frame house on the highest hill in the county. They remained there the rest of their lives. The area is known today as Goyens Hill; the crest is now the site of the Goyens Hill Baptist Church.

The couple was never fully accepted by Anglos, and social ostracism was probably the reason for their move to the country. In July 1834 Mary's two apprehensive brothers journeyed from Louisiana to meet her spouse and remarked that they were "well pleased" with both William and her situation; they no doubt envied the material success of their illiterate sister. By this time Goyens had started a new business activity, a sawmill and gristmill on Ysleta Creek several miles west of their home. When he sold part of the mill operation to Henry Raguet in December 1841, he received $7,000 for this thousand-acre Mill Tract.

William's most lucrative business dealings involved land speculation and money lending. He bought or sold more than fifty pieces of property. His real estate transactions required the services of such prominent Nacogdoches attorneys as Thomas J. Rusk and Charles S. Taylor. Goyens was a party to more than thirty lawsuits, most of them involving either efforts of white neighbors to take his property or failure to honor debts owed him. He also bought and owned slaves for strictly economic reasons but tended to quickly resell them. In 1835 he started the legal paperwork for the league and labor of land due him either as a Mexican citizen or for later service in the Texas Revolution — valid claims that were never honored. The Republic of Texas census of 1840 showed him as owning 5,067 acres of land, a town lot in Nacogdoches, fifty-five head of cattle, several horses, a silver watch, and a clock. By 1842 he owned 11,466 acres of land.

The white abolitionist Benjamin Lundy boarded with William while passing through Nacogdoches in 1832 and 1834. At the time, Lundy was hoping to found a colony of free United States blacks and runaway slaves near Tamualipas, Mexico; in fact, the Mexican government offered him some encouragement in the scheme but the project died with the coming of the Texas Revolution. In his diary entry of July 14, 1834, Lundy noted:

> I went about four miles into the country to the house of Wm Goyens, a very respectable coloured man, with whom I became acquainted here in 1832. He still takes a deep interest in my enterprise. He has a white wife, a native of Georgia. They appear to live happily together, are quite wealthy, and are considered as very respectable, by the people generally.

While on this visit Lundy was William's guest at a ball

115

held by some of the town's Mexican residents. Only Mexican women were present, but Goyens had no trouble finding dancing partners since *any* white blood made one socially acceptable according to Spanish law and custom. His mulatto host later obtained a pony from the Cherokees for Benjamin to continue his travels.

Goyens was also active in civic affairs. As early as September 1824, his name appeared on the voting list for the election of an alcalde for Nacogdoches. He developed a working knowledge of law and served as an attorney in Mexican courts, thus becoming Texas's first black lawyer. In the 1820s he practiced in the alcalde's court in Nacogdoches, where an examination of the town archives attests to his familiarity with Mexican law. William appeared as a witness in two lawsuits, took depositions, filed pleas, and issued judicial decisions while serving as arbitrator in the local court. His community standing was such that Nacogdoches chose him as a representative to the Consultation of 1835 that was to establish a provisional state government for Texas. Although he declined the honor out of fear that he might face racial discrimination in such unfamiliar surroundings, Goyens was to serve Texas in an even more important capacity.

In the 1820s he first began to act as an interpreter in Indian affairs for Mexican authorities. Since there was Cherokee blood on his father's side and his boyhood home in Moore County, North Carolina, was close to Cherokee lands, William knew their customs and could speak with them at a level above sign language. The Cherokees first entered Texas from Arkansas in 1819 and 1820 and settled near the Angelina, Neches, and Trinity rivers. As early as the summer of 1826, Cherokee Chief Richard Fields was using Goyens as his contact with the alcalde of Nacogdoches. In his role as Indian interpreter, William became a trusted friend and adviser to the Cherokees. He did some trading with them since Goyens Hill was on the edge of Indian country and a clear spring at its base was an Indian watering hole.

116

Upon the outbreak of the Texas Revolution, Gen. Sam Houston named Goyens as Texas Indian agent and interpreter to negotiate with and carry messages to the Cherokees. This assignment required William to make numerous trips into Indian country for the purpose of probing their attitude and sympathies regarding the war with Mexico. Evidently, both Houston and Gen. Thomas J. Rusk placed considerable faith and trust in Goyens; in a letter sent to Chief Bowles on September 24, 1835, the two said:

> Your talks have reached us by the hands of your friend William Goings [Goyens] . . . We have heard that you wish Mr. Goings to go with you and hear the talk. We are willing that he should go because we believe him to be a man that will not tell a lie either for the White man or the Red man.

Houston's dependence on him is revealed in the following note sent to Dr. Robert A. Irion of Nacogdoches on January 23, 1837: ". . . Give my respects to Mr. Guyons [Goyens] Agent, and tell him how much I rely upon him. Tell him to write me often." William's writing proficiency is shown in the following report to General Houston dated May 10, 1837:

> Sir: During the week last past I was notified by Bowles of his return, and of his wish that I should attend a talk at his village on Saturday last. Pursuant to his invitation, together with Colonel Millard, I arrived at Bowles' town. . . . The substance of his speech in relation to his journey is as follows. . . . I have the honor to be with respect, your obedient humble servant, William Goyens.

When the Consultation of 1835 met at San Felipe, they authorized the provisional state governor and the general council to negotiate with the East Texas Cherokees with the aim of defining Cherokee land boundaries and guaranteeing their claim to it in exchange for a Cherokee promise to remain at peace during the revolu-

117

tion. General Houston and John Forbes were sent to negotiate such a treaty in February 1836, with Goyens serving to interpret all messages at the meetings. The Houston-Forbes Treaty subsequently set the boundaries for Cherokee land as the area northwest of El Camino Real between the Sabine and Angelina rivers. The Indians kept their part of the treaty terms, but President Houston was angered and distressed when the postwar Republic of Texas Senate balked at ratifying the treaty. Once again, Houston pressed his friend, William Goyens, into service as an Indian agent with the objective of bringing the two sides to an amicable agreement. In August 1838 General Rusk sent several messages to Chief Bowles through William, assuring the Cherokees of his good, peaceful intentions and promising that they need fear no attack.

Despite the agent's best efforts, the Texas Senate declared the wartime treaty null and void on December 16, 1837, clearing the way for the eventual tragic and bloody Cherokee eviction from lands promised them. Goyens was greatly saddened at hearing of the Battle of the Neches in July 1839, which resulted in a Cherokee defeat and their forced removal from East Texas. It now seemed as if all his years' efforts as Indian agent had been in vain.

William faced an uncertain future after the Texas Constitution of 1836 required all free Negroes to get congressional approval to remain in the Republic of Texas. Even though this limitation was lifted in June 1837, the Ashworth Law of February 1840 gave "free persons of color" two years to leave Texas; those who stayed beyond that time without congressional permission were to be arrested and sold as slaves. Leaving Texas would forfeit twenty years of effort and achievement for William Goyens, who was saved by a host of white friends. In September 1840 Gen. Thomas J. Rusk drew up a petition signed by fifty-four Nacogdoches residents requesting permission for William to remain in Texas; the signers, including such prominent citizens as Charles S. Taylor, Adolphus Sterne, Henry Raguet, Bennett Blake, S. M. Orton, and H. H. Edwards, attested that Goyens "had conducted himself as an honest, industrious citizen and has accumulated considerable property in land, etc., and has been of great service to the country in our Indian difficulties." Congress approved the appeal on November 25, 1840, and passed legislation that December allowing free Negroes and their families who resided in Texas at the time of the Declaration of Independence to stay in the republic. This intervention on behalf of Goyens paved the way for 397 free Texas Negroes to remain and be listed in the federal census of 1850.

Texas was to give a final rebuff to Goyens. Ever since the state colonization law of 1824, free blacks had been unable to obtain the Mexican land grants automatically given to white settlers. In January 1852 William attempted to get the headright of land (one league and one labor) from the state legislature that was due him for service to the Republic of Texas. His petition was referred to the Committee on Private Land Claims, but the Senate tabled the bill and he never received the headright. It seems that Goyens had all the qualifications for the land claim except one: he did not have white parents. Never one to give up easily, he hired attorney James S. Gillett of Austin in September 1853 in an attempt to collect monetary claims against the old republic. The effort resulted in a piddling $100 being awarded William for four beef cattle he had sold to the Texas army in 1839.

William Goyens's last business transaction occurred on January 17, 1856, when he sold 200 acres of land at $1.50 an acre. His wife Mary died that February and was buried two miles from their home in a small Mexican cemetery on Moral Creek. Deeply grieved by the loss, her husband became ill at home on Goyens Hill that June and was attended by Dr. William Tubbe for four days.

119

The medicines charged at Raguet's store on June 18 and June 20 indicate that William had some type of congestive fever; he was treated with whiskey, quinine, alterative pills, soda powders, a blister plaster, and an expectorant. After muttering the words "splendid and triumphant," the sixty-two-year-old Goyens died on June 20, 1856, and was buried beside his wife. Upon hearing the news his friend, U.S. Senator Sam Houston, remarked, "I would rather have lost the best man in my power than to have lost a counselor as William Goyens."

On August 19, 1856, an inventory and appraisal of Goyens's property revealed that he owned 12,423 acres of land in Nacogdoches, Angelina, and Houston counties. He also owned six slaves, and his executor estimated his wealth to be $11,917.60. The only heirs to the Goyens estate were Henrietta and Martha Sibley, the two minor daughters of his deceased stepson Henry. One-half of the estate was awarded to the two girls, with the rest being sold at auction or divided to pay possibly dubious claims against the estate. Incidentally, it should be noted that a Nacogdoches realtor in 1967 appraised the Goyens land as being worth $1,863,450.

During his life, William Goyens never held a high office; he thought of himself as simply an average member of society, yet he was the most important Texas black leader of his time. In 1936 the Texas Centennial Commission erected a granite monument over his grave, making Goyens the first black man to be so recognized. The marker concludes with a succinct tribute: ". . . His skin was black; his heart, true blue."

Portrait of Robert Potter
Courtesy North Carolina Department of Cultural Resources,
Division of Archives and History, Raleigh, North Carolina

121

VI

Robert Potter:
The "Baddest" Man in the Republic

Robert Potter was the Casanova and bad boy of the Republic of Texas. A North Carolina writer called him "one of the most outstanding characters" who ever appeared in that state, but his promising political career ended there after Robert, in a fit of jealous rage, castrated ("potterized") two men he suspected of being his wife's lovers. After serving a prison term, he joined a notable list of those who had "Gone to Texas" to escape an unpleasant past. This brilliant but erratic man became a signer of the Texas Declaration of Independence, the first secretary of the Texas navy, and a senator in the Texas Congress. Two presidents of the Republic viewed him quite differently: Sam Houston said Robert's "infamy was wider than the world and deeper than perdition" while David Burnet claimed that Potter's "heart was open to melting charity and his patriotism is of the purest kind." This amorous statesman left much of his estate to Austin paramours rather than to the woman who thought she was his legal wife. When Robert's brave and long-suffering widow was eighty-three, she told her side of the story, memoirs which provided the grist for a best-selling novel. Genius, courage, love, suffering, vengeance, deception, depravity, insanity, and violence are recurring themes as Harriet Page Potter Ames recounts her life with a man ranked as ". . . next to Houston and Rusk, the striking figure of East Texas."

Rob Potter was born in June 1799, in Granville County, North Carolina, an area then known as a haven for fugitives, outcasts, squatters, and poor whites. On March 2, 1815, the fifteen-year-old lad was appointed as midshipman in the United States Navy. There was no naval academy then, so young officers received their education on board ship. During his six years in the navy, Potter served on six ships and was schooled by the ship chaplains in Latin and English, *Plutarch's Lives,* and Shakespeare's plays. He also became an expert in the manly arts of boxing, wrestling, and fencing. After being stuck in the grade of midshipman for five years, Robert resigned from the navy on March 26, 1821, while serving on the frigate *United States* at Norfolk, Virginia. He would later claim he quit the service because both parents died, leaving him responsible for raising three orphaned family members. However, there are other plausible motives for his leaving the navy: He had fought a duel on board ship and was miffed at not being promoted to lieutenant at the eligible age of eighteen.

After his resignation, Robert returned to Halifax, North Carolina, where he studied and read law in the office of Thomas Burges and lived with the Willie Jones family on their 10,000-acre plantation, "The Grove." The Joneses were the foster parents of Potter's hero, John Paul Jones. After a few months residence, young Rob took his bar exam and was licensed to practice law. By then he had acquired an exceptional English style with a crisp and biting use of sarcasm, ridicule, and invective as his stock in trade.

In 1824 Potter took on Jesse A. Bynum, a conservative Whig and the Halifax representative to the North Carolina House of Commons. The issue was poverty and unqualified democracy against riches and rock-ribbed conservatism. Although Rob lost the election, his reputation for daring and recklessness was enhanced when he challenged Jesse to a duel, most likely because of a romantic rivalry between the two. When Bynum declined because Potter was not a gentleman, the frustrated loser posted a sign on the courthouse door calling Jesse a "poltroon and coward." Such bad blood resulted in the 1825 election being cancelled after a full-scale brawl between the two bitter factions. The next year Rob finally defeated Bynum for the House of Commons seat and served in that body through 1828. The political forum added to his reputation as a magnetic orator; when this short, stocky, bull-necked man with the flashing dark eyes and melodious voice spoke in his deliberate, bombastic style, *all* stopped to listen.

While in the House of Commons, Robert unsuccessfully sponsored a Political College bill that would have provided a free education for poor farm boys. During the Depression of 1828, he flayed the twelve-percent interest bankers (the "plunderers") and those lawyers ("extortioners") who charged such high fees. His bill to revoke the charters of the state banks failed by only one vote, 59–58, while another of Potter's legislative battles was an attempt to slash salaries and fees of judges and attorneys.

In December 1829 Robert Potter took his seat in the United States House of Representatives as a Jackson Democrat. Following the lead of his political mentor, President Andrew Jackson, Congressman Potter on May 10, 1830, offered resolutions to dissolve the Bank of the United States. Like Jackson, Robert was a "hard money" man, believing that only specie was safe money and suspicious of all paper money banknotes. His resolutions were tabled, however, by a vote of 89 to 66.

Although Potter was reelected to the Twenty-Second Congress, a heinous crime was to end his Washington career before he could be seated again. It seems that his bride of three years, the former Isabella Taylor of Granville County, had two cousins who frequently visited their Oxford home; Reverend Louis Taylor, age fifty-five, was a Methodist minister and Louis Wiley was only seventeen. For some time her possessive husband had suspected Isabella of being intimate with both men. On Sunday afternoon, August 28, 1831, Reverend Taylor visited Mrs. Potter and they took a buggy ride together. When Rob came upon the two, a jealous rage overcame him; after accusing Taylor of adultery, Potter beat him senseless, then whipped out his keen, sharp knife and castrated the prone preacher. Afterwards, he tenderly put the hapless victim to bed, boasting that he had been merciful in sparing his life. The congressman then went looking for young Wiley and treated him to the same punishment.

Both men survived the gruesome ordeal while Potter was jailed the next day and held without bail until his trial at Oxford in September 1831. Rob chose to serve as his own defense attorney. His plea was the unwritten law: the sanctity of the marriage bed. No evidence was entered except his own, and the avenging husband was convicted of the charge of maiming the younger man; the case of Reverend Taylor never went to trial. After Potter was sentenced to the maximum of two years in jail and fined $1,000, he resigned from the U.S. House of Representatives. When the next legislature met that November, they promptly passed a law making criminal emasculation ("potterizing") a capital felony punishable by death "without benefit of clergy."

Isabella Potter was granted a divorce on December 12, 1834, received custody of their two children, Susan and Robert, Jr., and gave them the maiden name of her mother, Pelham. After Rob was released from jail, he announced that he would again run for the North Carolina House of Commons. The fall campaign of 1834 was termed "Potter's War." It seems that the central issue was a bitter debate about the relative character of husband, wife, and the two victims. After a heated contest

125

that included several brawls and one shootout, Robert won back his old seat, only to confront a legislature controlled by his enemies, none of whom would dare fight him a duel or with talent enough to beat him in debate. On Christmas night of 1834, Potter and R. C. Cotten played an all-night game of cards called "Thirteen the Odd." After losing all three hands and all his money, Robert claimed he had been cheated, drew his pistol, and made off with all the booty. On January 2, 1835, the House of Commons by a vote of 62 to 52 expelled Potter for playing a game of cards unfairly. Most likely, the real motives for this action were the old maiming incident and a rumor that he was sympathetic to the plight of free Negroes in North Carolina. Robert Potter was about to join the ranks of others such as William Barret Travis and Sam Houston who had "Gone to Texas" to rebuild their ruined lives.

He first laid over in New Orleans, spending much of his time at Banks' Arcade, a three-story building on Magazine Street, where several abortive filibustering schemes had been planned to liberate Texas from Mexico. In the spring of 1835, the ever-gallant Potter responded to the letter appeal of a Colonel James, who needed some "gentleman of quality" to escort his beautiful, twenty-year-old bride to Texas. Succumbing to Rob's charms, Mrs. James fell in love with "Brother" en route but was reluctantly reunited with her husband in East Texas. Potter chose to remain in Nacogdoches after arriving there on July 1, 1835, a time when Texas revolutionary politics was coming to a boil. Robert was listed as a captain when he joined Thomas J. Rusk's company of Nacogdoches Independent Volunteers on October 9. After helping Dr. James Grant arm and equip the Texian army for the Siege of Bexar, Potter was elected a delegate to the Consultation meeting at San Felipe for November 3–14, but his military duties kept him from attending.

It was during this period that someone from New Orleans planted a phony obituary in *Niles Weekly Register* announcing Rob's death in a Texas skirmish around November 15; was he trying to cover his old tracks once and for all? On November 21, 1835, Potter resigned from the Texian army with the intention of joining the fledgling Texas navy. On November 27 the General Council and Governor Henry Smith agreed on an ordinance to legalize piracy. The provisional state government was to issue letters of marque and reprisal to men of character with tactical skill who had ships of eighty tons carrying at least four twelve-pounders. They were authorized to cruise the Gulf, blockade any port of Mexico, and take as prizes any ship flying the flag of Mexico. The provisional government was to receive twenty percent of all prize money. The flag flown by these privateers was to be that of the Republic of Mexico with the figures "1824."

On November 31, 1835, Potter wrote to the governor and General Council, saying that he was

> . . . desirous of serving the country in the present emergency and believing from his experience in naval service, he could render more effectual service at sea than elsewhere, [he] has already apprised the government of Texas . . . of his readiness to serve them whenever they can procure an armed ship — in the meantime, he solicits . . . a commission with a letter of Marque to cruise on the coast of the enemy.

Both requests were approved by the provisional state government the next day, December 1. Frustrated by lack of a ship to command, Robert spent January and February of 1836 helping the provisional government formulate plans for an official Texas fleet. Private funds were used to purchase four schooners: the *Liberty,* the *Independence,* the *Brutus,* and the *Invincible,* which had been used in the African slave trade and was the strongest and fastest of the ships; it carried eight guns, two of which were eighteen-pounders. In all there were twenty-eight guns in this first Texas navy with another vessel, the *Flash,* operating under a letter of marque.

Friction between Governor Smith and the General Council developed after the Consultation failed to clearly spell out their respective powers. As a result of this political in-fighting, the council deposed Smith as governor on January 11, 1836, leaving Texas in effect without a government until March 1, when a plenary convention met at Washington-on-the-Brazos. Nacogdoches, a town of 500, was entitled to four delegates to this convention. There were seventeen candidates, with the central issue being loyalty to the Mexican federal Constitution of 1824 *or* independence. In the midst of the heated campaign, Capt. Sidney Sherman's company of Kentucky and Ohio volunteers rode into town and presented themselves at the polls. At first the election judges denied them the ballot; then Potter passionately exhorted the newcomers to "persevere in their determination to vote." In his journal, William Fairfax Gray, a Virginia speculator and money lender, notes that Robert was "courting favor with all his art and succeeding to a wonderful degree. He can only float on troubled water." After the angry company was drawn up in front of the Old Stone Fort, First Lieutenant Woods issued an ultimatum: the soldiers would either vote or riddle the polling place with rifle balls. The election judges were thus "persuaded" to relent, and Robert Potter received the fourth highest number of votes, beating out John K. Allen, a future founder of Houston, by a margin of three ballots. He owed his victory to the new soldiers and late arriving votes from outlying districts. Surprisingly, Sam Houston finished sixteenth out of the seventeen contenders; however, his name was also on the ticket at Refugio and he won there.

When fifty-nine delegates met in convention at Washington-on-the-Brazos on March 1, 1836, Potter was the only representative present from Nacogdoches. The meeting took place in an unfinished gunsmith shop rented from Noah Byars. The crude structure lacked doors and windows, so cotton cloth was stretched over the openings to shield the founding fathers from the blasts of

128

a fresh norther and the thirty-three-degree temperature. Delegates had to compete for space with chickens and pigs who wandered into the hall.

En route to this gathering, Robert and some other East Texas delegates met in secret caucus for the purpose of nominating convention officers. As the first order of business, his choice for president, Richard Ellis of Pecan Point, was elected to that position as were Isham Parmer as sergeant-at-arms and John Hizer as doorkeeper, whose main task was keeping out the livestock.

Although Robert and Sam Houston served together on committees charged with drafting rules of order and the writing of a constitution, they clashed frequently during the convention due to their opposite natures: the North Carolinian was a classicist while Houston was a humanist who considered Greek and Latin "a waste of time" and the domain of "graduated fools." On Houston's birthday, March 2, the convention approved the work of committee chairman George Childress, the author of the Texas Declaration of Independence and a recent arrival from Tennessee. Most likely, he brought the document in his saddlebag; according to his descendants, he "wrote it, phrased it, and penned it with his own pen, without assistance." One can imagine a stylist such as Robert Potter grimacing at the "grammatical monstrosities" of a document whose first sentence rambled on for 322 words.

On March 3 a Potter motion to raise a regiment of rangers was approved. The next day James Collinsworth, a Brazoria delegate and chairman of the military committee, moved that Sam Houston be appointed "Commander-in-chief of all the land forces of the Texian army, both regulars, volunteers and militia . . . " It met with little opposition except from Robert, who urged many objections in a "long and animated" speech. This motion was adopted on March 5, with Potter casting the one dissenting vote. On Sunday morning, March 6, President Ellis called the delegates into special session to read a March 3 dispatch to the convention from Alamo commander

William Barret Travis. In making his last appeal to this "honorable body" for reinforcements, ammunition, and provisions, Colonel Travis said in part:

> ... I look to the *colonies alone* for aid: unless it arrives soon, I shall have to fight the enemy on his own terms. I will, however, do the best I can under the circumstances; and I feel confident that the determined valor, and desperate courage, heretofore evinced by my men, will not fail them in the last struggle; and although they may be sacrificed to the vengeance of a gothic enemy, the victory will cost the enemy so dear, that it will be worse for him than a defeat. . . .
>
> "God and Texas — Victory or Death!!"
>
> William Barret Travis

An inspired Robert Potter jumped to his feet and made the following motion:

> Resolved, That the safety of the country is threatened in a manner which makes it the duty of all her citizens to hasten to the field.
>
> Resolved, That the members of the convention, . . . will, in the present emergency, adjourn to meet in the camp of our countrymen [the Alamo], there or elsewhere to complete the business of the convention. . . .

His nemesis, Sam Houston, quickly took the floor and delivered the following stinging rebuke during an hour-long speech:

> This proposal is mad. We have declared ourselves independent but we have no organization. There must be a government. It must have organic form. Without it we would be nothing but outlaws, and can hope neither for sympathy nor the respect of mankind. The country is in peril. I advise you to sit calmly and firmly and cooly pursue your deliberation. Be wise. Be patriotic. Feel no alarm. I pledge myself to proceed at once to Gonzales where we hear that a small corps of militia have rallied. I will interpose them between this convention and the enemy. While you choose to sit in convention I promise you the Mexicans will never ap-

130

proach unless they march over my dead body. If mortal
power can avail I will relieve the brave men in the
Alamo.

Robert's rash resolution to march to the relief of the
Alamo was then voted down after Collinsworth, Childress, and Rusk also spoke against its passage.

On the morning of March 8, delegate Potter brought
the land question to the convention floor by proposing
that the following provision be included in the Republic's
constitution: "No claim of eleven leagues of land or more
shall be valid; and all titles issued . . . for more than one
League and a Labor of land (empresarios excepted) shall
be null and void and of no effect. . . ." His real target was
the huge, questionable "quickie" land grants to specula-
tors made by the state government of Coahuila-Texas at
Saltillo. For example, Jim Bowie had received twelve of
these eleven-league grants in 1830, while the New York-
based Galveston Bay and Texas Land Company at one
time claimed title to twenty million acres of Texas land.
Robert was hoping to nullify such scandalous operations,
but his resolution was rejected in committee of the whole.
On March 11 he met defeat again after proposing that
those Mexicans who had been declared citizens of Texas
should be segregated in the Texian armed forces. Joining
forces with George Childress on March 13, he pushed
through a constitutional provision prohibiting any imprisonment for debt.

On the night of March 16, the convention received
word that the Alamo mission at San Antonio had fallen
to Santa Anna's army and that General Houston's
Texian army was retreating eastward from Gonzales.
This alarming news prompted Chairman Richard Ellis to
call a late session for 10:00 P.M. Shortly after midnight,
the delegates adopted a constitution and passed an ordinance to organize an ad interim government. Since the
front runners for the presidency — Austin, Houston, and
William H. Wharton — had other assignments and were
unavailable, the convention turned to the choice of the

131

Potter bloc, darkhorse David G. Burnet. At 2:00 A.M. on March 17, Burnet was elected ad interim president by a 29–23 vote margin over Samuel Carson, who was selected secretary of state. Potter's nominee for vice-president, Lorenzo de Zavala, was elected to that post with no opposition. In view of Robert's past experience in the United States Navy, the convention elected him ad interim secretary of the navy. Thomas J. Rusk was chosen secretary of war. The new administration was sworn in at 4:00 A.M., with President Burnet making a stirring inaugural address.

When the convention met in a morning session on March 17, Burnet issued a proclamation transferring the capital to Harrisburg "as the place of more safety than this." Shortly thereafter, a rider appeared shouting, "The Mexicans are coming!" It was rumored that Santa Anna's cavalry had crossed the Colorado River only sixty miles away. As President Burnet adjourned the convention, the delegates scattered in all directions to look after their families, triggering hysteria and a panic civilian retreat known as the Runaway Scrape. However, the president, Secretary of War Rusk, and Secretary of the Navy Potter stayed behind for two days to wind up convention business.

By the time they left on Friday afternoon, March 18, the village of Washington had become a ghost town. That night the three officials of the "horseback government" arrived at the home of Jared Groce, who was to be their host for three days. Groce, a cotton planter and the largest landowner in the area, lived in a "big house" called "The Retreat" in present Grimes County. When Burnet's party departed the morning of March 21, they followed an oversized cow trail as they headed for Harrisburg. The ad interim government reached Buffalo Bayou after dark on Tuesday, March 22, and were put up in the home of the attractive widow Mrs. Jane Harris. This most pretentious house in Harrisburg was to be the capitol of Texas until April 13. Protocol dictated that the president, vice-president, and secretary of state make use of the available beds while the rest of the cabinet slept on the floor. Potter's navy flag, a blue field with a star in the center and thirteen stripes in alternate red and white, was flown as the Texian flag from a pole in front of the Harris home.

While the capital was at Harrisburg, President Burnet knew nothing of General Houston's plans. On March 28 the retreating Texas army reached the west bank of the Brazos at San Felipe and turned north to Groce's Landing, where Houston camped and drilled his troops for two weeks. On April 2 Burnet wrote the following dispatch and ordered Rusk to take it to Houston's camp:

> General Sam Houston:
> Sir — the enemy are laughing you to scorn. You must fight them. You must retreat no farther. The country expects you to fight. The salvation of the country depends on you doing so.

By this time the president's friend, Potter, had sent a navy spy, Lt. James Hazard Perry, to watch the army's movements. Perry was a New Yorker who had joined Houston's camp at Beason's Ferry on the Colorado with a letter of endorsement from Robert. General Houston, impressed by papers showing Perry to be a graduate of the U.S. Military Academy, made him an aide-de-camp. On April 9, the general intercepted and read a derogatory twelve-page letter from Perry addressed to Secretary of the Navy Potter. This spying report read in part:

> Agreeable to your request, I embrace the earliest opportunity of giving you the information you desire with respect to the army. . . .
> We are within striking distance of the enemy, and there are no signs of moving; our men are loitering about without knowing more of military tactics at evening than they did in the morning, while the General, either for want of his customary excitement (for he has entirely discontinued the use of ardent spirits) or, as

133

some say, from the use of opium, is in a condition between sleeping & waking which amounts nearly to a constant state of inanimity . . . men are leaving us every day, by tens and twenties, dissatisfied with the unhealthy situation of the Camp & disgusted with the inactivity & want of energy in the General. . . . (P.S.) I should not be surprised if we are not ordered to retreat still further.

General Houston summoned Lieutenant Perry to headquarters and read parts of the letter to him. Claiming to be undisturbed by the spying of his enemies, the magnanimous Sam was content to put Perry under guard so as to keep an eye on him; the informer was eventually released after being kept out of the Battle of San Jacinto. Houston later said that Perry had "acknowledged himself his [Potter's] spy and pimp upon the general [Houston], and they were a most worthy pair."

In early April President Burnet ordered Potter to Velasco to supervise its defenses. After discussing the situation there with Commandant Warren D. C. Hall, the two decided to send all civilians — many of whom were already in flight — to Galveston for safety. Among these refugees were Mrs. Solomon C. Page and her boy and girl, a forlorn threesome who had trudged through nine miles of mire before Robert found them on Bailey's Prairie. When he first saw her, Harriet Page was wearing a mud-splattered black silk dress and a velvet-trimmed black hat. She would remember Rob as riding a grand black stallion, "Gadolphin," and carrying a sword and brace of pistols; he wore a blue coat, polished boots, had black, styled hair, and a voice with a "magic quality." When the smitten cavalier rode up, he said, "My servant will see to both the children if you will condescend to mount with me." As they rode back toward Velasco, Robert asked, "I make bold to inquire what brings such beauty to this wilderness?" Mrs. Page then poured out the tale of woe that brought her to this sorry state of affairs[1] Her sympathetic listener had Harriet "won to full trust and loyalty" by the time they reached Velasco; as she later recalled:

Never was a woman treated in a more kind and thoughtful manner, than was I by Colonel Potter. Himself a perfect gentleman, he treated me with all the deference due a queen, and I began to look up to him as a protection. Somehow he heard that I said I would never

---

[1] The beautiful Harriet was the daughter of Dr. Francis Moore, Jr., who was living five miles from Brazoria in 1835. At age seventeen she first met Solomon Page, a handsome gloved dandy who always dressed in black and gray. The twenty-two-year-old wholesale distributor had come to her father's Nashville office to have an injured hand treated. On Solomon's third visit, he told Harriet, "You are the woman I need," but was an hour late when he first called at the Moore home, an omen of things to come. Soon after their marriage in February 1829, he began to come home at all hours. Business reversals caused Solomon to hock Harriet's pearl ring while the family carriage and horses went to satisfy a gambling debt. A creditor who could have sent him to prison, a jeweler named Howard, was mysteriously murdered and robbed with all of his papers burned.

By the time little Joseph Page was six months old, his moody father was gambling again and decided to seek better business opportunities by moving to New Orleans. After trading their house for a coach and cash for the trip, the Pages were in the Crescent City by summer's end in 1830. While Solomon turned to drink and sampled the night life of the city, Harriet had a baby girl, Virginia ("Ginny"), and opened a dress shop on Camp Street to support the family. When the neglected, overworked wife came down with yellow fever, it was Dr. Anson Jones who cared for her and offered to reunite her and the children with her father in Texas. One day, after hearing the ship captain of the *Amos Wright* describe the rich, free land around Brazoria, Solomon burst into Harriet's shop and announced, "We're going to Texas!" His dutiful spouse closed the shop the next day and used her earnings to pay for their passage to Velasco; she was also farsighted enough to tie all her savings around her waist.

Shortly after reaching the Texas Coast in the spring of 1835, Solomon lost most of their furnishings and provisions at a card game while Harriet was visiting her sick father. The outraged Dr. Moore insisted that his daughter leave Page, offering her half a section of land and twenty cows to do so. Harriet continued to defend her deadbeat husband, contending that a steady job would settle him down. But

135

again live with my husband, Mr. Page, and from the time he learned this incident in my life he was most kind and attentive to my little boy, until I thought that there was nobody like the Colonel.

Harriet and the children were assigned a private cabin on board the armed schooner, *Flash*, the navy secretary's flagship, and placed under his personal protection. The night the vessel sailed for Galveston, Rob proclaimed his love for "Hatty" and said he wanted to marry

---

Solomon was dazzled by the prospect of getting the land bounty due war heroes. In the late summer of 1835, he moved his family to a dilapidated house near Chocolate Bayou, then relocated them on Austin Bayou in a good but isolated cabin owned by a Mr. Merrick, who was to be his employer. The Pages were running low on food, so Harriet gave her husband ten dollars for groceries; he returned empty-handed six days later, saying he needed more of her money for a suitable uniform so he could go to war. A frustrated wife then unleashed an angry, bitter tirade against her "coward" husband and said he would get no more money. When Solomon Page deserted his family the next morning at dawn to join the Texas army, Harriet's parting words were, "If you go off and leave us to starve, I hope the first bullet that's fired, pierces your heart! God smite you dead."

At first Mrs. Page and the children survived by eating the rich fruit of the sweet parsley-haws. Even though Ginny had been weaned for two years, the hungry little girl instinctively tried to breastfeed one night; the sharp pain caused her dry mother to awaken from a deep sleep. Leaping from the bed, the desperate Harriet ran to the bayou and almost drowned trying to grab a fish. After nine days, the widower Mr. Merrick visited, remarking that some awful dreams about the old home place had brought him there. He left them with meal, coffee, and some wild game, but after a solid week of rain, and no sun to dry it or salt to cure it, the meat rotted. By this time Virginia was pale, listless, and sleeping most of the time. Seeking some diversion, little Joe made a fire from some broom corn, and the smoke was seen by a Reverend Cloud, who had been sent by a dying neighbor, Mrs. Abit, to search for Harriet. The preacher gave them some of Mrs. Abit's choice stores, sent for two wagons from Brazoria, and Mrs. Page paid the teamsters in cash to move her family into an empty cabin in town.

In late March 1836 a drunk named Old Norton spread the false alarm that the Mexicans were coming, to "run for your lives." What he thought to be gunfire was actually the popping sound of exploding reeds: some runaway slaves had set fire to some canebrakes. This

136

her. The ship commander, L. A. Flanell, later testified that it was common gossip concerning their relationship with whispers about "public scandal," "Colonel Potter's paramour," and "illicit love." During this interval, little Ginnie Page developed a high fever and her despairing mother called in a young physician. However, he could do nothing to help, blaming the child's deteriorating condition on exposure and hunger. After the little girl's death, she was laid in a wooden coffin bearing the inscription "Of Such Is the Kingdom of Heaven" and buried on Galveston Island.

In the meantime, President Burnet on April 13 ordered his cabinet to leave Harrisburg and go to Galveston, the safest place to carry on the government and run the blockade for supplies. It was Potter who sent the *Flash* to retrieve the cabinet members, a decision that impressed the grateful president. After gathering his family at New Washington (Morgan's Point), Burnet joined the other members of the ad interim government on Galveston Island on April 19. Potter was on board when the president sent the steamboat *Cayuga* with a load of volunteers and provisions for Houston's army on Buffalo Bayou. On April 20 Robert was ordered to take command at Galveston, the home port of the four second-hand ships of the Texas navy. By this time a thousand refugees were sleeping on the crowded beach on the east end of Galveston Island where the government set up the capital. When it was rumored that the Mexican army was closing in, some panic-stricken adventurers plotted to seize all the small boats and escape across the bay to Bolivar Point on the mainland. Upon hearing of the cowardly scheme, President Burnet called a mass meeting on the beach. After he and Vice-President de Zavala spoke, Robert Potter addressed the throng. Pointing to the forlorn-looking women, he said:

"Norton Panic" led to the evacuation of Brazoria, and Harriet fled with Ginny and little Joe. It was in such dire circumstances that Harriet Page was rescued by Robert Potter on Bailey's Prairie.

137

Someone has said "a lady's tears are silent orators." Therefore I shall be brief. We have before us the flower of American womanhood, hardy souls who have come west to rear their families in peace and tranquility. It is a cruel fate, dictated by a merciless invader, that finds them upon the strand here, almost driven into the sea by the *rapacious* Mexicans.

Rob then proceeded to shame the host of able-bodied men standing before him and concluded a powerful oration by saying, "And now, let all who desire to leave Texas, step to the front." When none did, the spirit of rebellion was broken.

It was not until Saturday, April 23, two days after General Houston's stunning victory in the Battle of San Jacinto, that Secretary of War Rusk detailed three soldiers to carry the news to President Burnet. When David finally received the report on April 27, he was fuming because he was not the first to be officially notified of the great victory. The president and Potter took the steamboat *Yellowstone* and arrived at the battlefield on May 1. A fresh source of friction between Burnet and Houston was the dispensing of the $12,000 in Mexican gold found in Santa Anna's treasure chest. The interim government bluntly demanded delivery of the booty, only to find that the general had already distributed the money among his men in lieu of salaries. Claiming to need the funds for his navy department, an incensed Potter proposed dismissing Houston as major general of the army for this alleged misconduct but nothing came of it. Sam airily brushed off the episode by saying that Rob simply "wanted the handling" of the specie and continued to berate the navy secretary at every opportunity.

Allies Burnet and Potter had two other opportunities to slight the wounded hero of San Jacinto. After the battle, the government initially refused permission for Houston to sail for Galveston on the *Yellowstone* but the skipper, Captain Ross, declared that his ship would not leave without him! When the vessel started for Galveston on May 8, old Sam was carried aboard only *after* prisoner Santa Anna and his officers were already on board. Upon their arrival, General Houston was denied passage on the *Liberty,* a Texas navy schooner bound for New Orleans. Instead, he was assigned cramped quarters in a small, dirty, leaky American trading schooner, the *Flora.* In fact, the captain of the *Liberty* was so worried about the seaworthiness of the *Flora* that he decided to leave harbor the same time and serve as its convoy. Thus, in circumstances reflecting no glory on Burnet or Potter, a feverish and semidelirious Sam Houston on May 11 sailed for New Orleans, where he was to have twenty bone fragments removed from his ankle.

On May 14, 1836, President Burnet and General Santa Anna signed both public and secret treaties at Velasco. The public treaty included a pledge by the provisional government for the immediate safe return of Santa Anna to Mexico. In the secret document, the Mexican dictator pledged to use his influence with the Mexican government to secure the recognition of Texas independence with its southern boundary as the Rio Grande. It was Burnet's decision to spare the "Napoleon of the West," then wring concessions from him in return for his safety. However, two of his cabinet members, Potter and the new secretary of war, Mirabeau B. Lamar, opposed the strategy. Robert was particularly bitter about releasing Santa Anna, preferring instead to hang him as a war criminal without showing him even the courtesy due military men, death by firing squad.

In late April Rob moved Mrs. Page and her son Joe to the prize American brig *Pocket* in Galveston harbor.[2]

---

[2] The most eventful and historic naval engagement occurring during Potter's stint as secretary of the navy was the capture of the *Pocket* on April 10, 1836. That day the Mexican brig *Bravo* lost a rudder and went aground at the mouth of the Rio Grande off the port of Matamoros. The *Bravo* was assigned the task of keeping ships from slipping out of Matamoros to inform the Texians of a Mexican army plan to land a division of 2,000 at Copano Bay on the Texas coast.

There the detained Captain Howes and his unhappy American crew denounced Potter at ever opportunity. Harriet found herself shunned by other women, while the *Pocket* crew played a card game called "Potter's Privilege": the high man was to have first chance at *her* (the "little charmer") if Rob should be killed. Hatty was

---

That very day the Texas schooner-of-war *Invincible* sailed into view, and Capt. Jeremiah Brown ordered four broadsides fired into the hull of the helpless Mexican ship. With the *Bravo* reduced to wreckage and the crew overboard, the *Invincible* then stood off to continue the Texian blockade in the Gulf. Soon one of Captain Brown's lookouts spotted another sail approaching, the American brig *Pocket* of Boston, commanded by Capt. Elijah Howes. This ship was running contraband with a cargo of goods bound for the enemy port of Matamoros. When Captain Brown sent a prize crew to hoist the Texas flag on the mast of the *Pocket*, Captain Howes said, "This is an outrage," and vowed to complain to the United States government. After searching the American vessel, Brown's suspicions were confirmed. He found dispatches for Santa Anna and a manifest that did not square with the cargo, which consisted of powder, ammunition, and provisions for the Mexican army. There was also a descriptive map of the Texas coast in the ship's papers, while a passenger volunteered the information that the *Pocket,* on her return trip, was to transport Mexican troops to Texas. Captain Brown thus had ample reason to take the American brig as a legal prize and sail her to Galveston, where $8,000 of Mexican provisions were unloaded and fed to Texian troops after the Battle of San Jacinto.

After first keeping Mrs. Page and her son Joe on his flagship the *Flash,* Robert Potter transferred them to an elegant cabin on the *Pocket* in Galveston harbor. On April 24 Captain Howes was released to New Orleans, where he denounced the *Invincible* crew as pirates. During a cruise to New Orleans, the *Invincible* was detained there by the United States sloop-of-war *Warren.* The Texas crew was arrested; while on their way to jail, they were applauded by Canal Street locals. When testimony at their trial revealed that part of the *Pocket*'s cargo was indeed contraband, the Texians were found innocent of the piracy charge. After being released from custody, they were given free tickets to the theater before the *Invincible* returned to coastal patrol duty. Eventually, the Republic of Texas paid $11,750 in damage claims to passengers and members of the *Pocket*'s crew simply to retain American goodwill. In June 1836 the *Invincible* was ordered to Velasco for the purpose of returning Santa Anna to Vera Cruz, but volunteer newcomers from the United States took him off the schooner and forced him to remain in Texas.

140

shaken when Jethro, the black servant Robert had assigned her, suddenly left after hearing wicked words about his master's past. While Potter was off visiting the San Jacinto battlefield with Burnet, Harriet spent some time in his cabin mending shirts. One day this chore was interrupted by a knock on the door: it was her husband Solomon. This dirty, smelly, sickly man had come to get his wife but first accused her of disgracing the family and causing a scandal by running off with Potter. Hatty would later recall the confrontation as follows:

> We all stayed on the ship until after the battle of San Jacinto had been fought, and then I wanted to go to my grandmother's in Kentucky. I had parted forever from my husband, for he came on board the ship and begged me to return to him, but no inducement could turn me from my purpose, to go away from him and Texas forever. He had left his innocent, helpless little babies and young wife [in Brazoria County] to perish with starvation. No, never, never, would I trust myself nor them to his mercy again.
>
> When Col. Potter found how anxious I was to go to my grandmother, he told me that he had promised Mr. Moore to take his daughter [Martha] to Kentucky where she was to live with her grandmother, and go to school, and that he would take charge of both of us that far.

When Rob returned and was told of Solomon Page's visit, he avoided Harriet for a week. After being granted a leave of absence on May 8, Mrs. Page and Joe were with him on the *Pocket* when he sailed to New Orleans "on business" for the navy department. While he brooded during the voyage, thirteen-year-old Martha Moore shared Hatty's cabin. When they reached New Orleans, Harriet stayed with an old friend on Camp Street. Ironically, Rob and Sam Houston were in the Crescent City at the same time for a few weeks. While the general was heralded by the newspapers, Potter seems to have been totally ignored with no mention of him engaging in any public speaking. Although there is no record of his resigning as navy secretary, he did not return to Texas until the demise of the interim government; technically he drew pay and held office until October 22, 1836, when Sam Houston was installed as president of the Republic of Texas. His services as secretary of the navy cost the taxpayers $2,148, figured at five dollars a day from March 18 until October 22.

During the hiatus in New Orleans, Potter's conduct as a cabinet member came under severe criticism. Romantic, not naval, affairs took much of his time; his official duties consisted of spending $172 for some fancy uniforms while he privately ran the Republic into debt and found relaxation in the arms of his lady love. Maj. Charles E. Hawkins, the blunt-spoken commodore of the Texas navy, said this of Potter in writing from Galveston on May 19, 1836: "One of two of his appointments, I must say, without any feeling of disrespect toward that gentleman, I consider highly prejudicial to the Naval service. . . ." On October 26, 1836, Robert's neglect of his duties led S. Rhoades Fisher, the new secretary of the navy, to report: "That arm [navy] of the national defense appears to be in a most deplorable and crippled condition." Indeed, during the summer and autumn of 1836, only Hawkins's flagship, the eight-gun schooner *Independence,* and four small privateers were available to defend the Texas coast; of the other three ships in the Texas navy, the *Invincible* and *Brutus* had sailed for New York while the *Liberty* was tied up in New Orleans unable to pay a repair bill.

Late one June evening in 1836, Rob informed Hatty that a steamboat leaving the next day would take her and Martha Moore to Kentucky. This hurried departure was supposedly due to a predicted outbreak of yellow fever in New Orleans. Once they were under way, Harriet awoke one morning to find the vessel on the Red River bound for Texas. Claiming to be "indignant" over Potter's ruse, she demanded to get off at Alexandria and travel overland to Kentucky, but her lover vetoed that as

142

being very dangerous. When they reached Shreveport, Robert proposed marriage and asked her to live on his headright, the league and labor of Texas land due him as head of a family. This land was on the eastern edge of present Marion County, a peninsula on the north shore of Caddo Lake he called Potter's Point. Mrs. Page first spurned the proposal since she had never been legally divorced from her first husband. Undaunted, Rob argued that her first marriage was not legal in Catholic Texas since she and Solomon had not been married by a priest. Weakened by his persuasive powers, Hatty would later explain her change of heart as follows: "He loved me very devotedly, and the more I thought about it the better way it seemed out of my difficulties." With neither judge nor clergy present, three mapmaker guests witnessed a simple marriage-by-bond uniting the two lovers on September 5, 1836, in Shelby County.[3]

Rob first built a house for his bride at Potter's Creek near the Sabine River. As the new Mrs. Potter later recalled, "For one beautiful idyllic season we lived on the Sabine, and planted and harvested our crops there, living a happy, peaceful life." That October Robert took his hired hand Hezekiah with him to the lakes and built a permanent home at Potter's Point, a promontory overlooking Ferry Lake.

Hatty was left alone with Martha Moore and little Joe, but she soon had a visitor. Martha's brother-in-law

---

[3] In 1872 Harriet would testify that the marriage bond with Robert Potter was lost; thus there was no record of the act nor could witnesses be produced who had seen the bond. She testified that she felt free to marry Potter after hearing that her husband, Solomon Page, had been killed in the Battle of San Jacinto. Actually, Page was guarding army baggage at nearby Harrisburg when the battle was in progress. One fact is certain: Harriet was a bigamist from September 5, 1836, the date of her alleged marriage-by-bond, until May 11, 1840, when Solomon Page was granted a divorce in Harris County in order to remarry. Solomon sold his headright land certificate for $2,000 in February 1838, a time when *both* he and Robert Potter were claiming to be head of the same family. Page died in Texas about 1850.

Ed Crueber came for her and cruelly castigated Mrs. *Page* (as he called Hatty) for her "sinful ways" before he left. A few weeks later, Chief River Wolf and a band of thirteen braves approached Harriet's cabin. It seems that the chief's herd of horses had been stolen; after hearing of Robert Potter, he had come seeking "lawyer's help" to recover them. When River Wolf first approached her door, Hatty met him with a cannon, a loaded gun, and a pistol. Her temper flared when the hungry young warriors began to trample her melon patch. Impressed by her bravery, the chief ordered the boys out of the garden and referred to Harriet as "Kishi [panther] woman" before leaving. When Rob returned and heard of the stand-off, he boasted of being "married to the bravest little woman in the whole Republic of Texas."

Potter brought his wife a special gift, a little gray mare named "Sukey Blueskin" and a fine sidesaddle. Since he already owned a red-roan stallion called "Shakespeare," the couple decided to take a ride together and visit their nearest neighbors, the Slidells, who lived fifteen miles away. While the men were playing cards, the two ladies took a stroll, at which time Hatty first learned of her husband's checkered past. It seems that the dour Mrs. Slidell asked if she wasn't afraid to marry a man who had so mistreated his first wife. The stunned Harriet was informed that she was married to a criminal, an insane man. She was told that the first Mrs. Potter was a good, respected woman falsely accused of being a whore. Mrs. Slidell's version of the double castration had Reverend Taylor and young Wiley confessing their guilt only after Rob scared them out of their wits. According to this scenario, Isabella Potter was converted during a revival and her husband came home to find her and the minister innocently kneeling in prayer by her bed. Unaware that his secret was known by Harriet, Robert exploded in anger on the way home when he discovered that he had won some counterfeit banknotes from Mr. Slidell.

144

When Hatty confronted her husband back at the cabin, he pulled out a pamphlet for her to read — the whole story about the castration incident. Potter had written this vitriolic "Address to the People of Granville County" from the Hillsborough prison in 1832. In this remarkable eighty-six-page tract, he had defended his crime and asserted that being jailed and denied bail was simply a "foul game" played against him by two groups of political enemies motivated by either envy or, in the case of the "Bank Gentry," revenge. After verbally assaulting his persecutors, Potter used the last twenty pages of his booklet explaining the full story of his crime, including numerous biblical quotations and a discourse on religion and creed. Rob charged that Louis Taylor was the father of his youngest child, a dim-witted little boy. He admitted not actually seeing any adulterous act between Isabella and the preacher but claimed his wife confessed to him, and that four others approved of his actions. While Hatty was reading this spirited defense, she felt emotions ranging from pride and sympathy to heartache and sickness. She later wrote that the full knowledge of this terrible episode did not affect her love for or loyalty to her husband.

In December 1836 Robert moved his family forty miles to the new pine log cabin he had built at Potter's Point on Ferry Lake. For the next four years, he was to be a political recluse, planter, and hunter. Such a contemplative life allowed him to renew his study of poetry, the classics, and ancient history. His new bride was the first white woman in an area surrounded by some 300 Caddo Indians; there was also a Coushatta Village only three miles away. Hatty described Potter's Point as follows:

> . . . I never tired of admiring the scenery that lay about my new home. Our home stood upon a jutting promontory, that rose into a hill set in the midst of one of the grandest timber belts in Texas. The level timber lands circled about us, while for more than two hundred feet a steep bank overlooked the most romantically beauti-

145

ful lake that I've ever beheld. For eight miles one would look across to the opposite shore over a great sheet of sparkling water that washed up onto the white beach below the cliff. . . . My home was indeed set in the midst of lovely and romantic surroundings. I often wonder if ever so many flowers grew in any other woods. . . . Nature had spared no pains to make complete the beauty of this spot, and I felt that at last I must be happy. . . .

The romantic Rob soon penned a poem for Harriet in which he dubbed her "Lakeann" and first recited it to her from a treetop island in the lake.

Potter was carrying trade goods when he made a trip to Shreveport in June 1837. He planned to return within a week, bringing a servant woman to care for the pregnant Hatty. Shortly after his departure, she was bathing down at the spring when she heard little Joe calling for help. In her rush to respond, she slipped on the steps leading to the rock basin. The fall was accompanied by an intense pain; she was about to have her baby. Although Harriet managed to reach her bed, the newborn son died at her feet during the night and she tenderly wrapped the lifeless form in dressed deerskins. The next morning a stranger appeared at Potter's Point, a trader named Charles Ames who had been a wood carver and trunk maker in Massachusetts, and he buried Hatty's babe. This sad encounter with Harriet was love at first sight for Charles; however, he vanished soon after Robert returned with a mulatto woman named Delia. Summer found Charles in New Orleans, where he wrote "Profit and Loss on Love" in a small account book. Years later Hatty would read this heartfelt confession of a man yearning for her love and companionship. Pining for a dear one far away, Charles concluded:

. . . I will see you again — be certain of your welfare and happiness — anything that I can do through another to add to your pleasure or happiness, I will do. My love is a good love and forever a part of me. The

146

burden is secrecy, not shame. The torture is restraint, not regret.

So I hereby accept the love inevitable, with its touch of glory and its prod of pain. . . .

When Rob returned from Shreveport, he was preoccupied with legal problems affecting marriage and land, not grieving for a lost son. During his stay there, he had obtained a copy of the laws just enacted by the Texas Congress. Foremost in his mind was the bigamy law:

> Be it further enacted that all persons who have married agreeably to the customs of the country having another wife or husband living and should continue to live together as man and wife sixty days after the passage of this law shall be considered guilty of the offense of bigamy and shall upon conviction be punished as such.

Potter told Hatty there was only one way to keep her from being punished as a bigamist: their bond marriage contract must *not* be recorded. The land laws provided the other horn of his dilemma. The constitution of the Republic of Texas plainly stated that a league and labor of land (4,605 acres) was due any *head of family* in Texas before March 2, 1836. Technically, Rob was a single man on that date and thus qualified for only one-third that amount, 1,476 acres. He would have to lie in claiming Harriet and little Joe as family to get his full quota of land. In March 1838 he made application for a certificate covering the land due a *family* man; he also appeared in person before the Board of Land Commissioners of Red River County and took the required oath concerning citizenship and family status. Once the land certificate was approved and issued at Clarksville, the jubilant Potter was off on a spring jaunt to Shreveport for supplies.

One rainy day while Rob was gone, Harriet watched helplessly as some Coushatta "bad boys" drove off all of their horses. Late that evening Chief Prowling Bear came calling, just as Hatty had predicted he would. After inviting him inside she referred to the chief as a friend who surely would not steal from her. When she asked him to make the boys return her horses, Prowling Bear pretended not to understand. The riled housewife then grabbed a double-barreled shotgun and proclaimed that her husband would surely use it to get his livestock back unless the chief helped her. After she gave him presents of salt and flour, Prowling Bear smiled and said he wanted to spend the night with her, a proposition she firmly rejected. As he departed the pouting chief said, "You good woman with no-good man." The next morning, all of the stolen horses were returned from the Indian village, which was Prowling Bear's way of proving his true regard for the brave Mrs. Potter. When her husband returned he was furious about the whole episode. Although Hatty admonished him not to blame the chief, Rob remarked, "That will have to do for now, I suppose, but there'll come a time — "

Colonel Potter's oratorical skills were soon to bring him back into Texas politics. In April 1838 he and Hatty were en route to their old camp on the Sabine to gather livestock when they met a runner at the crossroads. Young Jim Page (of no relation to Harriet) shouted, "I've come after you. They're about to hang my father!" The boy then begged Robert to rush the hundred miles to Clarksville and save his dad, who had been accused of murdering a man named Boxer. It seems that the two had gone hunting and been jumped by Indians. Old man Page escaped, but his companion was severely wounded; just before he died, Boxer kept muttering Page's name to some rescuers. When they caught up with Page, he was carrying counterfeit money, proof to the mob that he had killed Boxer to keep him from talking about a counterfeiting ring over in Shelby County. When Potter arrived at the Page home, he found a tearful family proclaiming their father's innocence, that it was Indians who murdered the victim. Mrs. Page was cheered by Rob's promise to do all in his power to get a lawful trial for her husband. Leaving Hatty behind, Potter and young Jim dashed for Clarksville at daybreak. An angry mob of 300 men and boys were about to lynch Mr. Page when Robert pushed through the crowd and demanded a chance to speak. Jumping up on the same wagon where Jim's dad was tied with a noose around his neck, he delivered an impassioned speech demanding a trial and exhorting the mob not to blame Page for the counterfeit money, that no white man should die for an Indian killing. Some of the folks even wept out loud when Potter talked about Page's family. When he finished, Rob's voice was breaking and he was wet with sweat. Although the throng had paused to listen in rapt silence, their leader demanded to know if Potter could prove the Indians killed Boxer. He then asked, "What right have you to discuss proper punishment for crime, Robert Potter of North Carolina. *You* should know well enough that the law don't always fit the crime." That reference to his past took all the starch out of Rob, and the mob proceeded with their own brand of lethal justice at sundown, making "Page's Limb" a future landmark. However, the "good people" of Clarksville were so impressed by Potter's oratory powers that they soon elected him to the Fifth Texas Congress as senator from the Red River district, Fannin and Red River counties.

Leaving Harriet with the grieving Page family, Robert detoured from Clarksville by way of Potter's Point to find that all his horses had been stolen by Coushatta braves. After gathering an armed party of six white men, he marched on their village but found only women and children there. When they refused to talk, Potter took Prowling Bear's wife, the old squaw Tall Flower, as his prisoner and locked her up overnight. Although he released her the next morning, his action infuriated the villagers. Soon after the white men went searching for the horses, they came upon an armed war party of thirteen;

149

in the bloody struggle that followed, seven warriors and two white men, Mead and Johnson, were killed. Potter suffered a severe head wound in the melee, but the Indians finally retreated after he killed their old chief, Prowling Bear, exacting some personal vengeance in the process. Fearful of Indian retaliation, Rob took his wife to the safety of Shreveport, where they lived six months before daring to return home. During the sojourn at Shreveport, Potter suffered from throbbing pain and recurring fever caused by the head wound; Hatty relieved the boredom with constant sewing.

While her husband busied himself with legal services, Harriet came to feel neglected and depressed, particularly after Rob continued to put off recording their marriage. Her unhappiness increased after a Houston newspaper in effect indicted Potter for the Indian battle, claiming that his horses had simply strayed away to be found later by the servant Hezekiah. Robert dismissed the article as being "malicious political slander." One day down at the river, Hatty's melancholy turned to joy when she happened to see Charles Ames. The chance encounter seemed to fluster him; Charles hurriedly untied his boat and departed, saying he would visit their home at Mulberry Shore and send her a letter report. When Robert decided it was safe to take his family back to Potter's Point, he enticed two other settlers, Stephen Peters and Sandy Miller, to follow him there.

Evidently, the newly elected senator was still mad at Indians when he arrived at Austin in November 1840 to renew his political career. Both Potter and President Mirabeau B. Lamar hated Indians and contended that these "intruders, depredators and thieves" must be routed. In contrast, Robert was revolted by Sam Houston's "red brother" attitude. Potter promptly introduced a Senate resolution commending the raid of Col. John H. Moore. With a company of ninety volunteers from Fayette County, Moore had destroyed a Comanche camp on the upper Colorado some 300 miles northwest of Austin on October 27, 1840. In his report, Colonel Moore told of killing 128 and capturing thirty-four Comanches along with 500 horses; he wrote that "the bodies of men, women and children were to be seen on every hand, wounded, dying and dead." In offering the "thanks of Congress" for this massacre, Potter's resolution read of hearing "with admiration but not with surprise of the brilliant and decisive victory of Col. John H. Moore and the volunteers under his command."

During the first session of the Fifth Congress, Robert served on three committees: military affairs, naval affairs, and public lands. The committee on naval affairs recommended land bounties for all men who had served the republic on land *and* sea, but the proposal did not become law; its passage would have entitled Potter to three headrights of 640 acres each. The joint committee on naval affairs also proposed that the Texas navy be laid up and "resuscitated" if needed; evidently, the cost of maintaining an operational navy was simply too high. In January 1841, Robert, as chairman of the committee on public lands, pushed through legislation allowing the Roman Catholic church to use public lands for religious and educational purposes within fifteen acres of their missions. Motivated by the one-man-one-vote principal, Senator Potter introduced a bill to provide a census of the Republic, but it failed in the house. In February 1841 a Potter proposal became law which validated marriages and legitimized children of marriages performed by persons other than the clergy; this law making such illegitimate children capable of inheritance obviously applied to the Potter-Page marriage in September 1836. Robert was also successful in carving three more counties out of Red River — Bowie, Lamar, and Paschal — so that his senatorial district embraced these four plus Fannin County.

On January 18, 1841, Rob wrote a letter requesting the hiring of Charles Ames to help prepare for a crop at Mulberry Shore. Hatty was elated when Charles arrived late that month, even though he looked thin and seemed

151

very tense. Two-year-old Lakeann Potter immediately took a liking to him, bringing Ames a bouquet of white flowers. While Robert was still in Austin, he learned that the traveling Board of Land Commissioners would soon be in Red River County to examine land certificates and reject fraudulent ones. In mid-February he celebrated his return to Potter's Point with a moonlight violin serenade for Hatty, while the ever-more-uncomfortable Charles rushed back to Clarksville to settle down as a furniture maker. Rob was quick to assure his wife that the recently passed Marriage Act had removed any question about the legality of their union. When their son was born on February 26, 1841, Potter insisted that he be named John David for Harriet's older brother.

Within a month Robert was called to Clarksville to appear before the land commissioners. Upon his arrival a friend, Amos Merrill, broke the bad news: the board had rejected his certificate on March 5, due to insufficient evidence that he was indeed the head of a family on March 2, 1836. Potter bristled at this "indignity" caused by his enemies conspiring against him. Merrill informed him that local opposition was led by Capt. William Pinckney Rose, a dangerous neighbor who lived at Caddo Bend, only ten miles from Mulberry Shore. Old Rose was loudly proclaiming that Rob was a single man, that his lady was not his wife. He had even accused Potter of paying court to a woman in the Rose family and vowed to file on a portion of Potter's land claim for a relative. Merrill suggested that the best way out of this sticky situation was to take the case to district court, which would cause Robert to be gone for weeks during the court's spring session. During this interval, he prevailed upon Charles Ames to leave his work bench, manage the farm, and share in the profits. Once again Charles and Hatty were thrown together, working side-by-side outdoors. One spring night the curious Harriet finally worked up the courage to ask if he had a true love. Charles replied that he did, that his loved one had black curls and dark eyes.

His blushing companion thought he meant her until he said, "Here she comes" — it was little Lakeann! The crestfallen Hatty considered the episode a cruel prank, and Charles quickly walked away with a pained expression on his face. Ames would soon return to Clarksville.

After a district court jury confirmed Robert's land claim in April 1841, his popularity increased. That summer, John B. Denton opposed Potter in his bid for reelection to the Senate. The campaign took a vitriolic turn with Captain Rose supporting Denton and blasting Rob as a notorious, infamous criminal; his target of abuse in turn vowed to *personally* see Old Rose prosecuted if he won.

In order to squelch the old rumors pertaining to Rob's marital status, Amos Merrill suggested that he put his family and home life on public display by inviting everyone in his district to a barbecue. The enthusiastic Potter considered such a "frontier frolic" a perfect political trick and set out on a long personal tour of invitation. Over 200 attended the barbecue; many came so far that they had to spend the night with their host. To add a final touch of domestic bliss, Rob played his violin as Harriet and little Lakeann sat nearby in rapt adoration. Such a public show silenced many a gossipy tongue. Potter won the election and was back in Austin by early November 1841, when the Sixth Congress convened.

Robert and President Lamar, an old revolutionary ally, were the social lions of the capital. Potter toasted Lamar as "Culture's champion and the redman's foe!" while the president contended that no other member of Congress was so well read or could quote the classics with such wit and application as Senator Potter. In writing to some Clarksville friends, the senator remarked that Austin was "a lovely place. . . . the society is beyond all expectations." Lamar's private secretary, Major B. Ransom, observed that Robert was "born for action" and was "decidedly the most popular man in the two houses of Congress." According to Major Ransom, the striking Potter was

low in stature, slightly corpulent; his address bold and

graceful; his voice musical and distinct; his hair, much inclined to curl, dark amber in color, and worn very short, and dark hazel eyes.

Evidently, more than one government wife found him irresistible. Rob was often seen squiring the wife of Secretary of State James S. Mayfield around town, an affair that resulted in Sophia Ann Mayfield being the first and chief beneficiary in his will dated February 11, 1842; to assure her possession, Robert deeded Sophia the same land on February 5 just in case the will was contested. Another of Rob's favorites was Mrs. John G. Chalmers, the wife of the secretary of the treasury. A sadder-but-wiser Harriet Potter later wrote

> . . . of my husband's unfaithfulness to me, when he would write me every week long, affectionate letters full of love for his children and myself, and yet he would be riding about Austin with a married woman. I remember the home which he had ruined there and the sorrow I must suffer because of it, . . .
>
> He had always been kind and loving to me when he was at home, but, oh, how he had deceived me; . . .

President Lamar was extremely unpopular by the end of his term. His bloody Indian campaigns had cost $2.5 million, the public deficit was $6 million, and he was held totally responsible for the abortive Santa Fe Expedition. In the election of 1841, Sam Houston, who had been representing San Augustine County in the House of Representatives, was opposed by Lamar's vice-president, David G. Burnet. The enmity between the two led to a spate of accusations and name-calling during a bitter campaign. The victorious Houston made an issue of retrenchment and economy in government; when he took office that December, he proposed a ninety percent reduction in government spending. During a congressional debate in November 1841, Senator Potter made this caustic comment about Houston's agenda: "There is an idea in vogue that this is a two-horse government. . . . They

154

would soon have it regulated so as to work with one mule." At Lamar's farewell ball on the night of December 22, Robert made a sensational speech; in reminding his entranced audience of Lamar's role as cavalry leader during the Battle of San Jacinto, he noted:

> Need I remind an assemblage of Texans that in our darkest hour of our revolutionary struggle — "when our need was the sorest" — he [Lamar] came from other climes, like a knight-troubador of the days of romance and chivalry, and rushing into the lists where the fate of Texas was to be decided by the sword, with his good blade he essentially contributed to turn the disastrous tide of war. . . .

The *Austin Daily Bulletin* rhapsodized about the "graceful flow" and "beauty" of this Potter tribute.

In rebuking President Houston for his pessimism over the Republic's financial woes, Robert observed that the president ought to take the advice of an animal show keeper: whenever the monkey rode the pony, his keeper told him, "Always hold a high head in hard times."

One of Potter's pet projects in the North Carolina General Assembly was the promotion of public education. This philosophy led him to propose the creation of Marshall University at Marshall in Harrison County in December 1841. The institution was to be literary, scientific, and nonsectarian in nature, with the Republic of Texas donating four leagues of land for its benefit. Surprisingly, the measure was signed into law by President Houston on January 18, 1842. Two weeks later, however, the president vetoed a Potter joint resolution authorizing land bounties to navy veterans. Perhaps he was thinking of Robert's navy which had denied him passage to New Orleans when the general wrote the following venomous veto message:

> The seaman has no interest (except a transitory one) on shore. His professional pursuits forbid that attention to the use and improvement of grants of this kind,

155

... To make such grants then, would, in a large majority of cases, be the very perfection of prodigality. The harpies that are generally found in seaports and to whom seamen usually become indebted are those only who would profit by the bounty ... of the government.

Congress adjourned on February 5, 1842, but Potter tarried a few days and made out a controversial will in Austin. When he started a leisurely trip home, he was carrying an open invitation to disaster in his saddlebag: a Lamar proclamation of November 15, 1841, offering a $500 reward for the capture of William P. Rose, accused of murdering Sheriff John B. Campbell of Panola County on January 31, 1841. Robert Potter was riding to a date with death.

The origins of this tragic showdown date from the winter of 1839, when Capt. William Pinckney Rose brought his family from Louisiana to live eight miles east of Marshall. Rose was a legendary figure who claimed to have led a company under Andrew Jackson in the Battle of New Orleans. He and Potter first clashed over some lakeside land in Panola County that Rose wanted for his widowed daughter. Tension between the two heightened when Captain Rose backed John B. Denton in his losing Senate race against Robert in 1841. While serving in the Sixth Congress, Senator Potter worked for the official control over Rose's vigilante efforts in Harrison County. During the period between 1839 and 1844, a series of bloody clashes occurred in the counties east of the Sabine River along the Texas-Louisiana border. The violence and lawlessness in this strip of land, a part of the old Neutral Ground (1806–1819), resulted in Shelby, Panola, and Harrison counties being called "The Slaughter Pen." When the Regulators were formed to suppress crime and punish evildoers, "Old Rose" became a self-anointed warrior and leader of this vigilante group in Harrison County; this bully and killer reveled in the title "The Lion of the Lakes." Minor offenders were given ten days to leave the county, but the prescribed penalty might be thirty-nine lashes or lynching. The Regulators executed several suspects, and Captain Rose was indicted for murder by a Harrison County (Marshall) grand jury. However, none would dare arrest him. After the Moderators fought back to control these excesses, the strutting, preening Robert Potter (the "Peacock of the Pines") became their leader in the Caddo Lake area. He loudly boasted of going after Rose once Congress adjourned and even wrote letters to recruit a company of men for that purpose. In one such letter he said:

> I want Rose tried in court — forced to respect the laws and legal machinery of this country. If he resists arrest, then he should be killed — like any outlaw! If the duty finally falls on me to make this arrest, chastise this ruffian, I'll welcome the opportunity — and the five hundred dollars!

When Robert returned to East Texas in early February 1842, he was armed with a warrant for the arrest of "Old Rose" along with a Lamar proclamation urging citizens to help him bring the culprit to justice.

On March 1, 1842, the bone-tired Potter reached home and quickly gathered a posse of seventeen men to help in arresting Rose. After surrounding his house, eighteen-year-old Preston Rose informed Rob that his father was not there. Actually, Old Rose had been supervising some slaves clearing ground for planting when he noticed the Potter band approaching; he managed to hide by having brush piled on him, although a curious and noisy old rooster almost gave him away by circling the spot. Preston Rose insisted that only his mother and young bride were in the house, but Robert ordered his reluctant servant Hezekiah to search the place. Pointing a gun at Mrs. Rose, Hezekiah used the two women as shields, ransacked the house, and took her treasured pin-on watch when he left. Young Rose then promised on his

157

honor as a gentleman to bring his father in and to warn
Rob if he got out of hand. Before the duped Potter rode
off, he assured Preston that his dad would not be harmed
if he would agree to stand trial. Nine of his companions
then rode home with Robert, supposedly to guard his
house during the night. Once the Potter force departed,
Captain Rose obtained a warrant for the senator's arrest
on a complaint of trespassing on his property. When Rob
reached home Hatty warned him, "When Old Rose hears
that you have been hunting for him, he will come here to-
night and try to kill you." Her angry husband only
laughed at her fears, asked for some brandy, demanded
to be left alone, and went to bed.

That very night Rose and nine henchmen surrounded the Potter house. When the apprehensive Harriet heard the dogs barking, she awakened her husband;
seemingly unconcerned, he went back to sleep. Toward
dawn Mrs. Potter sent the slave boy George to grind some
cornmeal for breakfast. When he did not return, she ordered old Hezekiah to check on George before feeding the
hogs. Just as Hatty was halfway to the detached kitchen,
the Rose posse shot Hezekiah down as he crossed the
fence stile; Old Rose later said he gave him a dose of
buckshot for manhandling his women. Harriet managed
to dash back into the house to find her wide-awake husband asking, "What does that [the gunfire] mean?" She
replied, "It means that the house is surrounded, and that
we will have to fight or die." When Robert asked where
all *his* men were, she answered, "I suppose the men are
all killed; they have just killed one." Unnerved by this
news, Rob decided to escape by making a run for the lake;
he was a fine swimmer and would be safe there. Ignoring
his wife's pleas to stay and fight, Potter was shot at six
times as he bolted from the house and jumped the fence.
He raced down the hill and along the beach under a cliff,
then carelessly propped his shotgun against a cypress
tree and dived into the lake. Ironically, among those who
fired at him were two supposed friends, Sandy Miller and

Stephen Peters. In hot pursuit was Rose's son-in-law, John W. Scott, who ran down the bank, grabbed Potter's gun, and shot him once in the back of the head when Rob came up for air.

Meanwhile, back at the house, Old Rose leveled his gun on Hatty and tried to force her inside. Refusing to move even a step, the brave woman told her tormentor, "If only I had a match to touch off this cannon, I would shoot your tongue down your throat." When Scott returned after killing Rob, he dressed down his father-in-law, saying, "What are you abusing Mrs. Potter for? She has never done you any harm; come on, let's go, we have done what we came to do." With a cruel sneer on his face, Captain Rose asked Harriet as they left, "Now what do you think of your pretty Bobby?"

Before the Rose party departed, they released the slave boy George and Hatty's brother John. After dressing the wounds of old Hezekiah, who eventually recovered, Mrs. Potter spent the rest of that sad day rowing the lake, spyglass in hand, in a futile search for her husband's body. That night a fierce thunderstorm stirred up the lake; the next morning she found the corpse floating on the surface near the spot where his tracks left the sand. In his pocket was the big match needed to light the cannon. Two neighbors, Dr. Pearce and Mr. Meredith, helped Harriet bury Robert under a tall tree on a knoll in front of their house, the spot he had chosen as a burial site. There was no eulogy, no songs.

As the only witness to the shooting, Hatty feared for her own life and the safety of her three children. She even armed her slaves after realizing that her house was being watched night and day. Convinced that the Rose gang would kill her if they even suspected her of seeking vengeance, she determined to play the role of a meek, terrified widow. If she traveled to Daingerfield, the county seat, to seek justice for her husband's killers, the only road would take her right by John Scott's house and farm. Finally, after two weeks of posturing, Harriet, her brother Abraham, and a Mr. Parsons took three horses and a pack mule, wrapped themselves in big Mexican blankets, and plodded unchallenged by the Scott home, disguised as newcomers to Texas. Expecting to be gone only a week, the pregnant widow left her children in the care of her Negro slave Hannah at Potter's Point.

At Daingerfield the justice ordered the constable to bring Scott in for questioning, but the accused man did all the talking. Claiming to be part of a legal posse armed with a trespass warrant, Scott insisted that Potter had resisted arrest and fired on a deputy constable. Harriet was absolutely stunned when the justice ordered him released. As he was leaving, Scott admitted that Mrs. Potter was a "plucky little woman" and promised to leave her alone if she would just go home. Undeterred, Hatty went on to Clarksville, where a stranger informed her that District Judge John T. Mills was holding court forty miles away at Boston in Bowie County. On March 25, 1842, she went before Judge Mills to prefer murder charges against all ten members of the Rose gang. The next day Judge Mills ordered Sheriff Edward West of Red River County to arrest Captain Rose, John W. Scott, and eight others for the murder of Robert Potter. After Hatty rode all night to carry the order to Sheriff West, he took a posse of twenty and arrested the accused with no bloodshed.

On April 6, 1842, the grand jury of Red River County returned a true bill against William P. Rose, Preston Rose, John W. Scott, Samuel Petters, Samuel Perkins, William Smith, and Calvin Fuller. The bill of indictment said that Potter was shot in the back of the head with the wound being five inches deep and two inches wide. The prisoners were jailed at Nacogdoches on April 27 but were granted bail on May 4 after their attorneys, Thomas J. Rusk and J. Pinckney Henderson, brought copies of Potter's will and deed and sued out a writ of habeas corpus. At Nacogdoches Harriet was bewildered when she encountered open hostility and vulgar curiosity and was pointedly referred to as "Mrs. Page." District Judge William Ochiltree granted bail after "certain documents" (the Potter will and deed) came to light and refused to hear Hatty's testimony as "Mrs. Potter."

One night, in a drab little boardinghouse room, Rob's friend, Amos Merrill, explained the sudden turn of events to the shocked widow. Calling it the "most difficult task of his life," Merrill slowly read the disgraceful will and deed to the incredulous Harriet. When he finished, she first labeled the will a deceit of some kind. Surely Rob would have changed it if he had not been killed; she remembered him trying to tell her something three times before dashing for the lake. Then reality set in and she asked Amos to take her home, saying she had had enough. Hatty would *not* be sworn in as a paramour; at least she could spare herself and the children that recorded shame. Thus the murder case was scheduled for trial at Nacogdoches on May 6, 1843, only to be dismissed due to insufficient evidence.

During the trip to Potter's Point, Harriet admitted that Rob had left a long trail of deceit during their six years of married life. Twenty miles from home they stopped to spend the night at a neighbor's house. For some reason the whole family acted sad and strained; Amos and Abraham actually looked ill. Once they continued their journey and were almost home, Hatty stopped to pick Lakeann's favorite flowers, the white blossoms from the black hawthorne. Suddenly, one of her escorts, Mr. Parsons, sternly advised her not to pick the flowers before blurting out, "Little Lake is dead — dead and buried." When Amos rushed to her side, the anguished mother cried out, "Kill me, somebody. Let me die!" It seems that the slave Hannah had started a pot of soap, then left little Lakeann asleep on a pallet near the fire while she did some washing and ironing out in the shed. The tyke awoke and tried to stir the hanging pot; it overturned and the soap poured all over her, scalding Lakeann to death.

161

In recalling this latest calamity, the agony of her life, Harriet later wrote: "It would be impossible to describe my feelings. It has seemed strange to me since that I did not become a maniac on the spot." The grieving mother took some flowers to the fresh grave and sat there for a long time, silent and alone. Then she felt a hand on her shoulder: it was Charles Ames. Harriet whispered to him, "Charles, your true love is dead," then she began to sob wildly. Holding her tightly, he replied, "No, my darling. My true love is right here. Safe in my arms. And I shall never let her go."

In the summer of 1842, Congress met in special session at Houston and the Senate passed the following resolution concerning Robert Potter's death:

> WHEREAS the Senate have heard, with deep and sincere regret, of the death of Hon. Robert Potter, . . . and whereas the country has suffered a great loss in that able statesman, whose place will not be easily filled with a man of equal capacity to fill the place he occupied.
> RESOLVED, that we deeply deplore the loss of the talented Senator.
> RESOLVED, that in further testimony of respect, the Senators wear crape on the left arm for thirty days. . . .

The beloved English novelist Charles Dickens was making his first visit to the United States during the time Potter was killed. In his volume of essays entitled *American Notes* (1850), the outspoken idealist later lashed out against slavery and the barbaric American way of life; as an example of the brutalizing effects of slavery, he chose to quote the Shreveport *Caddo Gazette* story of the "Terrible Death of Robert Potter."

On August 21, 1876, the Texas legislature created Potter County in the Texas panhandle "in honor of Robert Potter, a distinguished Texan in the days of the Republic." Amarillo is the county seat of Potter County. On

October 9, 1928, the remains of Potter were reinterred in the State Cemetery in Austin, a place set aside for heroes and distinguished Texas figures.[4]

And what of the long-suffering widow, Harriet Page Potter? After the murder case against her husband was dropped, a court-appointed escort of seventeen men helped her move to Clarksville. Less than six months after Robert's death, she married Charles Ames on August 23, 1842.

The revolting will of Robert Potter was probated at Clarksville on January 10, 1843. Referring to her as Mrs. Harriet A. *Page,* the will finally mentioned Hatty in section four. In section two, Robert left 1,920 acres of land on Ferry Lake, including the Potter home place, to his Austin lady friend and playmate, Mrs. Sophia Ann Mayfield. This gift was for ". . . my gratitude for her friendship, and the happiness I have derived from her converse [defined as having sexual intercourse with], . . ." In section six,

---

[4] In the 1960s the state of Texas again made use of Robert Potter before the United States Supreme Court. Specifically at issue was jurisdiction over part of the continental shelf and minerals such as oil and gas deposits beneath the ocean floor. Around the United States is a shelf of comparatively shallow water which slopes into the ocean depths. This continental shelf extends some 140 miles off the coasts of Texas and Louisiana. In 1945 Texas pushed her seaward boundary to the edge of this shelf. However, when Congress passed the Submerged Lands Act of 1953, a Justice Department interpretation held that the Gulf states were restricted to within three miles of shore. Texas, Louisiana, and Florida, on the other hand, claimed their historic boundaries stretched to three leagues (ten and one-half miles). Texas had the strongest such claim due to the capture of the American brig *Pocket* during Potter's tenure as secretary of the navy. When the United States attorney general sought to break down the Texas claim by asserting that it "does not appear that the Texas Republic took any steps to effectuate its claim of jurisdiction over three leagues of the marginal sea," the state of Texas resorted to the Texian blockade in the Gulf of Mexico and the *Pocket* incident, an argument that apparently carried some weight. In the 1960s the U.S. Supreme Court held that the Texas boundary *did* extend three leagues seaward, partially because of the Texas navy's Gulf operations under Robert Potter and his successors.

163

Potter sarcastically bequeathed his favorite stud horse, Shakespeare, to Sophia's cuckolded husband, Col. James S. Mayfield. Another Austin companion, Mrs. Mary W. Chalmers, received some 1,500 acres, also in gratitude for her "friendship" and "converse." Well over half of Potter's real estate went to people other than his wife. In section four, Potter finally got around to Hatty:

> I give and bequeath to Mrs. Harriet A. Page all that part of my headright, . . . lying north of Section Twelve before mentioned and west of Section Six as mentioned, except one thousand acres to be set apart by Mrs. Page and reserved for her brother John D. Moore. I also give and bequeath to her, two mares to be chosen by herself, my stock of cattle, and three Negroes to wit George, Hannah and Matilda, and also my household and kitchen furniture, and farming utensils.

Small wonder that in May 1843, Harriet and Charles Ames petitioned the probate court of Bowie County to break at least part of Robert Potter's will; specifically, they asked that the land left to Mrs. Mayfield should be turned over to the Ameses and John D. Potter, the child of the deceased. On June 14, Judge James B. Smith of Bowie County granted the Ames petition. Content to let well enough alone, the Mayfields never contested this action before both died in 1852, leaving six children. However, the heirs of Mrs. Mayfield later sued the Ameses for the property willed to their mother. This suit on trespass to try title was tried in 1872. Finally, the Texas Supreme Court rendered final judgment in 1875, reversing part of a district court judgment, and awarding all three sections (1,920 acres) to the Mayfield heirs. Chief Justice Oran M. Roberts, in upholding the Potter will of 1842, based his decision on the critical factor that Harriet was *not* the legal wife of Robert Potter. In his ruling, Chief Justice Roberts concluded: "it can hardly be held that it has been clearly shown that a real marriage in good faith has been established, as the facts appear in the record." To use the court's own words, their living together was a "merely conventional arrangement for illicit intercourse and mutual assistance in living, she being the willing mistress and he the protecting paramour."

Harriet Page Potter Ames later made the following bitter comment about the court ruling:

> As the years went by and my happiness and prosperity increased I thought that I would at last end my days in peace, but that was denied me. I lost my dear husband, and after a man who had bought my land for the sum of seventeen dollars, from the woman to whom Col. Potter had deeded it, went to court with his claim and the court gave him my farm.
>
> I could never understand why the judge could grant such a claim. The property is surely mine, for I had lived upon it for forty years. None but the blackest heart could have done what that man did.
>
> He thought that he had a fortune when he received the deed to Potter's Point, and drove a helpless old woman out of her home. When these afflictions came upon me, I left Texas and went to New Orleans to live.

Charles Ames was to serve as judge of the probate court of Cass County. He and Harriet had thirteen children before his death in February 1866. After losing her homestead in the court decision of 1875, Hatty moved to New Orleans and lived in the beautiful home of her youngest daughter, Adeline ("Addie"), the wife of Dr. Frank Marreo, a skilled physician and member of a prominent local family. It was there at the age of eighty-three that she wrote her life story, "The History of Harriet A. Ames During the Early Days of Texas," in 1890. The date of her death is unknown, but Hatty's grave was located across Lake Ponchartrain in Covington, Louisiana, in the 1930s. Her handwritten manuscript was in the hands of family members in Florida when lawyer J. H. Benefield, Jr., of Jefferson, Texas, discovered it in the summer of 1936 while investigating land titles in the area of Potter's Point. Realizing its historical significance, Benefield had copies of the original manuscript typed in his Jefferson office. Harriet's remarkable memoirs were retold in the best-selling novel *Love is a Wild Assault* by Elithe Hamilton Kirkland in 1959. Dallas literary critic A. C. Greene chose this novel for inclusion in *The 50 Best Books on Texas,* a fitting tribute to the saga of the "baddest man" and the "bravest woman" in the Republic of Texas.

Painting of Rufus Burleson
From Barker Texas History Center, University of
Texas at Austin, Courtesy of University of Texas
Institute of Texan Cultures, San Antonio

Rufus Burleson's octagonal house.
Courtesy Texas Baptist Historical Center-Museum,
Independence, Texas

Mr. and Mrs. Rufus C. Burleson, 1853.
Courtesy Texas Collection,
Baylor University

VII

Rufus C. Burleson and Baylor University: Fifty Years of Toil and Triumph

From 1847 until 1897, the life of Rufus C. Burleson and the history of Baylor University were interwoven. For fifty years the two were dominant forces in providing the best education Texas had to offer. It was Burleson, the strong and steady-handed helmsman, who first headed Baylor on the course it has since followed, that of a Christian institution striving for academic excellence. During his administration, the Baylor influence gave the town of Independence the reputation as "The Athens of Texas," while the *London Times* in 1860 rated the university among the prominent institutions of learning in America. President Burleson was also the pastor and confidant of Sam Houston, and Baylor University became the general's adopted school and educated his children.

Rufus C. Burleson, the seventh of thirteen children of Jonathan and Elizabeth Byrd Burleson, was born at Decatur, Alabama, on August 7, 1823. On his maternal side he was a descendant of Sir William Byrd, the founder of Richmond and Petersburg, Virginia, and Governor William Adair of Kentucky. The precocious lad was only seven when he informed his proud father of his intent to

169

become a great scholar and lawyer. At age sixteen, however, Rufus was converted during a revival meeting held by Reverend W. H. Holcombe and resolved to prepare for the Baptist ministry. In 1840 he enrolled at Nashville University to study for entrance to a seminary, but health problems forced him to withdraw after eighteen months. After returning to his father's farm, he studied Greek, Hebrew, and Bible history until he accepted a teaching position at a private school in Mayhew Prairie, Mississippi, in 1842. During the next three years, Burleson also pastored four churches; but it was his experience as teacher that first led him to consider education as his life's work.

After resigning his position in 1845, Rufus returned home and entered the Western Baptist Theological Seminary at Covington, Kentucky, in 1846. While a student there, he was appointed as an agent of the infant, struggling Baylor University and collected money, books, and apparatus in Kentucky, Ohio, Alabama, and Mississippi. On June 21, 1847, the day he received his diploma, the young "preacher boy" faced West and vowed, "This day I solemnly consecrate my life to Texas."

Upon graduation Burleson volunteered for missionary work in Texas and was assigned to the Gonzales District in the fall of 1847. By then this tall, dignified young preacher was illustrating his direct and forceful sermons with stories from literature and history. While awaiting his departure date, he devoted his time to the study of Texas history and its eminent pioneers. En route to Texas Rufus visited his family near Decatur, where he learned that William Tryon, mission pastor of the First Baptist Church of Houston, had died of yellow fever in November 1847 and that he had been chosen as Tryon's successor by both the church and the Domestic Mission Board of the Southern Baptist Convention. At first the twenty-four-year-old Burleson felt inadequate to accept the calling; then, as he later recalled, "A small voice whispered in my ear, 'My grace is sufficient.'" Traveling

170

overland to New Orleans, he took a steamer for Galveston and landed there on January 5, 1848.

While serving the Houston church as pastor, Burleson was first prostrated by yellow fever and then cholera. His entrance into public life came in 1848, when he was elected a delegate to a general conference of churches meeting at Anderson which organized the Baptist General Convention of Texas. Among those who attended his Houston services was Susanna Dickinson, the only Anglo adult survivor of the Alamo assault. After preaching on the mission of the church one Sunday night in 1849, Pastor Burleson asked the packed congregation to join him in a prayer asking God to save the worst sinners in Houston. Mrs. Dickinson, nominally a member of the Episcopal church, was one of five to come forward weeping and asking to be saved the next Wednesday night during prayer meeting. She told the pastor she was aware of her lost condition, accepted Jesus Christ as her personal Savior, and was joyfully converted. A crowd of 1,500 lined the banks of Buffalo Bayou to see her baptized, after which she became a zealous church worker. In July 1851 Susanna's daughter Angelina, "the Babe of the Alamo," was married to John Maynard Griffith by Burleson. When her former pastor held a revival in Austin in 1862, Susanna was one of those coming forward to rededicate her life, admitting that she had been "erring and wayward" but wanting to do right and serve her Redeemer.

Burleson's highly successful pastorate at Houston ended when he responded to a challenging educational opportunity, the presidency of an undeveloped university. The acorn that grew into the Baylor University oak was planted on October 8, 1840, when messengers from Baptist churches at Independence, LaGrange (then Clear Creek), and Austin organized the Union Association, with Robert Emmett Bledsoe Baylor as corresponding secretary. Baylor, a lifelong bachelor, had distinguished himself in both law and politics before coming to Texas

171

from Alabama in 1839 at the age of forty-eight.[1] After years as an avowed atheist, he was converted to the Christian faith at Talladega, Alabama, in July of that year and was soon licensed as a Baptist minister. Upon his arrival in Texas, Baylor first taught a small school at LaGrange, then moved to Gay Hill a few miles west of Independence in 1841. That January, Robert was elected by joint ballot of the Texas Congress as judge of the Third Judicial District of the Republic of Texas. This position

---

[1] Robert Emmett Bledsoe Baylor, the sixth of twelve children, was born in Lincoln County, Kentucky, on May 10, 1793. His father, Walker Keith, was a captain in the Continental army and an aide to George Washington. Robert's mother, Jane Bledsoe Baylor, was the daughter of a Baptist preacher. Young Baylor studied law in the Paris, Kentucky, office of his uncle, Judge Jesse Bledsoe, a United States senator and law professor at Transylvania University. After serving in the War of 1812, Robert practiced law with brothers George Wythe and Walker Keith for several years and was elected to the Kentucky legislature. In 1820 he moved to Alabama where he was a state legislator, a director of the state bank, and served one term (1829–1831) in the United States House of Representatives. Baylor led Alabama volunteers against the Creek Indians in 1836, then emigrated to Texas three years later.

Judge Baylor was not only a founder of Baylor University at Independence; he was also a generous contributor, a professor of law there, and represented the president in his absence. One of his most ardent admirers was the noted Baptist minister, educator, and historian Dr. J. M. Carroll; when the eighteen-year-old Carroll and his young bride enrolled at the Independence school, Judge Baylor was the first person they met. After Texas joined the Union, R. E. B. Baylor served as a state district judge of his old, huge Central Texas district for twenty-five years, carrying both the laws of Texas and the Bible on his judicial circuit. This "parson judge" would administer the law and hold court by day, then organize churches and preach at night. He once baptized forty-one converts at the end of a revival. Baylor also served three one-year terms as chaplain of the Grand Lodge of Texas Masons.

In August 1853 he proudly acted as appointing judge in licensing his nephew to practice law; John Robert Baylor later won fame as a Confederate colonel.

Judge Baylor lived with his sister at his home, "Holly Oaks," five miles from Independence. In his twilight years, the Baptist State Convention requested that he write an autobiography which was dated

made him an ex officio associate justice of the Texas Supreme Court, where all cases involving constitutional questions were assigned to him.

When the Union Association met in October 1841 near Rutersville, William Milton Tryon, a New York City native and the missionary pastor of the Independence Baptist Church, suggested the need for a Baptist university in Texas.[2] His recommendation resulted in the formation of the Texas Baptist Education Society, with

---

April 13, 1871. Before dying at home on January 6, 1874, he asked to be buried on the campus of Old Baylor at Independence. His old home was torn down in 1925 and the state erected a granite marker on the site in 1936. When G. W. Baines, Jr., the son of the third Baylor president and great uncle of Lyndon Baines Johnson, visited Judge Baylor's gravesite early in this century, he was appalled by the neglected condition of the grounds and began to agitate for removing the remains to a more suitable location. As a result of Baines's efforts, the body of this renowned jurist, preacher, and educator was reinterred on the grounds of Baylor Female College (now Mary Hardin-Baylor) at Belton on May 6, 1917.

[2] Reverend Tryon was the second minister sent to Texas by the American Baptist Home Mission Society and had pastored three churches in both Georgia and Alabama before arriving at Galveston in March 1841. After reorganizing the disbanded church at Washington-on-the-Brazos, he ministered to four churches during his first year in Texas. Tryon led the Independence Baptist Church for almost five years and made it the strongest Baptist congregation in the Republic of Texas. He also persuaded seventeen other missionaries to go to Texas, including Rufus Burleson, who received a "powerful appeal" while attending the seminary at Covington, Kentucky. William was foremost in the organization of both the Education Society and Baylor University; Tryon Hall, the main building on the men's campus at Independence, was a memorial to him.

This "prince among Texas Baptist preachers" was still serving as a Baylor trustee when he became the mission pastor of the First Baptist Church of Houston. Under his leadership, sixty-seven additions were made to the church, and a new brick structure — only the third one in the city — was built on the site of the old Milby Hotel. The thirty-nine-year-old pastor died "in harness," succumbing to yellow fever on November 16, 1847, shortly after making visits to the sick and needy, and was buried in Houston's Glenwood Cemetery. Today the Baylor campus at Waco pays tribute to its founders with the Tryon and Huckins pillars which flank the Judge Baylor statue.

173

Statue of R. E. B. Baylor
Courtesy Texas Collection,
Baylor University

Judge Baylor serving as president and Tryon as corresponding secretary. The Society had two objectives: (1) to found a school to help support young men studying for the ministry and (2) to act as a statewide organization to place the entire body of Texas Baptists behind one institution for the education of a native ministry. The Society included several prominent political and military leaders. Richard Ellis had served as president of the Convention of 1836 which drafted the Texas Declaration of Independence. Noah T. Byars's unfinished building at Washington-on-the-Brazos served as the Texas "Independence Hall," and he was the armorer for General Houston's army. Noah was also the first missionary Baptist preacher ordained in Texas and the founder of over sixty churches. Society member Kenneth L. Anderson was the last vice-president of the Republic of Texas.

The Education Society was inactive until 1844 because of military and political turmoil with Mexico.

174

President William Carey Crane
Courtesy Texas Baptist Historical Center-
Museum, Independence, Texas

Judge R. E. B. Baylor
Courtesy Texas Baptist Historical Center-
Museum, Independence Texas

When the Union Association met that year, Baylor and Tryon were chosen as a committee of two for the purpose of securing a college charter. Tradition has it that Robert insisted on providing for a female department in the charter. It seems that he had recently visited a home near Independence with only girls in the family. The proud mother had expressed the opinion that her daughters had as much right to an education as did boys, and Judge Baylor was won over to her viewpoint. When he dictated the memorial to the Texas Congress requesting a charter, he also made it clear that the Society expected no financial aid from the government.

The space for the school's name was left blank when the charter was presented to the Congress then sitting at Washington-on-the-Brazos. It was Judge Baylor who first suggested that the blank be filled in with the name of Tryon, since it was his idea to establish a Baptist university in Texas and to apply for a charter. William declined because "he feared it might be thought that he was working for his own honor, and so it might injure the prospects of the school." He then took the charter and wrote "Baylor" in the blank, in spite of his coworker's vigorous protest. In explaining his own objections, Judge Baylor said, "First, I do not think I am worthy of such a distinction; second, my humble donation [he had subscribed $1,000 to the proposed university] might be misunderstood and the motives prompting it misconstrued." He was overruled, however, when Vice-president Kenneth Anderson joined Tryon in his efforts; Baylor later recalled that the two were "inflexible" and "determined upon it."

On December 28, 1844, the memorial of *R. E. B. Baylor et. al.* was presented by Senator George A. Patillo, representing Jasper and Jefferson counties. When Patillo introduced the original bill, he called the school San Jacinto University. On the second reading a week later, he marked out that title and inserted the name Milam University. When the time came for a third and final

176

reading, Patillo rose from his seat to ask that the name be changed once more, this time to Baylor University. The bill for said school was signed by President Anson Jones on February 1, 1845.

Both Judge Baylor and Reverend Tryon were appointed to the university's board of trustees, with Tryon being the unanimous choice as first board president. When the trustees met on October 13, 1845, to decide the location of the institution, four bids were considered. Each offered a bonus of land, oxen, cattle, horses, cotton, and days of manual labor to help locate the school. Independence, a town in Washington County on the main stage road from Houston to Austin, made the largest bid — $7,925 — and was selected by a trustee vote of ten to one over Huntsville, the second highest bidder.[3] That December the board voted to repair and use a two-story

---

[3] Independence was founded by John P. Coles, who was among the first forty of Austin's Old Three Hundred colonists. On August 19, 1824, Coles was granted eight and one-half leagues of choice land in adjoining corners of present Washington, Burleson, and Brazos counties. He then established a mill on Yegua Creek and built a "public house" around which developed Coles's Settlement. In January 1835 Miss Frances Trask opened a boardinghouse for young ladies on the Coles property. The school closed, however, during the Texas Revolution and was succeeded by the Independence Academy, chartered by the Republic of Texas on June 5, 1837.

After the Texas Declaration of Independence was adopted on March 2, 1836, at nearby Washington-on-the-Brazos, many of the signers came to Coles's Settlement to spend the night, celebrate, and hoist a Texas flag in the town square. This inspired local resident Dr. Asa Hoxey to suggest that the town's name be changed to Independence, which became the self-styled "Cradle of Liberty" and the "Little Williamsburg of Texas." With Independence and Washington as focal points, Washington County led the Republic in wealth, population, and influence by 1845. Several of the pioneer homes in Independence are now landmarks, and the Independence Baptist Church, organized in September 1839, is the oldest continuously operating missionary Baptist church in Texas. Four presidents of Baylor University — Graves, Baines, Burleson, and Crane — also served as pastors of the church. The original adobe structure built in 1849 was destroyed by fire. In 1872 the church was rebuilt of native stone and floored in cedar. That building is still used today.

frame house formerly owned by the Independence Female Academy, a girls' boarding school started by Miss Frances Trask in January 1835. This single building on Academy Hill had been included in the Independence bid and was to be used by both Baylor male and female students for the first five years.

On January 12, 1846, the trustees elected Reverend Henry L. Graves as president of Baylor and Henry Flavel Gillette as principal of the preparatory department. Graves was a graduate of the University of North Carolina, the Hamilton Literary and Theological Institute in New York, and a former math teacher at Wake Forest College. He first served as a Baylor agent and remained in Georgia raising funds until 1847, with the principal running the school in the interim. Gillette, who was Baylor's first teacher, opened school with twenty-four students on May 18, 1846; that number increased to seventy by year's end. The Graves family reached Independence on February 4, 1847, and set up residence in the Mose Hairston house, a stately two-storied, balconied home on College Hill. President Graves also served concurrently as pastor of the Independence Baptist Church and was elected as the first president of the new Baptist State Convention of Texas in September 1848.

The board decided that Graves and Gillette would be paid by sharing school profits at a ratio of three to two. Graves was to collect all tuition and pay teachers out of his own pocket. Evidently, such an arrangement resulted in quite a shortfall: at the close of the first Baylor term, the university owed Graves $1,200 and Gillette $800 — a year's salary for each, which was paid out of the trustees' own pockets! In December 1847 the financially hard-pressed college applied for state aid in the form of two leagues of land, an appeal which was rejected by the Education Committee of the Texas House of Representatives. At the June 1848 board meeting, it was decided to build a permanent stone building (Graves Hall) on Allen Hill at a cost of $6,000. The trustees also invested the

178

president with authority to handle all college disciplinary matters.

In 1849 Graves added lectures in law by securing the
voluntary services of Abner Smith Lipscomb and R. E. B.
Baylor. He was also responsible for the first chemistry
experiments conducted in Texas. After Baylor agent
James Huckins purchased a set of chemical apparatus
from the Chamberlain firm of Boston in 1851, President
Graves had J. A. Kimball assemble the pieces and perform numerous experiments at the Baylor June commencement.

Serious bronchial problems forced Graves to resign
as president of Baylor on June 17, 1851, and retire to his
farm near Brenham; he would later serve as president of
Fairfield College for ten years. He died at Brenham on
November 4, 1881.

Rufus Burleson always attended the annual Baylor
commencement exercises and thus was present at Independence the day Graves resigned; in fact, he opened the
board meeting with a prayer. After being nominated by
Judge A. S. Lipscomb to fill the vacant post, Burleson
was elected president of Baylor the next day. Before ac-
cepting the position, he insisted that the sexes must be
separated in all their schoolwork; thus male and female
departments were designated with a two-year course of
study in a preparatory school as a prerequisite for each
department. Entering freshmen were to be given an
exam on Latin and Greek grammar, Caesar, Virgil, Ci-
cero's orations, and algebra. Since a majority could not
pass these rigid exams, the preparatory division was offered for them.

An early objective of President Burleson was to lib-
eralize and broaden the Baylor classical curriculum. His
eight-point policy outline adopted by the trustees included the following goal: "In addition to the usual course
of college studies, give special attention to English literature, and the history of our own great men, . . ." Thus
the 1852 catalogue added lectures on modern history and

179

First faculty of the male department at Independence.
Courtesy Texas Collection, Baylor University

Graves Hall — Allen Hill (Independence)
Courtesy Texas Collection, Baylor University

Main Building, Women's Campus at Independence, ca. 1857.
Courtesy Texas Collection, Baylor University

181

a history of the United States. The new president also emphasized daily oral recitations and made compositions and declamations a semimonthly requirement. He took complete control of the male department and moved his charges into the new two-story stone building on Allen Hill in September 1851. The structure was thirty-six by fifty feet with the lower story serving as a one-room chapel and the upper floor containing two classrooms.

Horace G. Clark was named principal of the female department and served in that capacity for fifteen years. He had sailed around the world as a boy, spent four years at sea, and had been shanghaied and rescued at age fourteen. Clark was principal of the Henry Academy at New Castle, Kentucky, for four years before leaving for Texas. Upon his arrival, Horace showed his commitment by taking a wagon to Houston to buy needed flour and provisions. His female department remained in the old Academy Building, but the trustees did pay $1,230 for a house and eight acres for their use. Principal Clark soon purchased this property, and his boardinghouse became the only dormitory for girls while Baylor was at Independence. Although he was a gentle, affable man and less stern than President Burleson, Clark exercised total control over the ladies, even prescribing a complete student uniform for them. All letters to the girls had to be addressed to the principal, and they could not communicate with gentlemen or receive their attention. In the early years, the women had no social life; church attendance was their only contact with the outside world.

The first clash between Burleson and Clark came after Judge Lipscomb suggested that the state legislature endow all church colleges with land grants of 40,000 acres to each denomination. Early in his tenure, President Burleson went before the board requesting a petition to that effect. Even though the proposition failed, a similar plan was introduced at the Baptist State Convention meeting at the Independence Baptist Church. In a speech to that gathering, Rufus said that "he wanted it distinctly understood that this donation was to be for the male department of Baylor University." When a vote was taken, nine favored the resolution but ninety voted against its passage, including Horae Clark. The die was thus cast for a long-running, bitter feud between two strong-willed educators.

When Burleson moved to Independence, he found a college with a small enrollment, an inadequate physical plant, a tiny endowment fund, and few dedicated supporters. The efforts of the energetic young president were quick to bear fruit. His first step was an aggressive advertising campaign to bring new students to the campus. To that end he ordered Baylor circulars printed and sent six couriers on horseback to deliver them across the state. Rufus also wrote personal letters and talked to church groups as a method of promoting the fledgling Baptist school. The endowment fund increased from one to twenty thousand dollars, and a library was started. Baylor University was on the road toward offering genuine college work and graduating students with degrees. By 1855 the two Baylor departments had a total enrollment of 188, and the institution had advanced from the experimental stage to one with a statewide reputation.

President Burleson had a full schedule of teaching assignments in intellectual philosophy, moral philosophy, belles-lettres, Latin, Greek, and Spanish. He also conducted daily morning chapel attended by all students, taught a special theological class for ministerial students, and presided over faculty meetings. In late 1854 Rufus wrote to his brother Richard, offering him the position of professor of mathematics. The letter included the following self-appraisal:

> ... My dear brother there are more learned men, classic scholars, — regular graduates in this Association [Union] than in all North Alabama. ... You may ask how it is that I hold such a prominent position among such men. Well, I assure you it is not from superiority but from surplus vigilance and untiring energy. ...

183

Burleson was a self-centered, headstrong, tempera-
mental man of consuming ambition. He demanded excellence and was a stern disciplinarian and father figure
who was respected, admired, and loved by the male students. It was not uncommon for Rufus to first pray over a
young delinquent, then give him a sound whipping. In
1857 a student said of him: ". . . and while we were
shrinking back from the piercing glance, the hand of cor-
dial welcome was extended. He is courteous and polite,
yet we stand in awe. We do not dread him, for we love
him." This austere figure also took a special interest in
the sports and diversions of his pupils. In 1858 Burleson
was seen on campus gamely offering himself as a target
to a hundred boys playing "hot ball." Although the pelt-
ing from the solid rubber balls left many painful bruises,
he managed to leave the playground with a smile and a
salute. The president also made a hide-and-seek game
out of student pranks. It seems that he had a "detective
bird" that whispered in his ear, allowing him to ferret out
and foil such shenanigans. Sometimes, however, Rufus
came out the loser: in the spring of 1858, his renowned
carriage was found on top of the Female College building!

On January 3, 1852, Burleson married Georgia Jenkins, the daughter of Judge P. C. Jenkins, a distinguished lawyer who brought his family to Texas from
Georgia in 1836. Miss Jenkins was a high honor graduate of Judson Female Institution in Marion, Alabama,
and first met the young president during his frequent
visits to Independence. The newlyweds made a "bridal
tour" to New Orleans, where she busied herself "in social
recreation" while her ever-earnest husband improved his
Spanish during a five-week stay. Georgia was a cultured
and charming young lady who was to be an inspiration
and counselor to her mate and a beautiful character
model to thousands of Baylor students. Upon their return
to Independence, she tried to arrange a social for the girls

from Academy Hill, but Principal Clark would not allow them to attend. Her offended spouse termed Horace's refusal "disrespect to Mrs. Burleson."

On May 10, 1856, the couple's little daughter died at birth. That September the Burlesons moved into their new octagonal house just east of Graves Hall. This three-story home contained six rooms for family use and twenty-five other large rooms, each capable of accommodating four young men. A large chimney in the center of the house allowed for a fireplace in each room.

In 1856 President Burleson had a total income of $3,400 from tuition, preaching, an endowment, and boarding ten students in their home. When poor health and fatigue forced him to travel to the South and East for an extended period in late 1859, he rejected an offer to become president of Union University at Murfreesboro, Tennessee. In a letter to his wife, Rufus admitted that the position would be easier "and perhaps more honorable and profitable . . . and we should be clear of taking boarders . . ." But, he said, "I am bound to Texas, our church, and Baylor University by a thousand tender ties. . . ." He later turned a deaf ear to the same offer from Shreveport University in Louisiana.

In December 1854 Stephen Decatur Rowe became Baylor's first graduate by receiving an A. B. degree from the male department. During the next school year, he became an assistant professor of ancient languages and resident graduate. In December 1855 Principal Clark recommended that a diploma be given to Mary Gentry Kavanaugh, the first graduate of the female department. Mary was the daughter of Baylor trustee Nelson Kavanaugh and had first enrolled there as a seven-year-old student in 1846. In 1856 Baylor awarded a degree to the first transfer student, Oscar Leland, a former teacher in Georgia who attended Baylor for five months. Another significant milestone was the school's first publication, the *Texas Literary Journal*. This monthly magazine of sixty pages was devoted to education in Texas, science, and history. The first issue appeared on February 1, 1857. A law department was added that year, and the 1859 catalogue announced a new theological department with courses to begin in the winter of 1860.

The course of study at Baylor was rigorous indeed. A student in the male department could choose a four-year course of study leading to an A.B. degree, a three-year scientific course, law school, or preparation for the ministry. The A. B. requirements included algebra, plane geometry, Latin and Greek grammar, ancient history, trigonometry, natural philosophy, natural history, surveying and navigation, Spanish or French, German, Greek and Roman history, analytical geometry, chemistry, astronomy, intellectual philosophy, English history and literature, the United States Constitution, moral science, political economy, geology, differential and integral calculus, elements of criticism, reading from the great authors, and evidences of Christianity. The A.B. for women included arithmetic, mental philosophy, chemistry, Latin grammar and readings, English composition, French readings, algebra, natural philosophy, anatomy, physiology, geometry, meteorology, logic, astronomy, rhetoric, trigonometry, elements of criticism, intellectual philosophy, vocal music, drawing, painting, embroidery, and evidences of Christianity.

Both men and women students had four one-hour classes each day with ten minutes of "recreation" between classes. Immediately after each class, the professor assigned a numerical grade for each student ranging from a zero for not being prepared to a ten for a perfect recitation. Instructors kept daily records of attendance, conduct, and recitations for each student, with a weekly report going into a permanent file. Examinations were conducted by a visiting examining committee; those of 1855 lasted four days. The examinations included student speeches, essays and addresses, and ended with a commencement exercise. Holding concerts was a favorite diversion of the female department, while the men preferred debates. Nancy Anderson, a proud student in the female department, wrote a letter to her sister on November 1, 1859, in which she said, "When I come there you will all have to haul down your dictionary and dust it. I am in a very good society. I don't think it can be beaten." In recalling her days as a Baylor student at Independence, Mrs. Ebbie Higdon Ozburn said that

> . . . Housekeeping was a part of our education. Conveniences? We knew them not. Kerosene lamps, bare floors, crude furniture, but oh, how spotless clean these rooms were kept! Bath rooms, did you say? No indeed!
>
> The world was shut out and we had an earnest student body. If there was ever a failure, no second chance was given. Our reports were printed in black or gold, signifying our general average. A black report was more to be dreaded than the plague. . . .

Each Sunday a solemn procession of Baylor men and women would march down their respective hills to attend services at the Independence Baptist Church, where they sat on opposite sides of the aisle. Mail call and picking berries were the main amusements for the ladies; in 1885 the trustees of Baylor Female College banned "holidays and night sociables" from the campus as being "destructive alike to scholarship, good order and good habits." Their catalogue of that year prohibited slang expressions, chewing gum, borrowing, lending, trading, or reading books not approved by the president. From the very beginning, all young ladies from out of town had to board on campus and were not allowed to be off campus at night. Baylor women also had a strict dress code: they could wear only plainly trimmed white straw bonnets with no gay or expensive ribbons. Rings were prohibited, and the only jewelry permitted was a plain breast-pin. Students also could not be connected with a dancing school without faculty approval. Even in this spartan atmosphere, however, there were frivolous moments. Mary G. Kavanaugh recalled that she and four roommates had a dormitory room just above the kitchen. At prearranged times the hungry scholars would lower a basket by a line and the Negro cook would fill it with "feasts" for their between-meal snacks. Mary also remembered how the resourceful ladies produced "homemade" cosmetics. They were told that an effective overnight beauty mask could be made from a mixture of flour and honey. Such a mask hardened like plaster and had to be cracked off the next morning, but it did give the girls rosy cheeks!

Baylor had its share of regulations for males. No profane language was allowed on campus, boys could not carry pistols and knives or use ardent spirits, and no gambling or visiting of "dramshops" and "drinking houses" was permitted. A student could not leave his room after 9:00 P.M. or leave school without faculty permission. A system of demerits was used for disciplinary purposes, with 100 demerits being grounds for dismissal from school. For example, a young man received five demerits if he was absent from his room after dark or ten demerits if he came in after 9:00 P.M. All students were required to attend daily opening religious exercises which included scripture reading, prayers, and singing of hymns. Even though Baylor was a Baptist school, only twenty-four of the 102 male students in 1855 professed to be church members; holding periodic revivals for the non-Christian students was the college's remedy for such a problem.

President Burleson was called as pastor of the Independence Baptist Church in February 1854. Before he resigned from that position in 1856, a famous newcomer was added to the church rolls. U.S. Senator Sam Houston moved his family to Independence from Huntsville on October 25, 1853, after purchasing the Thomas Barron house from Mr. Hines. There were several reasons for the move. Ten-year-old Sam, Jr., and seven-year-old Nancy Elizabeth (Nannie) were already studying Latin and approaching school age; for them the Baylor preparatory school offered the best educational opportunities in Texas. It was also hoped that the higher elevation might improve Margaret Houston's asthma condition. Nancy Moffette Lea, Margaret's widowed and aging mother, also lived at Independence in a cottage across the street from the old Baptist church. Her home was a social center for Baylor students and only two blocks from Houston's house.

Sam Houston had become notorious for his drinking and vulgarity in his early Texas political career, but he pledged to abstain from liquor after his marriage to Margaret in May 1840. His wife also exerted great spiritual influence on her wayward husband. During his early years in the United States Senate, Houston started attending the fashionable E Street Baptist Church of Reverend George Whitfield Samson in the capital, telling the pastor that he came out of respect for his wife, whom he described as one of the best Christians on earth. Sam soon became a regular at the services, sitting in the same pew well toward the front and all the while whittling toys for children during the long sermons.

Margaret realized that she had a powerful new ally when her spouse began to summarize Samson's sermons in his regular Sunday afternoon letters to his wife. Senator Houston particularly liked sermons on the Proverbs text, "Better is he that ruleth his spirit than he that taketh a city." When he realized that Sam was under conviction, Brother Samson preached on several examples of saving faith, and sought to erase his doubts by giving Houston a copy of Nelson's *Cause and Cure of Infidelity*. However, there was still one basic problem to overcome. As a boy the senator had attended a Presbyterian meeting with his mother and heard a Dr. Blackburn preach; this revivalist made an indelible impression on Sam by quoting from Corinthians to the effect that eternal damnation was promised the unbeliever who took communion. Thus Houston hesitated to be baptized or take part in

The Nancy Lea Bell
Photo by J. C. Hoke, Wharton, Texas

Independence Baptist Church
Photo by J. C. Hoke, Wharton, Texas

any other sacrament for fear of making a "sad and awful mistake."

After the move to Independence, Margaret wanted her pastor, Rufus Burleson, to serve as a spiritual adviser to her husband, who knew just enough about the Bible to be argumentative and relished debating Rufus into the late evening hours. At one point the educator continued an argument in a sermon, causing the angry Houston to stand up, interrupt, and attempt to correct the preacher. At first the two merely tolerated each other; it was Reverend George W. Baines, who lived at Anderson and was to become Baylor's third president, who became the senator's best religious friend.

Sam was back in Washington when he received the blessed news that his second son, Andrew Jackson, had been born on June 21, 1854. Shortly thereafter, he told Reverend Samson that he was ready to profess his faith. By the time Sam reached home that October, Margaret knew that Judge R. E. B. Baylor would be conducting a four-day revival at Independence in November and would be preaching his famous "Jesus Wept" sermon. Years before, Judge Baylor had saved Margaret Houston from drowning at Marion, Alabama, and she regarded this revival as the opportune time for her husband's conversion. One November night at sunset, Sam made a profession of faith to Margaret over her open Bible; they no doubt attended the Baylor revival, but Houston chose to make a public profession during regular church services. In his memoirs, Pastor Burleson recalls preaching on the senator's favorite passage from Proverbs. According to Rufus, "When I had finished my sermon, General Houston arose and came down and extended his hand to me and when I grasped it he said, 'I give you my hand and with it I give my heart to the Lord.'"

The senator's reluctance to be baptized was overcome by his close friend, G. W. Baines, who corrected Sam's lifelong misunderstanding about the book of Corinthians. Brother Baines pointed out that Paul's complaint about the abuse of the sacraments was aimed at those who mocked holy symbols by giving in to feasting and drinking to satisfy animal desires. After rereading that book of the Bible, Houston was satisfied with Baines's explanation. Pastor Burleson had earlier built a special coffin-shaped baptistry in Kountz Creek north of town and he intended to use it for Houston's service. However, vandals filled it with mud, tree limbs, and stones the night before, so Rufus baptized the general in Rocky Creek two miles south of Independence at noon on November 19, 1854. It was a bright, cold day and a crowd of 225 from as far away as Austin, Brenham, and Washington-on-the-Brazos gathered on the creek banks to watch the baptismal service. According to those present, Burleson seemed unsure of his footing as he trudged deep enough into the pool to dip a man of Houston's height below the surface. When he lifted him up and out of the water, Rufus said, "Now Sam, your sins are all washed away." The senator saltily retorted, "God help the fishes!" He also remarked to Burleson that his pocketbook had been baptized and agreed to pay half of the minister's salary after joining the Independence Baptist Church. Shortly after the baptism, Houston was riding with John H. Reagan when his mount suddenly stumbled. He first blurted out, "God damn a stumbling horse!"; then the contrite Christian dismounted, knelt in the dusty road, and prayed for forgiveness. The conversion of this spectacular sinner was such a national event that a leading church periodical, *America's Own,* was moved to make the following comment on December 23, 1854:

> The announcement of General Houston's immersion has excited the wonder and surprise of many who have supposed that he was "past praying for" but it is no marvel to us. . . . Three thousand and fifty clergymen have been praying for him ever since the Nebraska outrage in the Senate! [A reference to Houston's vote on the Kansas-Nebraska Act of 1854: Houston was the

only Southern senator to vote *no* on this law, which opened slavery territory that had been closed by the Missouri Compromise 36° 30' dividing line in 1820.]

In late 1854 Senator Houston became an active patron of Baylor University by offering the use of his large library and serving on an advisory board. He followed up in April 1855 by making the first gift of $330 to the Baylor Department of Ministerial Education. Houston began to buy and dispense large numbers of religious books, to lead in public prayer, and became a regular in attending both preaching and prayer meeting services. He talked publicly on the temperance question, became a leader in missionary work among the Indians, and began to end all of his political documents with a devout recognition of the Diety. Texas Congressman L. D. Evans, who occupied the room under Senator Houston in a Washington, D.C., boardinghouse, later recalled that a creaking sound each morning and night always signaled that the general was kneeling in prayer. Although this humbled new Christian did partake of the sacrament of the Lord's Supper, he told Margaret that he felt unworthy to do so.

President Burleson became Houston's confidant after the senator's conversion. During the secession crisis of January-February 1861, Governor Houston conducted a one-man campaign to keep Texas in the Union and made a spacial trip to Independence to seek the help of Rufus in "saving Texas" from secession. The two agreed to make their fight within the Union and prayed over it. After Baylor students debated such a series of resolutions and the affirmative side won, they ran up the Stars and stripes on a fifty-foot-high liberty pole. Political opinion in Austin ran to the contrary, however, and Sam sent word to the Baylor president that "all is lost!" A few days later, Independence Mayor Task Clay cut down the pole, and the torn flag was trampled in the dirt.

After being deposed as governor of Texas on March 16, 1861, for refusing to take an oath of allegiance to the Confederate States of America government, Houston re-

193

turned to Independence to visit and pray with Burleson, telling him that "our only hope now is God. Let us kneel down and pray to the God of Liberty." When he wrote his memoirs, the educator told of Houston's revealing his real military objectives in the 1836 retreat before Santa Anna. According to Burleson, the general had a secret agreement that if the Texian army was forced to retreat to the Sabine, they would be joined there by 4,000 United States Army troops commanded by General Gaines. This combined force would have then repulsed the Mexican army, marched to the Rio Grande, and demanded that Texas independence be granted or else Mexico would face invasion. The impressed Rufus remarked in his memoirs that "a grander campaign was never planned."

Sam Houston, Jr., gave the school's San Jacinto Day speech in April 1856 and attended Baylor's academy until the summer of 1859. After service in the Confederate Army, he returned to the male department for further study. By 1861 Houston's three oldest daughters — Nannie, Maggie, and Mollie — were enrolled in Baylor's female department. During her student days, Nannie was reprimanded for talking during a lecture; she told her father of the incident in a letter, but not her mother. When she was fifteen Nannie was given a Steinway piano by her doting father; in 1903 she gave the beloved instrument to Baylor University's Texas Collection. In 1866 the Baylor campus newspaper, *The Violet,* was produced by four students, including two Houston daughters: Margaret Lea ("Maggie") was the "editress" and Mary William ("Mollie") was publisher. Mollie and a younger sister, Antoinette Power ("Nettie"), the most accomplished poetess of the family, were among the graduates in the Baylor Female College class of 1868. Temple, the last of Sam and Margaret's eight children and the first child to be born in the Governor's Mansion at Austin, received a bachelor of philosophy degree from Baylor at Independence in 1878.

The seemingly bright future of Baylor University was clouded in the 1850s by the Burleson-Clark feud. When Burleson accepted the presidency in 1851, he considered the male department to be of primary importance and took over the new stone building for his charges. The female department of Principal Horace Clark was to play a secondary role so was located in the decaying old wooden Academy Building. At first the younger and more ambitious Burleson devoted all his time and energy to the men while giving Clark a free hand with the women. New friction between the two developed in 1853 after the girls outgrew their "crazy old building" and requested a new home. Principal Clark became a direct competitor of the male department for financial support. In July 1855 the trustees closed a contract with John P. Collins to erect a female department building at a cost of $8,000. In 1857 the women moved into this large new "elegant" three-story stone structure, a "handsomely furnished" facility forty by seventy feet with a portico, cupola, and dome. It housed a spacious audience hall, school room, library and apparatus room, five ample recitation rooms, and was described as "the best school building in all Texas." The board had initially cut Clark's elaborate design to two stories, but when he persuaded Dr. Asa Hoxie to donate $1,000 for the basement, the trustees authorized him to proceed with the original plans. Trustee A. C. Horton, the first lieutenant governor of Texas, donated a large, costly bell that could be heard five miles away. This personal, imposing college edifice of Clark was larger and better equipped than Burleson's building; in fact, the president grumbled that maintaining it was beyond the financial capabilities of Texas Baptists. Today the four lonely fronting columns of this main building of the female department are the only remains of the twelve buildings on the two hills making up the "Old Baylor" campus at Independence.

President Burleson was jealous of the obvious success of the female department and began to take a more

195

active interest in the affairs of Principal Clark, who resented this sudden attention and interference. By December 1857 friction between the two increased to such a point that the board of trustees appointed a committee of four "to wait on each of them, separate and apart and make known all the rumors afloat." After finding the rumors of unpleasant feelings between the two to be true, the board reacted by separating the two departments, with Burleson having no authority over the women and the trustees supervising both divisions. In settling one of their "petty difficulties," the trustees warned Clark not to prevent young women from attending Burleson's revival meetings at the Independence Baptist Church.

Yet another point of contention arose when the president moved for freedom of social contact between men and women on the two hills, a concept the principal opposed. The two Baylor departments were a mile apart, and the small creek splitting the campus was "the Jordan" separating the men from "the promised land." Clark even contended that Burleson let offenders off too lightly when they crossed over to pull pranks on the female grounds. When R. T. Wheeler resigned as a Baylor professor of law in February 1860 and began competitive law lectures at nearby Brenham, Rufus and Horace conducted a heated debate in the *Texas Baptist* as to whether or not there were ulterior motives behind Wheeler's decision. The festering quarrel between the two came to an open clash on Sunday, June 17, 1860, at the evening service of the Independence Baptist Church, where Pastor Michael Ross suggested that the congregation come together as a prayer meeting. After a troubled Judge Baylor bemoaned the dissensions and jealousies within the church body, Burleson rose to state that he had felt the "fraternal dagger." At the close of the meeting, Clark said it was "needless to affect ignorance of the insinuations of President Burleson." He then claimed that he had made continued efforts to make peace and had even written a letter to effect reconciliation. This prompted

196

Tryon Hall at Independence
Courtesy Texas Baptist Historical Center-
Museum, Independence, Texas

Female Dormitory at Independence
Courtesy Texas Baptist Historical Center-
Museum, Independence, Texas

Columns of Female Building, Old Baylor at Independence.
Photo by J. C. Hoke, Wharton, Texas

Rufus to retort that the letter had charged him with "in-sincerity and hypocrisy" and thus "placed a wall of fire" between them.

On June 27, 1860, the board of trustees ordered both men to either adjust their differences by the following Saturday or lay before the board their grievances in writing for an adjustment; both should either comply with said request or resign. On June 30 each man read a list of six charges to the trustees, who decided on the relative merits of the accusations that evening. Four of Clark's charges were sustained, with the board "disapproving" of either Burleson's conduct, actions, or remarks. Finally, on July 1, 1860, the governing body issued a formal statement to the effect that their patience was exhausted and that no more compromises were to be needed. The official outcome distressed proxy-trustee Abner E. Lipscomb, a Burleson supporter who cast the only vote opposing the board decisions. Lipscomb contended that his colleagues had been unfair to the president and condemned Principal Clark because "the settlement was not based on Gospel principles." On July 14, 1860, Lipscomb took the matter before the regular conference of the Independence Baptist Church. With Clark's friends demanding a church trial, Reverend Ross served as moderator at a fiery meeting attended by armed church members. When the conference voted that Lipscomb had not sustained his charges and he refused to withdraw them, he was expelled from church fellowship by a four-vote margin. The shaken, unnerved Burleson then "lost his balance," shook his finger in the moderator's face and bitterly proclaimed, "You have been guilty of unfairness, and have used . . . your official position to adopt this motion, and nothing but your gray hairs protect you from the punishment you . . . deserve." After this tirade, Pastor Ross adjourned the meeting without a reply. Church member Sam Houston witnessed the proceedings and was visiting in a friend's law office later when Rufus came by and offered his hand. Exploding in anger, the general said that Burleson's conduct was the worst he had seen in all his public life and announced that he would not shake hands until the president sincerely repented. Although these two old friends soon reconciled, the disruptive feud between Burleson and Clark left lasting scars.

Competition for President Burleson's services developed after November 1860, when nine Central Texas Baptist churches organized the Waco Association and took over sponsorship of the Waco Classical School, the only school for boys in Waco since 1857. In January 1861 school board president Joseph W. Speight, a former pupil of Rufus in Mississippi, began attempts to recruit Burleson and his male department faculty. The Baylor leader had been stung by the sharp words of the trustees and announced on April 29, 1861, that he and his entire faculty were going to resign at the end of the school term. The group resigned en masse on June 28, Burleson was named president of the newly chartered Waco University (formerly the Classical School), and the four members of the Baylor male department also joined the Waco faculty. Yielding to the influence of their former mentor, the seven seniors of the Baylor male department refused to present themselves for graduation. They instead transferred to and applied for diplomas from the month-old Waco University, a school with no academic standing where they had never attended classes, and graduated there on September 4, 1861. In the book *Centennial Story of Texas Baptists,* Dr. Frederick Eby refers to this maneuver as "an academic monstrosity."

During the early phases of the Civil War, President Burleson left Waco University in charge of his brother Richard and joined Colonel Speight's regiment near Milican. In a fervent letter to the *Houston Telegraph,* Rufus proclaimed that "all of our professors capable of performing military service and all our students over eighteen are now in the army." Waco University was not suspended, but the University Guard did require military training of the 123 male students registered there during the 1862 spring semester. Baylor University also contributed its share of manpower to the war effort: 151 Baylor students enlisted in the Confederate Army, including two who became brigadier generals, Lawrence Sullivan Ross and Felix H. Robertson. During the 1866 commencement service, President Burleson struck a melancholy note when he remarked that about 100 of his students at either Independence or Waco had died during the war.

Under his leadership, Waco University became the most prosperous of all Texas Baptist schools. For the first five years, the institution served males only; then Burleson introduced the new concept of coeducation, where men and women were instructed in the same classes. He was a true pioneer in this progressive movement, and Waco University was among the first coeducational colleges in the country. Women graduates, however, were awarded the maid or mistress of arts rather than the

200

bachelor of arts degree. By 1867 the male department enrolled 172, while the female department had eighty-one students. Waco University had an enrollment of 300 by 1873 and graduated eighty-five students between 1874 and 1881. The sponsorship of the college was transferred from the Waco Association to the new Baptist General Association in 1868.

In 1867 the degree of D. D. was conferred upon Dr. Burleson by Howard College, Alabama. In 1882 Keachi College, Louisiana, conferred on him the degree of LL.D. After *The Texas Baptist Herald,* the only Baptist journal in the state, was established in December 1865, Dr. Burleson contributed religious articles to the weekly publication. In 1867 he called a conference of pastors to suggest that they welcome Sunday schools into their churches and successfully quieted their fears that such schools might detract from preaching and prayer meeting services. In his later years, he served as president of the Baptist General Convention. President Burleson was also active in off-campus secular activities. He was a member of the Texas State Historical Association and wrote many Texas history articles which were published in the *Waco Guardian* in the 1890s. While serving as agent of the Peabody fund for Texas, he canvassed 127 counties and talked to 60,000 young people about education. A strong advocate of specially trained teachers for public schools, Dr. Burleson was instrumental in the founding of Sam Houston Normal Institute at Huntsville. In 1870 he addressed the meeting of the National Education Association at Niagara Falls, New York, served as one of its vice-presidents, and presided over some meetings of the Texas State Teachers Association.

And what of Baylor at Independence? George W. Baines succeeded Burleson as president on July 17, 1861, then relinquished the post to William Carey Crane in September 1863. Crane was a cofounder and vice-presi-

201

dent of the Mississippi State Historical Association, a coeditor of the *Mississippi Baptist,* and served as president of two Mississippi colleges in the 1850s. This noted and competent scholar was to serve as president of Baylor University for twenty-two years.

Baylor at Independence was doomed to failure, and his heroic struggle to maintain the school cost Crane his fortune and his most productive years. Baptist historian J. M. Carroll called him "the best equipped college man that had ever been in Texas." According to Carroll, Dr. Crane could teach any college course, "all the languages, ancient or modern, all the sciences. . . ."; in fact, he taught six or seven hours daily. His private library of 2,500 volumes was twice as large as that of Baylor University. During Crane's tenure at Baylor, he was the first president of the Texas State Teachers Association, founded in January 1879, and was also chairman of the committee which recommended the founding of Sam Houston Normal Institute, the first state-supported teacher training college west of the Mississippi.

Dr. Crane came to know Margaret Houston as her pastor at the Independence Baptist Church. She and her children moved back to Independence from Huntsville after the death of her husband in July 1863. Margaret's cash poverty at the time left her hard-pressed to pay the Baylor tuition; evidently her dead husband's past generosity to the school had been forgotten. She soon asked Reverend Crane to write a biography of Sam Houston and gave him access to the trunks of letters, speeches, and mementos stored in her attic. Quite often Crane would work through the night on the project, then put in a full day's work at his Baylor office. In March 1866 he sent an inquiry to a Philadelphia publisher, only to be informed that there was "no pressing urgency" for the project and that it was not an "opportune time" for such a biography. The stung Margaret spitefully burned handfuls of the precious letters in her fireplace and did not live to see the Crane work published in 1884; in the preface to

The Life and Select Literary Remains of Sam Houston of Texas, the author notes that Mrs. Houston instructed him to include at least one chapter on her husband's religious character. After Baylor was closed down by a yellow fever epidemic which hit Independence in September 1867, Margaret died of the dread disease on December 3. It seems a cruel irony that Pastor Crane refused to conduct her funeral for fear of contamination even though he had performed the marriage ceremonies of her two oldest daughters, Nannie and Maggie, and was living rent-free at the time in the Houstons' former home, the old "Hines Place."[4]

In August 1863 Rufus Burleson wrote a welcome letter to Reverend Crane, thinking that he had accepted a call to become pastor of Burleson's old church, First Baptist of Houston. The two were old friends and William had preached the ordination sermon when Burleson was ordained as a minister in Mississippi on June 8, 1845. However, when Rufus heard that Crane had accepted the Baylor presidency instead, his mood turned nasty. Bitter memories resurfaced, and the Waco president fired off a tactless, blunt warning to William, advising him that Baylor was dead and that his efforts would be in vain. The new educational rivals met in Texas in October 1864

---

[4] Margaret was buried beside her mother in the small cemetery directly across the street (now Farm Road 50) from the Independence Baptist Church. The cemetery is actually a part of Mrs. Lea's homestead lot, where she built a steep-roofed cottage about 1850. In honor of Sam Houston's conversion to the Christian faith, his mother-in-law sold the Moffette family silver and used the funds to donate a 500-pound bell to her beloved church in 1856. Nancy Lea died on February 7, 1864, and was buried in a little stone vault on her lot; today the plaque on the bell tower says that "she sleeps within its sound." The Nancy Lea Bell cracked in March 1969 and is now on display in the Texas Baptist Historical Center-Museum attached to the Independence Baptist Church. In May 1965 the Washington County Historical Survey Committee sponsored a dedication service for the restored Houston-Lea Family Cemetery. At that time an official Texas Historical Marker and a large, Texas pink granite monument were placed at the burial sites of mother and daughter.

at Providence Church in Burleson County. At that time, Rufus announced that "he could not consent that Waco University should be ignored as a Baptist school." Crane replied that he could not accept the new university under the Convention on an equal basis; as an alternative he suggested that some new Northern organization might sponsor the Waco school. Burleson responded by persuading the East Texas Convention to dissolve in 1868 and surrender its authority to the new Baptist General Association, which included the Waco and Trinity associations. Rufus was both a leader and officer of this new body, whose real reason for existence was the fostering of Waco University.

The Burleson-Crane rivalry turned personal and testy in March 1869, when the Baylor trustees determined to give President Crane land in lieu of salary. The board then offered to surrender to Burleson a $56 note they held against him if he would turn over an eighty-acre tract of land in McLennan County to Crane. This transaction prompted a brusque letter from Rufus to William on May 23 which read in part:

> . . . I rejoice that you have accomplished so much; for I had never regarded you as a successful preacher or teacher. . . . But the impression prevails . . . that your extraordinary *claims* and your most unfortunate way of manifesting them fearfully lessens your influence and defeats your incessant toils and necessitates frequent removals on your part.

Crane is to be admired for his circumspect reply dated July 4, 1869:

> . . . I am content that history and my contemporaries . . . may say when I am gone whether your statements as to my self have any foundation or not. . . .
>
> I shall not undertake to imitate your candor in giving an estimate of your personal character. I *have* understood some things. I understand more now. . . .

On September 28, 1866, the Texas legislature created Baylor Female College as a distinct institution with its own board of trustees, while Baylor University became simply the male department.[5] During the Reconstruction period, the two colleges had a combined enrollment of less than one hundred. Waco University, on the other hand, was flourishing during this time. The contrasting fortunes of the two Baptist schools prompted Gen. J. E. Harrison of Waco to write a letter to President Crane in August 1870, proposing the creation of "a great

---

[5] In 1870 a distinguished artist joined the faculty of both Baylor University and Baylor Female College. Henry Arthur McArdle was born on June 9, 1836, in Belfast, Ireland, but came to America as an orphan at age fourteen to live with an aunt. After learning his craft at the Maryland Institute for the Promotion of the Mechanic Arts, he won the Peabody first prize and medal at the Maryland Academy of design in 1860. During the Civil War, McArdle served as a draughtsman for gunboats for the Confederate Navy and as a member of Robert E. Lee's engineering staff. His wife's tuberculosis brought the couple to Independence, Texas, in 1869 and Jennie died a year later. Soon after Henry arrived in Texas, veterans of Hood's Texas Brigade commissioned him to paint the historical canvas "Lee at the Wilderness" and posed as his models. The painting was lost when the old capitol burned on November 9, 1881.

Professor McArdle taught art and civil engineering for many years, and Baylor President Crane recommended him to the governor of Texas as being qualified to paint Texas heroes and historical scenes. After both Baylor colleges moved from Independence in 1886, the artist set up his studio in San Antonio. His patron was the frontier historian James T. DeShields, who attended Baylor University and encouraged Henry to paint large, authentic historical scenes of the Texas Revolution and the Republic. McArdle's classic canvas, "Dawn at the Alamo," was begun in 1876 and finished in 1883. The painting is seven feet high and twelve feet wide and reveals his penchant for intricate detail and cameolike vignettes within the composition. The Texas legislature paid his heirs $25,000 for this work and a twin piece, "The Battle of San Jacinto." The two hang in the Senate chamber in the Texas capitol. Another of the artist's large canvases, "The Settlement of Texas by Anglo-Americans," hangs in the hall of the House of Representatives in the capitol. Each of these paintings reflects McArdle's painstaking research into every detail, including topography, equipment, and costume. This renowned Texas artist died at San Antonio on February 16, 1908. Today the Texas Collection of Baylor University has seven McArdle paintings: portraits of Sam Houston, Judge Baylor, and presidents Crane, Andrews, Graves,

central Baptist University" for Texas. Since ambition, prejudice, and jealousy had divided Baptists in supporting the two colleges, Harrison saw one central university as the obvious solution. The Waco backers of Harrison's proposal secretly pushed for an arrangement whereby Waco and Baylor universities would merge in the new institution, with Burleson as president and Crane as professor of theology. Rufus no doubt knew this when he wrote a warm, enthusiastic letter to William on October 27, 1870, and said, "I would rejoice to be associated with you during our last days and mightiest struggles for our blessed Savior's cause." The Harrison plan first came up at the Texas Baptist State Convention held at Bremond in late 1870, triggering a controversy that would last for years.

By the late 1870s, several factors contributed to an accelerated movement to relocate Baylor and consolidate it with Waco University. Independence had become increasingly inaccessible by then due to poor roads and the bypass of town by the two railroads built in the area. Another threat was posed by the growth of Texas public schools, which in effect forced Baylor out of the elementary and secondary fields of instruction. Competition for students also came from nearby state-supported colleges such as Texas Agricultural and Mechanical College (1876), Sam Houston Normal Institute (1879), and the University of Texas (1883). Lack of funds and general financial depression after the Civil War put added pressure on Baylor. President Crane even had to cope with a natural disaster, a destructive cyclone that seriously damaged four major campus buildings on February 27, 1882.

With regard to the consolidation question, South Texas wanted Baylor left at Independence, North Texas favored one central university at Waco, while Dr. Burle-

---

Baines, and Burleson. On April 27, 1967, the Baylor Art Department opened the McArdle Art Gallery in honor of the university's first artist.

son stood aloof from the acrimonious debate; his position was that

> Waco and Baylor would sustain themselves, and if the denomination wanted anything bigger and better than either, the whole State was open, and the Baptists had a perfect right to undertake the work of establishing it; but that, if it was decided to change the location of Baylor, Waco University was ready to furnish her elder sister at Independence a domicile and shelter.

The precarious existence of Baylor at Independence was dealt a final blow when President Crane suddenly died of pneumonia on February 27, 1885. His death marked the practical end of the school; Dr. Carroll said that "the master mind, spirit and personality [of Baylor] had gone." After first being buried in the old cemetery at Independence, the remains of Dr. Crane were reinterred in the State Cemetery in 1937.

In November 1884 a committee created by the Baptist State Convention met in Temple and decided to remove Baylor Female College to Belton (the highest bidder), to consolidate Baylor with Waco University, and to locate the new university in Waco. These decisions were endorsed by resolution when the Convention met at Lampasas in October 1885. Baylor Female College opened at Belton in September 1886.[6] Baylor University at Waco also opened its doors in 1886 with a student enrollment of 337; the first building constructed on its new campus

---

[6] Special mention should be made of three former students and graduates of Baylor Female College. Rebekah Baines Johnson, the mother of President Lyndon Johnson, went there for two years and ran the college bookstore. She had first attended Baylor University in 1901, then the University of Texas in 1902, but was dissatisfied with her elocution classes so transferred to the Belton school. Mrs. Miriam Amanda "Ma" Ferguson was elected governor of Texas in 1924 and 1932, making her the first woman to be elected to that office. Another former Belton student, Mrs. Oveta Culp Hobby, became only the second woman to serve in a cabinet post when she was appointed secretary of the new Department of Health, Education, and Welfare in 1953.

207

that year came to be known as "Old Main." There was also a partial consolidation of the two faculties, and Dr. Burleson was elected president of the merged universities. In 1887 a second building was added which was dedicated to female education and named the Georgia Burleson Hall in honor of the president's wife. A new Bible department was soon added, and the institution was out of debt by 1893. Even into his seventies, Burleson was the first to arrive on campus and the last to leave at night.

In the twilight of his life, Dr. Burleson starting writing a book titled *Fifty-three Years in Texas,* a project that was completed and published by his living wife in 1901. On June 11, 1897, the trustees named him president emeritus for life on full pay. He was also a member of the Texas Veterans Association and served as its chaplain from 1898 until his death. It was Dr. Burleson who first started collecting material and data for a proposed history of the association. This distinguished educational and religious leader died at his Waco home on May 14, 1901, and was buried in Oakwood Cemetery. The next day a *Galveston News* editorial read in part:

> . . . Dr. Burleson's work as a missionary in pioneer times led to the establishment of Baylor University, . . . There are in all portions of Texas men and women who will remember with a tear the earnest and zealous old man whom they learned to love during their college days. . . . Evidences of the zeal and energy of the deceased are to be found in many places, and thousands of living witnesses stand ready to honor the dead. It is set down that Baylor University is "a monument to his genius and industry."

Today all that remains of "Old Baylor" at Independence are four columns with a bronze plaque marking the site of the female department on Academy Hill and a granite slab which marks the site of the male department on Allen Hill.[7] The two hills stand about a mile apart, sloping gently toward each other until they reach the small creek the Baylor students used to call "Jordan." This pastoral scene offers a stark contrast to the Baylor campus at Waco and its central Burleson Academic Quadrangle, an area which includes the renovated landmarks, Old Main and Burleson Hall, as well as the W. Guy Draper Academic Building. This quadrangle complex was dedicated on September 10, 1976, and is a fitting monument to a pioneer religious educator.

---

[7] In June 1965 the Texas Baptist Historical Center-Museum was dedicated at old Independence. Owned and operated by the Baptist General Convention of Texas, the center-museum is headed by a pastor-director and includes the site and ruins of old Baylor Female College and the Independence Baptist Church (1839), which is Texas's oldest continuing missionary Baptist church. At one time it was the largest Baptist church in the state, and its early pastors were among Baptists' greatest leaders. Visitors to the lovely old church can still see the marked pew where Sam Houston and his family worshiped.

Suggested Sources
for Further Reading

I
Michael Muldoon:
That Other Father of Texas

Barker, Eugene C. *The Life of Stephen F. Austin, Founder of Texas*. Austin: Texas State Historical Association, 1949.

Flannery, John B. *The Irish Texans*. San Antonio: University of Texas Institute of Texan Cultures, 1980.

Freytag, Walter P., ed. *Chronicles of Fayette: The Reminiscences of Julia Lee Sinks*. LaGrange, Texas: LaGrange Bicentennial Commission, 1975.

Smith, Bennett L. *Marriage by Bond in Colonial Texas*. Fort Worth: Branch-Smith, 1972.

Smith, Henry. "Reminiscences of Henry Smith." *Quarterly of the Texas State Historical Association*, XIV (1910–1911).

Smithwick, Noah. *The Evolution of a State: Or, Recollections of Old Texas Days*. fac. Austin: The Steck Company, no date (ca. 1935).

Syers, William. *Off the Beaten Trail*. Waco: Texian Press, 1972.

Webb, Walter Prescott, ed. *The Handbook of Texas*. 2 vols. Austin: Texas State Historical Association, 1952.

Weyand, Leonie Rummel, and Houston Wade. *An Early History of Fayette County*. LaGrange, Texas: *LaGrange Journal*, 1936.

II
The De León Family:
Riches, Race, Rapine, and Rags

Brown, John Henry. *History of Texas; From 1685 to 1892*. 2 vols. fac. Austin: Jenkins Publishing Company, 1970.

Carsner, C. C., comp. *Abstract of Title to the Martín De León*

211

Survey, A-74, Conveyed to J. N. Keeran, in Victoria County, Texas. Victoria, Texas: unpublished abstract, 1957. (Prepared for Leonardo De León; property of Wence De León, Victoria, Texas)

Cole, Bettye Welborn. *A Passing of the Seasons, The Story of Marguerite Wright.* Mesquite, Texas: privately printed, 1985.

Grimes, Roy, ed. *300 Years in Victoria County.* Victoria, Texas: Victoria Advocate Publishing Company, 1968.

Hammett, A. B. J. *The Empresario, Don Martín De León.* Waco: Texian Press, 1973.

Hauschild, Henry, ed. *The Victoria Sesquicentennial "Scrapbook"; 1824–1974.* Victoria, Texas: The Victoria Sesquicentennial Inc., 1974.

Huson, Hobart. *Refugio: A Comprehensive History of Refugio County from Aboriginal Times to 1953.* Volume I. Woodsboro, Texas: The Rooke Foundation, Inc., 1953.

Linn, John J. *Reminiscenses of Fifty Years in Texas.* fac. Austin: Steck, 1935.

Lukes, Edward A. *De Witt Colony of Texas.* Austin: Jenkins Publishing Company, 1976.

Mitchell, Hugh C., comp. *The Mitchell Family in Texas.* Washington, D.C.: unpublished manuscript, 1954. (Property of Mike Mitchell, Edna, Texas)

Morris, Leopold. *Pictorial History of Victoria and Victoria County.* San Antonio: Clemens Printing Company, 1953.

Petty, J. W., Jr., ed. *Victor Rose's History of Victoria.* fac. San Antonio: Lone Star Printing Company, 1961.

Victoria Advocate. *Victoria's History Makers.* (Special Texas Sesquicentennial magazine section), April 21, 1986.

III

The Groces and the Whartons:
Two Generations of Texas Leaders

Abernethy, Francis Edward, ed. *Legendary Ladies of Texas.* Dallas: E-Heart Press, 1981.

Berlet, Sarah Wharton Groce. *Autobiography of a Spoon.* Port Arthur, Texas: LaBelle Printing Company, 1977.

Bryan, James Perry, ed. *Mary Austin Holley: The Texas Diary,*

212

1835–1838. Austin: University of Texas Humanities Research Center, 1965.

Carroll, John M., ed. *Custer in Texas.* New York: S. Lewis, 1975.

Carter, James D. *Masonry in Texas: Background, History, and Influence to 1846.* Waco: Committee on Masonic Education and Service for the Grand Lodge of Texas, A. F. and A. M., 1955.

Clarke, Mary W. "Elisabet Ney (1833–1907): An Independent Spirit." *Southwest Art* (April 1983), 104–111.

Creighton, James. *A Narrative History of Brazoria County.* Angleton, Texas: Brazoria County Historical Commission, 1975.

Fehrenbach, T. R. *Lone Star; a History of Texas and the Texans.* New York: Macmillan, 1968.

Flanagan, Sue. *Sam Houston's Texas.* Austin: University of Texas Press, 1964.

Fortune, Jan. *Elisabet Ney.* New York: Knopf, 1943.

Giles, L. B. *Terry's Texas Rangers.* Austin: Von Boeckmann-Jones, 1911.

Goar, Marjory. *Marble Dust: The Life of Elisabet Ney; An Interpretation.* Austin: Eakin Press, 1984.

Hasken, Corrie. *Historical Records of Austin and Waller Counties.* Houston: Premier Printing and Letter Service, 1969.

Holbrook, Abigail Curlee. "A Glimpse of Life on Antebellum Slave Plantations in Texas." *Southwestern Historical Quarterly* 76 (April 1973): 361–383.

Jones, Marie Beth. *Peach Point Plantation: The First 150 Years.* Waco: Texian Press, 1982.

Lubbock, Francis R. *Six Decades in Texas.* Edited by C. W. Raines. Austin: B. C. Jones, 1900.

Robertson, James I., Jr. "The War in Words." *Civil War Times* (April 1979), 41.

Stroebel, Abner. *The Old Plantations and Their Owners of Brazoria County.* Houston: Union National Bank, 1926.

Tolbert, Frank X. *The Day of San Jacinto.* New York: McGraw-Hill, 1959.

Welch, June Rayfield. *People and Places in the Texas Past.* Dallas: G. L. A. Press, 1974.

213

IV
Emily Morgan:
The Yellow Rose of Texas

Abernethy, Francis E., ed. *Legendary Ladies of Texas*. Dallas: E-Heart Press, 1981.

Bate, W. N. *General Sidney Sherman: Texas Soldier, Statesman and Builder*. Waco: Texian Press, 1974.

Biffle, Kent. "Yellow Rose Story Loses Its Bloom." *Dallas Morning News*, November 17, 1985, 45A.

Braider, Donald. *Solitary Star; a Biography of Sam Houston*. New York: Putnam, 1974.

Crawford, Ann Fears, ed. *The Eagle: The Autobiography of Santa Anna*. Austin: Pemberton Press, 1967.

Friend, Llerena. *Sam Houston, The Great Designer*. Austin: University of Texas Press, 1954.

Huston, Cleburne. *Deaf Smith, Incredible Texas Spy*. Waco: Texian Press, 1973.

Muir, Andrew F. "The Free Negro in Harris County, Texas." *Southwestern Historical Quarterly* 46 (July 1942–April 1943): 214–238.

Pena, José Enrique de la. *With Santa Anna in Texas; a Personal Narrative of the Revolution*. Translated by Carmen Perry. College Station: Texas A&M University Press, 1975.

Schwab, Elmo, Jr. "They Weren't Merely Fiddling Around." *Houston Post*, April 21, 1985, Sec. 3B.

Tolbert, Frank X. *The Day of San Jacinto*. New York: McGraw-Hill, 1959.

Turner, Martha Anne. *The Yellow Rose of Texas; Her Saga and Her Song*. Austin: Shoal Creek, 1976.

Tutt, Bob. "The Runaway Scrape: San Jacinto Landowner Takes Place in History." *The Houston Chronicle*, April 21, 1985, Sec. 1, p. 14.

Wisehart, Marion. *Sam Houston, American Giant*. Washington: R. B. Luce, 1962.

V

William Goyens:
A True-blue Black Texian

Barr, Alwyn. *Black Texans: A History of Negroes in Texas, 1528–1971.* Austin: Jenkins, 1973.

Barr, Alwyn, and Robert A. Calvert, eds. *Black Leaders: Texans For Their Times.* Austin: Texas State Historical Association, 1981.

Kubiak, Daniel. *Monument to a Black Man.* San Antonio: Naylor, 1972.

Nacogdoches (Texas) Jaycees. *The Bicentennial Commemorative History of Nacogdoches.* Nacogdoches: 1976.

Schoen, Harold. "The Free Negro in the Republic of Texas." *Southwestern Historical Quarterly* 39 (July 1935–April 1936): 292–308.

Welch, June Rayfield. *People and Places in the Texas Past.* Dallas: G. L. A. Press, 1974.

VI

Robert Potter:
The "Baddest" Man in the Republic

Dickens, Charles. *American Notes.* London: Chapman and Hall, 1850.

Dienst, Alex. *The Navy of the Republic of Texas, 1835–1845.* Temple, Texas: privately published, 1909.

Douglas, C. L. *Thunder on the Gulf: Story of the Texas Navy.* Rev. ed. Austin: Graphic Ideas, Inc., 1972.

Fischer, Ernest G. *Robert Potter: Founder of the Texas Navy.* Gretna, Louisiana: Pelican Publishing Company, 1976.

Gray, A. C., ed. *Diary of Col. William Fairfax Gray; From Virginia to Texas, 1835–1837.* fac. Houston: Fletcher Young Publishing Company, 1965.

Kemp, Louis Wiltz. *The Signers of the Texas Declaration of Independence.* fac. Salado, Texas: The Anson Jones Press, 1959.

Kirkland, Elithe Hamilton. *Love is a Wild Assault.* Garden City, N.Y.: Doubleday & Company, 1959.

Neu, C. T. "The Case of the Brig *Pocket." Quarterly of the Texas State Historical Association* 12 (July 1908).

Shearer, Ernest C. *Robert Potter, Remarkable North Carolinian and Texan.* Houston: University of Houston Press, 1951.

Tarpley, Fred. *Jefferson: Riverport to the Southwest.* Austin: Eakin Press, 1983.

University of Texas Library Archives. Kemp Collection. "The History of Harriet A. Ames during the early days of Texas" (written by herself in New Orleans at age 83). Typescript.

Winston, Robert Watson. "Robert Potter: Tar Heel and Texan Daredevil." *South Atlantic Quarterly* 29 (1930): 140–.

Wisehart, M. K. *Sam Houston: American Giant.* Washington: Robert B. Luce, Inc., 1962.

VII

Rufus Burleson and Baylor University:
Fifty Years of Toil and Triumph

Baylor, Orval W., and Henry B. Baylor. *Baylor's History of the Baylors.* Leroy, Illinois: Leroy Journal Publishing Co., 1914.

———, ed. *Baylor's Quarterly* (July 1930), entire issue.

Burleson, Georgia J., comp. *The Life and Writings of Rufus C. Burleson, D.D., LL.D., Containing a Biography of Dr. Burleson by Harry Haynes.* Waco: 1901.

Carroll, J. M. *A History of Texas Baptists.* Dallas: Baptist Standard Publishing Company, 1923.

Crane, William Carey. *Life and Select Literary Remains of Sam Houston of Texas.* Philadelphia: J. B. Lippincott and Company, 1884.

Dawson, Joseph Martin. *A Century With Texas Baptists.* Nashville: Broadman Press, 1947.

Dietrich, Wilfred. *The Blazing Story of Washington County.* Brenham, Texas: Banner Press, 1950.

Haynes, Harry. "Dr. Rufus C. Burleson," *Southwestern Historical Review* 5 (July 1901): 49–60.

———. Part I "Biography of Rufus C. Burleson," *The Life and*

Writings of Rufus C. Burleson. Compiled and published by Georgia J. Burleson, 1901.

King, C. Richard. *Susanna Dickinson: Messenger of the Alamo.* Austin: Shoal Creek, 1976.

Matthews, Harlan J., et. al. *Centennial Story of Texas Baptists.* Dallas: Baptist General Convention of Texas, 1936.

Murray, Lois Smith. *Baylor at Independence.* Waco: Baylor University Press, 1972.

Schmidt, Charles S. *The History of Washington County.* San Antonio: The Naylor Company, 1949.

Seale, William. *Sam Houston's Wife: A Biography of Margaret Lea Houston.* Norman: University of Oklahoma Press, 1970.

Shuffler, R. H. *The Houstons at Independence.* Waco: Texian Press, 1966.

Simmons, Laura. *Out of Our Past.* Waco: Texian Press, 1967.

Student League and Alumnae Association of Baylor College. *Baylor College After Seventy-Five Years: Diamond Jubilee.* Belton, 1920.

Toland, Gracey Booker. *Austin Knew His Athens.* San Antonio: The Naylor Company, 1958.

White, Michael. *History of Baylor University, 1845–1861.* Waco: Texian Press, 1971.

INDEX

A

Abit, Mrs., 136
Abraham, 161
Academy Building, 182, 195
Academy Hill, 178, 185, 208
Academy of Art at Munich, 83
Acordada prison, 10
Adair, William, 169
Adams, Frank, 8
*The Advocate of the Peoples
  Rights*, 57
Agua Dulce Creek, 37
Aguirre, Miguel, 98
Alamo, 37, 94, 97, 101, 106, 129,
  131, 171
Albany, New York, 92
Aldrete Candelaria, 41
  José Miguel, 36
Alexandria, Louisiana, 60
Allen, John K., 128
  W. Y., 69,
Allen, Hill, 209
Alley, John, 37
Almonte, Colonel, 65
  Juan, 95
Alston, Joseph, 19
Alvarez, Francisca, 39
  Teleforo, 39
Alvin, Texas, 55
Amarillo, Texas, 162
American Baptist Home Mission
  Society, 173
American Notes, 162
America's Own, 192
Ames, Charles, 146, 150, 151,
  152, 153, 163, 164, 165
  Harriet Page Potter, 123, 165
Amos Wright, 135
Anahuac, 59
Anahuac insurrection, 9
Anahuac, Texas, 93
Anderson, Kenneth L., 174, 176
  Nancy, 187
Andrews, 205

Angleton, Texas, 4
Anna Elizabeth, 36
Aransas Pass Railroad, 11
Aransas River, 16
Archer, Dr. Branch T., 56, 57,
  67, 72, 79
Arenosa Creek, 22, 32
Arlington National Cemetery, 88
Arnold, Hendrick, 106
Artiaga, Captain, 33
Ashworth Law, 118
Austin, Brown, 55
  John, 10, 57, 60
  Stephen F., 2, 3, 4, 5, 7, 8, 9,
    10, 11, 12, 19, 25, 27, 30,
    48, 51, 55, 56, 59, 60, 63,
    66, 67, 71, 88, 89, 131, 177
  William T., 57
Austin Bayou, 136
Austin County, 4
Austin Daily Bulletin, 155
Austin Parks and Recreation
  Department, 90
Austin, Texas, 88, 89, 153, 171
Autobiography of A Spoon, 79

B

Baines, G. W., 177, 191, 192, 206
  G. W., Jr., 173
Banita Creek, 113
Bank of the United States, 124
Banks Arcade, 126
baptism, 5, 6, 7, 192
Baptist General Association, 201
Baptist General Convention of
  Texas, 171, 201, 209
Baptist State Convention of
  Texas, 172, 178, 182, 207
Barnett, Thomas, 4
Barragan, Marcos, 96
Barrera, Melchora Iniega, 94
Barron, Thomas, 188
Battle Island, 57
battle of Coleto, 38

219

220

Burleson Academic Quadrangle, 209
Burleson County, 177
Burleson Hall, 209
Burnet, David G., 26, 38, 49, 50, 58, 61, 63, 65, 66, 69, 95, 105, 106, 122, 132, 133, 134, 137, 138, 139, 154
Burr, Aaron, 19
    Theodosia, 19, 20
Bustamante, Anastacio, 31
    President, 68
Byar, Noah T., 128, 174
Bynum, Jesse A. 123, 124
Byrd, Sir William, 169

C

Cabazos, Alvino, 22
Caddo Gazette, 162
Caddo Indians, 145
Caddo Lake, 143, 157
Caldwell, Angelina, 25
    J. P., 60
    James, 25
Calhoun County, 31
Calvit, Alexander, 49
    Mary Ann, 57
Camp Groce, 81
Cardenas, Francisco, 22
Carlos Ranch, 42
Caro, Ramón, 109
Carroll, J. M., 172, 202, 207
Carson, Samuel, 132
Caruso, Enrico, 89
Carvajal, José Luis, 21, 37
    José M. J. (J. M. J.), 19, 21, 35, 36
Casa Mexicana, 10
Cass County, 165
Castillo, Hipolito, 22
Catholicism, 3, 5, 6, 7, 11, 23, 60, 151
cattle, 29
cattle business, 14
Cayuga, 137
Cause and Cure of Infidelity, 189
Cenci, 88
Centennial Story of Texas Baptists, 200

Chalmers, Mrs. Mary W., 164
Chambers, Mrs. John G., 154
Chambers, Thomas Jefferson, 9
Cheltipin Creek, 16
Cherokees, 110, 111, 116, 117
Chicago World's Fair Columbian Exposition of 1893, 88
Chief Bowles, 111, 117, 118
Chief Buffalo Hump, 45
Chief Prowling Bear, 147, 148
Chief Richard Fields, 116
Chief River Wolf, 144
Childress, George, 129, 131
Chocolate Bayou, 136
Chocolate Creek, 42
Chovel, Rafael, 21
Cincinnati, Ohio, 59
Cisneros, Agatón, 22
    Estevan, 22
Civil War, 45
Clark, Horace G., 182, 183, 185, 195, 196, 198, 199
Clay, Task, 193
Clemens, Jeremiah, 42
Cleveland, Annie, 54
Clifton, 81
Cloud, Rev., 136
Clute, Texas, 53
coeducational colleges, 200
Cole, Bettye Welborn, 20
Coles, John P., 177
Coles's Settlement, 177
Coleto Creek, 17
College Hill, 178
Collins, Frances Spriggs, 81
    John P., 195
    Wharton, 8, 81
Collinsworth, James, 66, 129, 131
Colonels Sherman and Hockley, 69
Colonization grant, 3
Columbia, 59, 65
Comanche, 43, 45, 150, 151
Constitution of 1824, 36
Consultation, 63, 128
Consultation of 1835, 62, 116, 117
contested divorce suit, 44
contraband, 23, 28, 140

221

Eagle Pass, 45
East Texas Convention, 204
Eastern Internal Provinces, 16
Eastland, William Mosby, 104
Eby, Frederick, 200
Edwards, H. H., 119
Eighth Texas Cavalry, 75
El Camino Real (The Royal
    Highway), 112, 114, 118
El Sabinal, 19
Ellis, Richard, 129, 131, 174
Emanuel, M. 111
English, Bele, 112
Erath, George, 103, 109
Escalera, J. M., Jr., 21
    J. M., Sr., 21
    J. N., 21
Escoban, Manuel, 42
Escondida, 43, 44
Evans, L. D., 193
Evergreen, 49
Evergreen Cemetery, 46
Evolution of a State, 8

F

Fairfield College, 179
Fannin, 21, 37, 38, 39
Fannin County, 149, 151
Fannin, James Walker, Jr., 60
Father Deus, 114
Fayette County, 5, 6, 9, 11
female department, 182, 185,
    186, 187, 194, 195, 201,
    208
Ferguson, Miriam Amanda "Ma",
    207
Ferry Lake, 143, 145, 163
Fiddler's Bend Cemetery, 102
The 50 Best Books on Texas, 166
Fifty-three Years in Texas, 208
Filisola, General, 65, 99, 103
First Baptist Church of Houston,
    170, 173, 203
Fisher, S. Rhoades, 142
Flanell, L. A., 137
Flash, 92, 93, 95, 127, 136, 137,
    140
Flora, 139
Forbes, John, 111, 118

Formosa, 88, 89, 90
Fort Bend, 4
Fort St. Louis, 30
Fort Velasco, 59
Franklin, Isaac, 41
Fredonian Rebellion, 113
Freemason, 60
Fuller, Calvin, 160
Fulton, Courtney Ann, 58
    Sarah Grace, 26

G

G. P. Putnam's Sons of New
    York, 89
Gaines, General, 194
Gallardo, Pedro, 19, 22
Galvan, Estevan, 22
Galveston Bay, 92
Galveston Bay and Texas Land
    Company, 131
Galveston County, 9
Galveston News, 78, 208
Galveston, Texas, 79, 82, 171,
    173
Garay, Colonel, 39
Garcia, Desiderío, 21
    Valentin, 19, 21
Garcitas Creek, 22, 30, 38
Garibaldi, Giuseppe, 83
Gay Hill, 172
General Council, 26, 63
George, Dan, 108
Georgia Battalion, 40
Georgia Burleson Hall, 208
Giles, L. B. 76
Gilleland, Johnstone, 43
    Mary, 43
    Rebecca, 43
    William, 43
Gillette, Henry Flavel, 178
    James S., 119
"The Girl I Left Behind," 101
Going, William, 110
Gold Standard, 97, 98
Goliad, 36, 37, 39, 42, 43
Goliad Massacre, 21, 37, 38, 106
Gonzales, Pedro, 21
    Rafael, 26
Gonzales County, 4

Gonzales, Texas, 4, 20, 25, 26, 131, 170
Goyens, Mary Pate Sibley, 114, 119
    William, 110–120
Goyens Hill, 114, 116, 119
Goyens Hill Baptist Church, 114
Grand Lodge of Louisiana, 60
Grand Lodge of Texas Masons, 60, 172
Grant, Dr. James, 37, 126
Granville County, North Carolina, 123
Graves Hall, 178, 181, 185
Graves, Henry L., 177, 178, 179, 205
Gray, Mabry "Mustang," 40, 42, 43
    William Fairfax, 49, 128
Grayson, Peter, 9
Green Lake, 31
Greene, A. C., 166
Griffith, Angelina Dickinson, 171
    John Maynard, 171
Grimes County, 49, 50, 58, 132
Grimm, Jacob, 83
Groce, Courtney, 73, 82
    Edwin Waller, 57, 73
    Fulton, 73
    Jared E., 48, 49, 50, 52, 53, 57, 58, 72, 132
    Leonard, 52, 58, 72, 73, 75, 80, 81, 82
    Sarah Wharton, 79
    William Wharton, 73, 75, 78, 79, 81
Groce family, 48–90
Groce's Folly
Groce's Fort, 48, 53
Groce's Landing, 38, 58, 133
Groce's Retreat, 49, 50, 132
Guadalupe River, 17
Guadalupe Victoria, 19, 21
Guajardo, J., 21
Guion, David W., 108

H

Hairston, Mose, 178

Halifax, North Carolina, 123
Hall, Warren D. C., 134
Hamilton Literary and Theological Institute, 178
Hannah, 160, 161
Harris, Jack, 73, 78, 79
    Mrs. Jane, 132
Harrisburg, Texas, 93, 94, 95, 99, 132, 133
Harrison, J. E., 205, 206
Harrison County, 155, 156, 157
Hawkins, Charles E., 142
Hays, James William, 20
    Peter, 20, 44
Heard, W. J. E., 101
Hempstead High School, 89
Hempstead, Texas, 49, 75, 80, 82, 85, 87, 90
Henderson, J. Pinckney, 160
Henry Academy, 182
Henson, Margaret Swett, 109
Hezekiah, 143, 150, 157, 158, 159
Hidalgo uprising, 17
Hill, Allen, 178, 181, 182
    Diamond, 21
Hines Place, 203
Hizer, John, 129
Hobby, Oveta Culp, 207
Holcombe, W. H., 170
Holguin, Carlos, 21
Holland, John Henry, 60, 62
Holland Lodge, 60
Holley, Horace, 52
    Mary Austin, 70
Holly Oaks, 172
Holt, Jane Ballowe, 60
Holtzinger, Captain, 38
Hood's Texas Brigade, 205
Horton, A. C., 195
Houston, Andrew Jackson, 191
    Antoinette Power (Nettie), 194
    Margaret Lea (Maggie), 189, 191, 194, 202, 203
    Mary William (Mollie), 194
    Nancy Elizabeth (Nannie), 188, 194, 203
    Sam, 4, 11, 21, 38, 40, 42, 56, 58, 62, 63, 64, 65, 66, 68,

81, 88, 89, 94, 95, 96, 98,
99, 100, 102, 103, 104,
105, 106, 110, 111, 113,
114, 117, 118, 120, 122,
126, 128, 129, 130, 131,
133, 134, 138, 139, 141,
142, 150, 154, 155, 169,
188, 189, 191, 192, 193,
194, 199, 202, 203, 205,
209
Sam, Jr., 188, 194
Temple, 194
Houston-Forbes Treaty, 118
Houston-Lea Family Cemetery,
203
Houston Morning Star, 106
Houston Telegraph, 200
Houston, Texas, 69, 70, 72, 77,
106
Howard College, 201
Howes, Elijah Captain, 140
Hoxey, Asa, 177
Huckins, James, 179
Hunter, Bob, 104
Robert Hancock, 104
William A., 21
Huntsville, Texas, 177, 188

I

Independence, 67, 127, 142, 203
Independence Academy, 177
Independence Baptist Church,
173, 177, 178, 182, 187,
188, 190, 192, 196, 199,
202, 203, 209
Independence Female Academy,
178
Independence Hall, 174
Independence, Texas, 169, 171,
172, 173, 177, 178, 179,
183, 184, 187, 188, 189,
191, 192, 193, 194, 195,
197, 198, 200, 201, 202,
205, 206, 207, 208, 209
Inez, Texas, 30
Invincible, 127, 140, 142
Irion, Robert A., 117

J

Jack Phillips ranch, 57
Jackson, Andrew, 106, 124, 156
Abner, 49
Acenath, 81
Jackson County, 26
Jasper and Jefferson counties,
176
Jefferson, Texas, 165
Jenkins, Georgia, 184
P. C., 184
Jethro, 141
Johnson, David, 73
Frank W., 4, 11
Lyndon Baines, 173, 207
Penelope, 73
Rebekah Baines, 207
Johnston, Albert Sidney, 43, 89
Jones, Anson, 11, 60, 62, 66, 135,
177
E. A., 107
John Paul, 123
Willie, 123
Judson Female Institution, 184
Juergens, Mrs., 9

K

Kansas-Nebraska Act, 192
Karankawas, 30, 31
Kavanaugh, Mary Gentry, 185,
187, 188
Nelson, 185
Keachi College, 201
Keeran, John Newbanks, 30, 41
Keith, Walker, 172
Kerr, Ison, 25
James, 25, 26, 27, 28, 31
John James, 25
Mary Margaret, 25, 26
Thomas Richard, 27
Kerr County, 27
Kerr's Creek, 26
Kerrville, Texas, 27
Kimball, J. A., 179
King George V, 83
King Ludwig II, 83
Kirkland, Elithe Hamilton, 166
Kosciusko, 93
Kountz Creek, 192

225

L

La Bahía, 17, 22, 23, 28, 35, 37, 40
Lady Macbeth, 89, 90
Lafitte, Jean, 22
La Fou, Ramón, 17
LaGrange, Texas, 6, 171, 172
Lake Jackson, 49
Lake Place, 49
Lake Ponchartrain, 165
Lamar, Mirabeau B., 66, 72, 98, 100, 139, 150, 153, 155, 156, 157
Lamar County, 151
Lampasas, Texas, 207
Lane, Walter, 98, 101
Lapham, Moses, 8
Laso, Carlos, 22
Las Sabinas, 19
Lavaca Bay, 45
Lavaca County, 9
Lavaca-Navidad Meeting, 26
Lavaca River, 17, 26, 28
Lea, Nancy Moffette, 189
Leal, Sálome, 32
Lee, Robert E., 205
Lee at the Wilderness, 205
Leisewitz, Robert, 83
Leland, Oscar, 185
Libertador, 67
Liberty, 127, 139, 142
Liberty, Texas, 93
Liendo, 50, 71, 75, 76, 77. 80. 81, 82, 83, 85, 86, 87, 89, 90
Liendo, José Justo, 80
The Life and Select Literary Remains of Sam Houston of Texas, 203
Lincoln County, Georgia, 48
Lincoln County, Kentucky, 172
Linn, Alcalde, 38
    Charles, 22, 33
    Edward, 22, 33, 45
    J. J., 22
    John Joseph, 18, 22, 26, 33, 35, 37, 39, 40, 42, 45, 46
Linnville, 33, 41, 45
Lipan Comanche, 16

Lipantitlan, 26
Lipscomb, 182
Lipscomb, Abner E., 198, 199
    Abner Smith, 179
Little, W. W., 5
Llorca, Señor, 113
London Times, 169
Long, James, 22
    Jane, 49, 57
Longhorns, 29, 30
Lorenzo de Zavala State Archives and Library Building, 63
Louisiana Lodge No. 32, 62
Lubbock, Francis R., 76, 77
Lundy, Benjamin, 115
Love is a Wild Assault, 166
Lynchburg, 65, 95
Lynch's Ferry, 96

Mc

McArdle, Henry Arthur, 205
    Jennie, 205
McArdle Art Gallery, 206
McCormick, Arthur, 104
    Margaret, 104, 105
McHenry, John, 22
McKinstry, George B., 56
McLennan County, 204

M

Madeira, 83
male department, 180, 182, 183, 185, 186, 194, 195, 199, 200, 201, 205, 208
Manchola, Rafael, 19, 22, 28, 35, 36
Manso, Leonardo, 19, 21
Marion, Alabama, 184, 191
Marion County, 143
Marreo, Adeline (Addie), 165
    Frank, 165
Marriage Act, 152
marriage-by-bond, 3, 4, 5, 143
Maryland Academy of design, 205
Maryland Institute for the Promotion of the Mechanic Arts, 205

226

Masonic Charter Oak, 60
Masonic order, 60, 62
Matagorda Bay, 17
Matamoros, Mexico, 37, 68, 139
Marshall, Texas, 155, 156
Marshall University, 155
Masterson, Harris, 79
Mayfield, James S., 154, 164
  Sophia Ann, 154, 163
Mayhew Prarie, Mississippi, 170
Mayón, Ygnacio, 22
Mededith, Mr., 159
Merrill, Amos, 152, 153, 161
Mexican Citizen, 7
Mexico City, Mexico, 3, 10, 35,
  56, 59, 94
Mexican Federal Consititution
  of 1824, 63, 112, 128
Mier Expedition, 102
Milam University, 176
Miller, Sandy, 150, 158
  William P., 39, 40
Mills, John T., 160
Mina (Bastrop) County, 6
Mission Espíritu, Santo, 29, 43
Mission Valley, 17, 20, 29, 43
Mississippi Baptist, 202
Mississippi State Historical
  Association, 202
Mitch Miller and Chorus, 92, 108
Moderators, 157
Monterrey, Mexico, 4, 16
Montezuma, 36
Montgomery, Alma, 87
  Arthur ("Arti"), 83, 86
  Daisy Tompkins, 87, 88
  Edmund, 83, 85, 86, 87, 89, 90
  Lorne, 83, 87, 90
  Sarah, 88
Moore, Francis, Jr., 135
  John D., 164
  John H., 6, 150, 151
  Martha, 141, 142, 143
Moore's Fort, 6
Moral Creek, 119
Moreno, Regalado, 42
Morgan, Celia, 93
  Emily West, 91, 92–109, 95,
    96, 97, 99, 103, 106, 107

James, 92, 93, 94, 95, 106,
  107, 109
Morris, Leopold, 20
Mulberry Shore, 150, 151
Muldoon, Michael, 1–12, 54, 68
Muldoon, Texas, 5, 11
Murfreesboro, Tennessee, 75, 185
Mustang Gray; A Romance, 42

N

Nacogdoches Independent Vol-
  unteers, 126,
Nacogdoches, Texas, 111, 112,
  115, 126, 128, 160
Nashville Battalion, 39
Nashville University, 170
Natchitoches, Louisiana, 20, 112
National Education Association,
  201
Neill, James, 97
New Castle, Kentucky, 182
New Orleans Bulletin, 38
New Orleans, Louisiana, 17, 27,
  32, 33, 36, 40, 41, 126,
  135, 142, 165
New Washington, now Morgan's
  Point, 92, 93, 94, 95, 96,
  106, 137
Ney, Elisabet, 83, 84, 85, 86, 88,
  89, 90
Ney Museum, 90
Niagara Falls, New York, 201
Niles Weekly Register, 126
Norton Panic, 137
Nueces River, 16
Nuestra Señora de Guadalupe
  de Jesús, 17
Nursery, 32
Nutt, Conway, 86

O

Oakwood Cemetery, 208
Ochiltree, William, 161
O'Connor, Kate Stoner, 24
O'Donojo, Don Juan, 3
Old man Page, 148
Old Norton, 136
"Old Station," 26, 27, 28, 29, 30
Old Three Hundred, 26, 48, 104,

228

Reagan, John H., 192
Reconstruction, 82, 205
Red River, 9
Red River County, 147, 149, 151, 152, 160
Red Rovers, 37
Refugio County, 21, 128
Regulators, 156, 157
Reminiscences of Fifty Years in Texas, 45
Republicans, 17
Restwood Memorial Park, 79
Reyna, Juan, 21
Rios, Simón, 22
Roberts, Oran M., 88, 89, 164
Robertson, Felix H., 200
Robinson, James W., 36
Rocky Creek, 192
Rodriguez, Bonifacio, 22
Roosevelt, Franklin D., 108
    Theodore, 87
Rose, Preston, 157, 158, 159, 160
    Victor M., 19
    William Pinckney, 152, 153, 156, 157, 160
Ross, Lawrence Sullivan, 200
    Michael, 196
    Reverend, 199
    Sterling, 89
Rough Riders, 87, 88
Round Top House, 35, 46
Rowe, Stephen Decatur, 185
Royalists, 17
Runaway Scrape, 62, 104, 132
Rusk, Thomas J., 40, 65, 66, 98, 104, 115, 117, 118, 119, 126, 131, 132, 133, 138, 160
Russell, Alexander, 60

S

Sachem, 81
St. Charles County, Missouri, 25
St. Thomas Hospital, 83
Salcedo, Governor, 16
Saltillo, 4, 23, 131
Samson, George Whitfield, 189, 191
San Antonio and Mexican Gulf

line, 45
San Antonio River, 43
San Antonio, Texas, 3, 10, 11, 17, 23, 94
San Augustine County, 154
San Felipe, 3, 4, 8, 19, 26, 37, 55, 58, 60, 94, 117, 126
San Fernando Cathedral, 23
Sam Houston Normal Institute, 201, 202, 206
San Jacinto, 36, 37, 38, 65, 92, 104, 108
San Jacinto Day, 194
San Jacinto Monument, 41
San Jacinto River, 96
San Jacinto University, 176
San Nicolas mines, 16
San Patricio, 4, 16
Sanchez, José María, 49
Santa Anna, Antonio López de, 10, 11, 35, 36, 39, 62, 63, 65, 92, 93, 94, 95, 96, 97, 98, 99, 100, 102, 103, 105, 106, 107, 109, 131, 132, 138, 139, 140, 194
Santa Fe Expedition, 154
Santa Dorotea (Goliad), 29
Saucedo, Jośe Antonio, 3
Saucedo, 28
Saviriago, Captain, 37
Sayres, 89
Schopenhauer, Arthur, 83
Schulenburg, Texas, 12
Scott, John W. 159, 160
secession, 193
Seguin, Erasmo, 112
The Settlement of Texas by Anglo-Americans, 205
Shackleford, Captain, 37
Shelby County, 143, 148
Sheridan, Phil, 82
Sherman, Sidney, 63, 96, 98, 100, 102, 128
Shreveport, Louisiana, 150
Shreveport University, 185
Sibley, Henrietta and Martha, 120
    Henry, 114, 120
Siege of Bexar, 60, 126

229

Simath, Cresentia ("Cenci"), 85
Sinks, Julia Lee, 5
Six Decades in Texas,76
The Slaughter Pen, 156
Slidell, Mr., 144
    Mrs., 144
Smith, Henry, 4, 5, 6, 66, 127, 128
    James B., 164
    John, 112
    William, 160
Smithsonian Institution, 89
Smithwick, Noah, 8, 28
Solis, Manuel, 22
Soto La Marina, Tamaulipas,
    Mexico, 16, 41
Southern Baptist Convention,
    170
Spanish-American War, 87
Speight, Joseph W. 199, 200
Spriggs, Frances, 80
Stapp, Elijah, 26
State Cemetery, 56, 77, 89, 163,
    207
state colonization law, 17, 25
state colonization law of 1824,
    119
state colonization law of 1825, 4,
    21
state colonization law of 1830,
    113
Stephen F. Austin State Park, 2
Sterne, Adolphus, 119
St. Mary's Church, 23, 34, 43, 45
Submerged Lands Act of 1953,
    163
Swarthmore College, 87
Swartwout, Samuel, 106
Sylvester, James A. 105

T

Taft, Lorado, 89
Tall Flower, 149
Talladega, Alabama, 172
Tamaulipas Indians, 16
Tamaulipas, Mexico, 115
Taylor, Charles S., 115, 119
    Isabella, 124, 125
    Louis, 125, 145
    Rev., 144

Richard, 76
Zachary, 42
*The Telegraph and Texas
    Register*, 58, 95
Terry, B. F. (Frank), 74, 75
    Clint, 73
Terry's Texas Rangers, 75, 76, 77
Texana, 38
Texas Academy of Science, 90
Texas Agricultural and Mechan-
    ical College, 206
Texas Baptist, 196
Texas Baptist Education Society,
    173, 174
The Texas Baptist Herald, 201
Texas Baptist Historical Center-
    Museum, 203, 209
Texas Baptist State Convention,
    206
Texas Centennial Commission,
    46, 120
Texas Collection, 194, 205
Texas Fine Arts Association, 90
Texas Declaration of Indepen-
    dence, 26, 37, 63, 122, 129,
    174, 177, 185
Texas navy, 66, 122, 127, 137,
    139, 151, 163
Texas Revolution, 14, 20, 36, 58,
    65, 66, 67, 92, 93, 104,
    115, 117, 122, 177, 205
Texas State Historical Associa-
    tion, 201
Texas State Teachers Associa-
    tion, 201, 202
Texas Supreme Court, 44, 164,
    173
Texas Veterans Association, 79,
    208
Thomas, 79
Thomasville, Georgia, 83
Tolbert, Frank X., 107
Tonkawa Indians, 31, 32
Tower, John, 46
Transylvania College, 52
Transylvania University, 172
Trask, Frances, 177, 178
Travis, William Barrett, 9, 126,
    130

231

Wiginton, A. M., 43
Wiley, Louis, 125, 144
William Robbins, 36
Williams, Samuel May, 4
Wood's Settlement, 6
Wright, Emma Ann, 45
   John David, 20, 21, 44
   Margaret, 18, 19–21, 44, 45
"Will You Come to the Bower?,"
   101
William Bollaert's Texas, 107
Wyatt, Jim, 86

Y

Yaraborough, Ralph, 108
Yegua Creek, 177
The Yellow Rose of Texas, 107,
   108, 109
Yellowstone, 56, 95, 138
Yoakum, Texas, 102
Young, John, 46
Ysleta Creek, 114, 115

Z

Zacatecas, 44
Zarco Creek, 42